**MIMESIS
INTERNATIONAL**

POLITICS
n. 10

Spartaco Pupo

DAVID HUME
The Sceptical Conservative

© 2020 – MIMESIS INTERNATIONAL
www.mimesisinternational.com
e-mail: info@mimesisinternational.com

Isbn: 9788869772757
Book series: *Politics*, n. 10

© MIM Edizioni Srl
P.I. C.F. 02419370305

TABLE OF CONTENTS

Acknowledgements	7
Introduction	9
1. The Historical-Political Context of Hume's thinking	13
2. A Sceptical Political Essayist	19
3. At the Origins of Government: Interest, Justice, and Property	31
4. A Guide for Humankind: Custom	45
5. Political Realism	57
6. An Admirer of Machiavelli	67
7. Government is an Opinion	77
8. For Institutional Stability	91
9. Factionalism and National Interest	99
10. A Lesson of Moderation	119
11. Hume's Conservatism: The Historiographical Certainties	129

12. The Impossible Liberalism	141
13. A Sceptical Conservatism	151
14. Conservative Because Realist	167
15. A Conservative Among the Conservatives	175
Bibliography	199
Index of persons	217

ACKNOWLEDGEMENTS

It is a pleasure to thank the institutions and the people who have assisted me in preparing this volume. I must begin with a general word of thanks to the University of Calabria, particularly to the Department of Culture, Education, and Society, for providing a suitable academic home and generous funding. I am grateful to Ian Michael Robinson, my esteemed colleague at the University of Calabria, for the careful revision of the text. I am particularly indebted to the two anonymous reviewers for reading a draft of the book and providing helpful comments. I would also like to thank my friends of the Italian Association of Historians of Political Thought and the Eighteenth-Century Scottish Studies Society, for pointing me toward useful resources.

In the conception and drafting of this volume, I have benefited enormously from the conversation, encouragement, and insight of many students who have followed my courses with interest. To them, this book is dedicated.

INTRODUCTION

By focusing on David Hume's serious challenge to the intellectual standpoint informed by the arrogance of political rationalism, this book attempts to resolve some of the issues debated by his scholars and provides a structured interpretation of Hume's political conservatism.

The volume focuses on Hume's ideas on the origin of government political obedience, property, justice, opinion, moderation, continuity, and anti-fanaticism – all themes that are a valuable source of inspiration for the development of modern and contemporary political conservatism. As concerning the last issue, this book highlights the importance of a rediscovery of David Hume's political thought, focusing on his ideas on the origin of government and political obedience and his vision of ideals such as liberty, property, political stability, and moderation – all topics that are a precious source of inspiration for the development of political conservatism. The fourteen chapters of this book outline the main features characterising Hume's conservatism. These features are counter-revolutionary: political realism; mistrust of sudden and violent innovations; scepticism toward abstractions; opposition to rationalist arrogance; respect for custom and institutional continuity; need for the preservation of stability; rejection of ideological rhetoric, sectarianism, and dogmatism; constant denial of intellectual subsidies; and defence of national interest.

Starting from the analysis of the *Essays, Moral and Political* (1741-42) and subsequent *Political Discourses* (1752), it is possible to find a reliable conservative tendency in Hume's political thought, also permeating the letters, dispatches, and accounts relating to his work as interpreter of war, diplomat, and statesman (1745-68), and culminating in the *History of*

England (1754-62), and above all in the last of his political essays, *Of the Origin of Government*, completed in 1774, two years before his death, and published posthumously in 1777.

Hume's intellectual production entirely embodies a corpus of texts that are often revised, corrected, grafted, and upon which he continually intervened in order to investigate the overall meaning, the apparent contradictions, the consolidation of particular perspectives, in order to offer a framework as organic as possible, though always opened and never ended, consistent with his sceptical methodological attitude. The outcome of these continuous corrections and text revisions proved the increasing importance by Hume ascribed to the government as an embodiment of authority and the consequent development of his doubts about license, equalitarianism, radicalism, and fanaticism – all political doctrines descended from a single ideological matrix, that is that of political rationalism. Concerning this last point, which some scholars have glimpsed without investigating it to the hilt, this work focuses on the fundamental characteristics of Humean "sceptical" and "secular" conservatism, that is quite different from the Anglo-American conservatism. This will born some decades after his death as consequence of Edmund Burke's writings, but it is the first one to appear on the political scene of modernity.

The conservatives who followed Hume, perhaps because they were too attached to a religious and metaphysical dimension of conservatism, did not fully accept him as one of their own. Only since the twentieth century have some of the most representative conservative thinkers, self-avowed *conservative*, namely Robert A. Nisbet, Russell A. Kirk, Giuseppe Prezzolini, Michael Oakeshott, and Roger Scruton, from different perspectives, started to inscribe Hume's name in the tradition of political conservatism. And it is this inscription, as an unmistakable sign of ideological acknowledgment and identification, an irrefutable proof of Hume's conservatism. Another proof, to which great attention is paid in this book, is Hume's political realism, due to his disenchanted approach to the analysis of human nature, history, society, and political institutions, as a worthy continuator of Niccolò Machiavelli's political realism.

This book, ultimately, aims to fill what is a gap in critical literature concerning Hume's political thought, namely the lack of an organic monography on his conservatism. It aims to reconstruct the causal links between the various epistemological elements that characterise his conservative political doctrine, that in the evolution of his intellectual production always appear clear, coherent, and tuning with the most significant expressions of modern and contemporary conservatism.

1. THE HISTORICAL-POLITICAL CONTEXT OF HUME'S THINKING

The entire eighteenth century, in Britain, from the advent of the Stuarts to the Hanoverian succession, was characterised by a great conflict between the monarchic power, strengthened by the King and the Municipalities, which progressively progressed in a society that enjoyed a regime which was no longer monarchical in the same way as the Elizabethan one, and found the part reserved to them by the constitution inadequate. Religious fanaticism, under the banner of an ultimate freedom, gave way to the last campaign that with the monarchy would have overwhelmed true freedom, which was undoubtedly not the tyranny of Parliament or Oliver Cromwell's military despotism. The balanced development of civil society following the Restoration was not due to the initiative of the Stuarts. The two great English political parties, the Tories, supporters of the Crown's prerogatives, and the Whigs, advocates of Parliament's rights, agreed in placing on the throne a king who had to guarantee the balance of power between Crown and Parliament, namely the constitutional balance between the authority of the monarchical component and the freedom of the republican one; a balance that made the conflict between the two parties lose its original ideological character, so that Tories and Whigs would respectively become the Court Party and the Country Party.

The Stuart dynasty became extinct in 1714 after Queen Anne's death. The English throne was inherited by the German house of Hanover, whose first representatives, George I and George II, came to reign in a country of which they ignored traditions and language. However, George I managed to resist the forces of the restoration of the Stuart monarchy, leaning on Whigs and calling their leader, Robert Walpole, to the leadership of the government.

Walpole, for over two decades (1721-1742), created the conditions for widespread prosperity, thanks, above all, to the development of maritime and commercial activities. He also kept England outside of international disputes, although his antimilitarism ended up favouring competition from France and Spain over the seas and colonies. The national awakening movement which opposed Walpole's policy was promoted by William Pitt, who became head of the Cabinet, in 1757, and undertook a vigorous foreign policy of power and colonial extension of England in Asia and America, to the disadvantage of Spain and France. Pitt's withdrawal from the government (1761) shortly followed the advent to the throne of George III, who, instead of marrying his minister's imperialist policy, was concerned about restoring the prerogatives of the Crown before Parliament.

Although short of organisational energies, the parties persisted in the form of alliances around people and unforeseen problems. The government, for example, in 1757, was composed of politicians identified as Whigs, while the relative majority of the opposition was composed of Tories, that recognised themselves around two complexes of ideas: the succession and the social basis of the party. Proud to be the party of Church and Crown, the Tories, after having been supporters of the royal power of the Stuarts against the succession of the Home of Hanover, showed significant opposition to the authority of the Crown due to their mistrust of an undesirable king. The departure of the Tories from the Hanoverian political context led to a nostalgia for the golden times of Queen Elizabeth and a rejection of the new age. The base of their party being composed mainly of the low nobility, the Tories defended the interest of landed men and opposed any policy that could weaken it, fought against land taxation and the wars that caused it, feared banks and commerce, and hated the great Whig aristocrats and the middle class of the city who, through Walpole, controlled the nation. The Whig party, on the other hand, supported the Hanoverians establishment, accepted the modern era as the dawn of a better world, believed in the rule of the aristocracy, defended the interests of the mercantile classes, and supported wars waged in the name of such interests. The Whigs were more democratic than the Tories, although they greatly feared the irrationality of the masses and the continually looming danger of social anarchy[1].

As far as Hume's Scotland is concerned, until 1707, it was an independent kingdom, whose kings, from the Stuart dynasty, were also kings of England until the so-called Glorious Revolution (1688-89) and the subsequent ousting of the Stuarts. The traditional dominion of the great noble and feudal families was progressively replaced by a new class of officials linked to the English monarchy, and opposed to rebellions and radicalism. The last kings of Scotland were Catholic, and for this reason they lost both thrones. Presbyterianism dominated the country, heir to the ascetic and rigorous tradition of Calvinism and Puritanism, which rejected the centralised organisation of the Anglican Church, and recognised the local parish as the sole authority.

The closure and the ideological dogmatism of Presbyterianism covered Scotland with a cloak of intolerance of which Hume himself was a victim. He was never able to obtain a university chair precisely because of the intense ostracism enacted against him by the Presbyterian clergy, which controlled the whole cultural world, from parishes to universities, from publishing to press, and did not forgive him some heretical theses illustrated in his works. Hume received the harshest and most virulent attacks from the Scottish and English clerical spheres, which repeatedly accused him of atheism by mocking him in pamphlets published anonymously[2]. Some of his friends, including Henry Home, thought the work too "indiscreet", but by this point Hume professed that he could "see not what bad consequences follow, in the present age, from the

---

1   See George M. Trevelyan, *The Two-Party System in English Political History* (Oxford: Clarendon Press, 1926); John Brewer, *Party Ideology and Popular Politics at the Accession of George Third* (New York: Cambridge University Press, 1976).

2   In a series of books, published between the 1750s and 1770s, some religious polemicists, mostly English and Scottish, tried to offer an alternative interpretation to Hume's conception of religion. On these "zealots", who argued against his conclusions about the issue of the origin of popular religion, the possibility of a rational religion, providenfce, and miracles, see Corrado Giarratana (ed. by), *Contra Hume. The Eighteenth-Century Debate on Hume's Work on Religion* (Rome: Bonanno, 2017).

character of an infidel; especially if a man's conduct be in other respects irreproachable"[3].

The events consequent to the second English revolution gave the start of that process that shortly after would have decreed the Union, in 1707, between England and Scotland. For Scotland it meant the beginning of a process of sweeping institutional reforms[4]. At the time, Scotland was going through a period of deep crisis: the population languished in misery and was divided into factions perpetually fighting each other; agricultural techniques were deeply backward; there were few commercial outlets; the educational system was in awful economic conditions and dominated by religious fanaticism. In the Scottish Parliament, the majority of the deputies believed that the possibility of entering the British markets, with the consequent opening for agricultural and industrial products, would have helped Scotland to get out of an extremely precarious economic situation. England, then, had shown a growing interest in the Union because it needed a group to oppose the English magnates, in order to weaken the political power that the latter had gradually taken over. The Union was carried out in 1707 with the consent of the majority of the Scottish Parliament, but it opened a series of apparently unsolvable problems, among which the social division between the *Highlands'* backwardness and the *Lowlands'* accelerated economic development[5].

The relations between England and Scotland turned out to be complicated because of the intention of assimilating the former to the detriment of the latter, and the latter's desire to maintain some of the main peculiarities unchanged. This tension, however, had

---

3 Hume, *To James Oswald of Dunnikier (2 October 1747)*, in *The Letters of David Hume*, ed. by John Y. T. Greig (Oxford: Clarendon, 1932), vol. 1, p. 106.
4 The Union – Trevor-Roper has written – "enriched Scotland materially; it enlarged its intellectual horizons; it transformed its society"; Hugh Trevor-Roper, 'The Scottish Enlightenment', Studies on Voltaire and the Eighteenth Century, 68 (1967), p. 1637.
5 For a discussion on the political consequences of the Union, see John Robertson, *A Union for Empire. Political Thought and the British Union of 1707* (Cambridge: Cambridge University Press, 1995).

positive consequences in the following decades, because it induced the Scot, on the one hand, to harbour admiration for the English conquests and, on the other, to try to emulate and overcome them in the economic and cultural field[6].

It would be too long to dwell here on the religious climate in Scotland at the time of Hume. In the central decades of the century, the undisputed religious dominance in the Scottish cultural context was undermined by the debate within the Scottish Church thanks to the formation of two opposing factions: the traditionalist one, which intended to preserve the elective system of ministers from below, declaring itself opposed to any innovation; the reforming one, which called for a less oppressive presence of the Church in social and cultural life. Among the occasions of confrontation between these two camps, the decisive one occurred between 1755 and 1756 and had as its object the contest of the very ideas and personality of Hume, who could count on the support of many friends in the faction of reformers, who succeed in neutralising the attempts to sanction the sceptic or infidel Hume. However, he lived this situation in a somewhat detached manner, considering himself entirely unrelated to religious events, indifferent to sanctions, and always apart from the factional clashes. Moreover, he was a proponent of a thinking that reduces religious beliefs, as well as political beliefs, to the small fruits of personal choices, and that cost him cultural isolation.

---

6 For a masterful narrative that explores the major events of this period, see Trevelyan, *England Under the Stuarts* (London and New York: Routledge, 2002); Allan I. Macinnes, *Union and Empire: The Making of the United Kingdom in 1707* (Cambridge: Cambridge University Press, 2007).

2. A SCEPTICAL POLITICAL ESSAYIST

When David Hume's *Essays, Moral and Political* came out in British bookstores, between 1741 and 1742[1], presented themselves as the most vivid evidence of the intellectual equilibrium amid thought and action, theory and praxis, which distinguished their author as few other thinkers in the history of western social and political thought. This was due to the actual conciliation, audaciously experimented, between the historical and the philosophical perspective of the approach to politics. Their editorial success was immediate, contrasting his metaphysical and moral work, *A Treatise of Human Nature* (1739-40)[2], that, as he recalled in his autobiography written just before his death, "fell *dead-born from the press*; without reaching such distinction as event to excite a murmur among the zealots"[3].

This first collection of essays had a non-coincidental political characterisation. Political essays in this period were very much in vogue, although they were "fervently partisan" literature[4], which was what Hume aspired to overcome. According to a

---

[1] David Hume, *Essays, Moral and Political* (Edinburgh: printed by Robert Fleming and Alexander Alison, 1741-42).
[2] Hume, *A Treatise of Human Nature: Being an Attempt to introduce the experimental Method of Reasoning into Moral Subjects* (London: Printed for John Noon, 1739), vols 1-2; Hume, *A Treatise of Human Nature: Being an Attempt to introduce the experimental Method of Reasoning into Moral Subjects* (London: Printed for Thomas Longman, 1740), vol. 3.
[3] Hume, *My Own Life* (1776), in *Essays Moral, Political, and Literary* (1777), ed. by Eugene F. Miller (Indianapolis: Liberty Fund, 1987), p. xxxiv. Hume's italics.
[4] Cristopher J. Berry, *David Hume* (New York-London: Continuum, 2009), p. 13.

reasonably influential interpretation, his real intent was to endow the Hanoverian regime with an intellectual foundation[5] and exceed once and for all the dynastic and religious dogmatics[6].

Hume was among the few authors of modern times to deal with political problems in the form and style of the essay. Unlike the philosophical treaty, the essay was more for an ordinary reader, and also provided the idea that its content was far from being a final outcome. Instead, it appeared as the temporary account of research still in progress and free from any claim to be conclusive. The French philosopher Michel de Montaigne intended the essay as an editorial form more easily adaptable to the sceptical mentality that by himself was introduced in modern culture. He was the most influential interpreter of the ancient sceptical philosophers, such as Pyrrho and Sextus Empiricus[7].

Terminologically, *essay* means *test* or *experiment*, and as such, it was, by its nature, provisional, subject to further verification and confirmation, however utterly devoid of the ambition to give teaching, indoctrinating, and establish creeds, beliefs or dogmas. Significantly, Montaigne, so admired that he could be considered Hume's mentor[8], in his *Essais*, did not claim timeless certainties, but had a healthy scepticism about the ability to persuade those "men of intelligence" who, in the establishing and substantiating of their interpretation, cannot refrain from altering the facts a little, and

---

5   See Duncan Forbes, *Hume's Philosophical Politics* (Cambridge: Cambridge University Press, 1975), p. 136.
6   Forbes, *Hume's Science of Politics*, in George P. Morice (ed. by), *David Hume: Bicentenary Papers* (Edinburgh: Edinburgh University Press, 1977), pp. 39-50.
7   See, on this topic, Luciano Floridi, *Sextus Empiricus: The Transmission and Recovery of Pyrrhonism* (Oxford and New York: Oxford University Press, 2002); Richard H. Popkin, *The History of Scepticism: From Savonarola to Bayle* (Oxford-New York: Oxford University Press, 2003).
8   Montaigne is quoted in an essay that Hume brings to press in the second volume of his *Essays, Moral and Political*, emblematically entitled *The Sceptic*, in which he invites his reader, "when passion is awakened, fancy agitated, example draws, and counsel urges", because "the philosopher is lost in the man", to enjoy "the gaiety of Montaigne"; Hume, *The Sceptic* (1742), in *Essays*, p. 179, note 12.

"never present things just as they are, but twist and disguise them to conform to the point of view from which they have seen them; and to gain credence for their opinion and make it attractive, they do not mind adding something of their own, or extending and amplifying"[9]. In order not to fall into this trick, Montaigne entrusted himself to the essays, written in a subdued literary style, that was useful for "juxtaposing ideas and deliberately suspending judgment"[10]. Also, it was precisely the style chosen by Hume too, with which, by the mid-1750s, he spent a decade and a half preparing his intellectual guide for methodological scepticism in an extraordinarily creative path, that would lead him to stand out on the cultural scene of Western thought. For this reason, perhaps, Richard H. Popkin sees Hume as the "*only* living sceptic" in the eighteenth century, the "most aware man of the new predicament created by the Enlightenment – that there was no faith left to guide men"[11].

Almost all his scholars believe that Hume was a sceptic, so it will not be necessary to prove it here. There has been some debate about whether he is better understood as a Pyrrhonian or an Academic sceptic. Here it is not appropriate to intervene in the discussions on what kind of sceptic Hume was and on the answers to the questions on this aspect of Hume's thought[12], but only focus on how Hume's philosophy of custom can be seen as a sceptic response to rationalist dogmatism.

Hume's scepticism was not a preliminary methodology or a necessary means to create a *tabula rasa*, or "a mere set of rules that we should follow carefully so as not to be mistaken", it is

---

9   Michel de Montaigne, *On Cannibals*, in *Essays*, ed. by John M. Cohen (New York: Penguin, 1993), p. 108
10 Peter Burke, *Montaigne* (Oxford: Oxford University Press, 1981), p. 60.
11 Popkin, *The High Road to Pyrrhonism* (San Diego: Austin Hill Press, 1980), p. 58. Popkin's italics.
12 See Popkin, *David Hume: His Pyrrhonism and His Critique of Pyrrhonism*, in *Hume, A Collection of Critical Essays*, ed. by Vere C. Chappell (Garden City: Doubleday, 1966); John C. Laursen, *The Politics of Skepticism in the Ancients, Montaigne, Hume, and Kant* (Leiden: Brill, 1992); and Yves Michaud, 'How to Become a Moderate Skeptic: Hume's Way Out of Pyrrhonism', Hume Studies, 11 (1985), pp. 33-46.

"a *philosophical position* that creates absolutely new *objects* of thought"[13]. Hume recommended a mitigated scepticism against the impracticability of the Pyrrhonian programme and the use of an imaginative freedom to challenge every kind of belief. In other words, for Hume, people must get used to doubting, dealing with counter-arguments, avoiding hasty decisions on the issues that concern them and their questions on the empirical subjects. However, he did not mean "this philosophical doubt should turn us into neurotics forever having bones set because we do not know what to believe about oncoming traffic"[14].

Among the ancients, Sextus Empiricus had given a similar account of the life of the sceptic. He observed that in the absence of truth and while suspending judgment, the sceptics lived "a life conformable to the custom of our country and its laws and institutions"[15]. It was illustrated by four "rules for life", which a sceptic could follow not dogmatically and as a truth, but as a practice. They were: 1) follow the guidance of nature; 2) live subject to the constraint of the passions; 3) follow the tradition of laws and customs; and 4) learn an art. What Hume wrote about custom had much in common with these rules of Sextus, because it is a specification of the details of living with custom. For Hume, as for the ancient sceptics, the government which suggested that we lived much of our life following custom was as good a guide to life as we will ever have[16].

Some references to the sceptical tradition directly concern the conception of scepticism, as ability or mental attitude, temperament devoted to the doubtful formulas used to doubt oneself before the

---

13 Frédéric Brahami, *Criticism and Science in Hume*, in José R. Maia Neto and Gianni Paganini and Laursen (ed. by), *Skepticism in the Modern Age. Building on the Work of Richard Popkin* (Leiden-Boston: Brill 2009), p. 375. Italics in text.
14 David F. Norton, *How a Skeptic May Live Skepticism*, in John J. MacIntosh and Hugo A. Meynell (ed. by), *Faith, Skepticism, and Personal Identity: A Festschrift for Terence Penelham* (Alberta: University of Calgary Press, 1994), p. 130.
15 Sextus Empiricus, *Outlines of Pyrrhonism*, ed. by Robert G. Bury (Cambridge: Harvard University Press, 1933), p. 13.
16 See Alan Bailey, *Sextus Empiricus and Pyrrhonean Scepticism* (Oxford: Clarendon Press, 2002).

rest of the world, in a Pyrrhonian sense, as a lifestyle, a world view, a balancing principle of all that is subject to doubt. All these elements belong to a rhetoric of scepticism, inaugurated by Montaigne[17], of ongoing research, ambivalence, and ambiguous work, as such, in stark contrast to the rhetoric of affirmation, truth, and clarity. The sceptic does not give up on the ordinary business of life because he is incapable of finding any reasons to believe in one thing rather than its contrary. According to Pierre Bayle, the great French sceptic who was much admired and commented by Hume[18], society does not need to be afraid of sceptics, "for the sceptics do not deny, but that men ought to conform to the customs of their country, and practise moral duties, and resolve upon those things from a probable reason, without staying for certainty"[19]. And this conformism to the customs of a nation, this adaptation to the conventions of its inhabitants, this quietism with respect to its fundamental institutions, cannot but be aspects of a typically conservative attitude.

As a result of these assumptions, it is worth clarifying here what appears rather simplistic a juxtaposition of Hume to English empiricism, which is the one operated by the classic manuals of the history of philosophy. At the end of the 1990s, Donald W. Livingston openly maintained that Hume was not an empiricist precisely because he was sceptical and, above all, did not share the vision of social and political relations historically peculiar to empiricism[20].

---

17 See Victoria A. Kahn, *Rhetoric, Prudence, and Skepticism in the Renaissance* (Ithaca: Cornell University Press 1985).
18 Hume had an interest in Bayle before he went to France, at the libraries of Rheims and La Flèche (1734-37), but it may be supposed that his interest in modern scepticism deepened while he was in the country of Montaigne and Pascal, leading him on to François La Mothe du Vayer, Jean-Pierre de Crousaz, and Pierre-Daniel Huet; on this aspect of Hume's biography, see James A. Harris, *Hume. An Intellectual Biography* (New York: Cambridge University Press, 2015), p. 80.
19 Pierre Bayle, *The Historical and Critical Dictionary*, transl. anon. (London: J. J. and P. Knapton, 1734), vol. 4, p. 654.
20 Donald W. Livingston, *Philosophical Melancholy and Delirium: Hume's Pathology of Philosophy* (Chicago: University of Chicago Press, 1998), pp. 3-7, 11-13.

Modern scepticism implies, first of all, a decision, or rather a resignation: we do not know the essence of things, and therefore, we must be content with appearances. In its initial phase, Hume's *moderate* scepticism appears as something very similar, at times identical, to the empiricism devised by Locke, whose most significant contribution to philosophy, as is known, was the destruction of the idea of *substance*. The experimentalism by Hume inaugurated in the *Treatise*, his great epistemological work, appears to him, in the current and traditional use of the word, entirely "extravagant"[21], that is a term by Hume used to indicate all those conceptualisations not corresponding to the attitude of the authentically anti-dogmatic philosopher. Unaware as it is of the needs of science, the dogmatism of those who delude themselves into grasping the substance of objects is bound to lead to nothing but an extreme scepticism. On the contrary, the true sceptic does not have access to the interiority of things, their being, and their substance; therefore, he goes in search of the possibility of a well-founded science.

It is precisely the sceptical attitude, as suspension of belief and dogmatic truth, which informs Hume's choice of the essay as an editorial medium with which to convey his political thought.

Initially, Hume wrote the *Essays, Moral and Political* for a publication in widely circulated magazines, in the style of "The Spectator" and "The Craftsmen", aimed to combine "the world of society and letters, on the one hand, and that of politics, on the other"[22], and to introduce in Scotland cultured discourses on morality and politics. However, this attempt was destined to fail, as he said, "partly from Laziness, partly from Want of Leisure"[23]. That periodical publication never took place, and a good part of the writings converged in the collection of the *Essays* of 1741. The shift from the magazine format to the collective volume allowed Hume's political thinking to spread to the whole of Great Britain rapidly, and to acquire public intellectual notoriety throughout

---

21 See Hume, *A Treatise of Human Nature* (1739-40), ed. by David F. Norton and Mary J. Norton (Oxford: Clarendon Press, 2007), vol. 1.

22 Ernest C. Mossner, *The Life of David Hume* (Oxford: Clarendon Press, 1980), p. 139.

23 *Ibid.*, p. 140.

Europe. Hume wanted to convert the sectarian and biased disputes in some moderate, civil, and useful political debates. The same reasons that led him to deal with the problems of politics were to be sought in his ambition not so much to affect the British society's policy, but to solicit and direct the public opinion[24].

The distinctive features of Hume's political essays, which represent a sort of political supplement to the *Treatise*, are clarity, objectivity, depth of observation, and critical insight, with which Hume addressed the most relevant political themes. Hume was a rare example of a modern sceptic and anti-dogmatic author who, while considering politics as an important sphere of human action, preferred to remain always detached from the fascinating passions generated by it. Experience having taught him that "the Whig party were in possession of bestowing all places, both in the state and in literature", he was "so little inclined to yield to their senseless clamour"[25]. Hume's intellectual autonomy, which guaranteed him full freedom of criticism against all the political and religious factions of his time, reached maximum levels in several of his political writings, in which he "very liberally abused both Whigs and Tories" and "enjoyed the favour of both parties"[26].

For Hume, some complicated issues, such as the ancient constitution, the theory of natural rights, and the monarchy by divine right, could never lead to a unity of opinion. They always imposed unsurmountable beliefs, destined to kindle the public clash, and to poison the public. He invited political writers of his time to recognise that any political process, be it of conservation or innovation, restoration or reform, was a matter of consciously formed opinions, and the politics could have led to a calm conversation, a polite exchange of views that was free from any

---

24 See Carl Wennerlind, *David Hume as a Political Economist*, in Alexander Dow and Sheila Dow (ed. by), *A History of Scottish Economic Thought* (London and New York: Routledge, 2006), pp. 46-70; Roger L. Emerson, *Essays on David Hume, Medical Men and the Scottish Enlightenment* (Burlington: Ashgate, 2009), p. 117.
25 Hume, *My Own Life*, p. xxxviii.
26 Hume, *To John Clephane (4 February 1752)*, in *The Letters of David Hume*, vol. 1, p. 167.

sectarian prerogative and projected to the empirical-historical foundation of the practice of government.

Given the success of the first collection of political essays, Hume brought to the press, ten years later, another collection, *Political Discourses*[27]. The majority of these discourses focused squarely on issues related to what was then called *political economy*. They denoted a conception of commerce founded on a historical perspective that disdained petty national prejudices and hatreds. The discourses were intended to attract the attention of the most influential European representatives of the Enlightenment, an intellectual movement that reached the highpoint of its vitality in the 1770s, when the nascent political economy offered solid foundations for any empirical study plan of the political institutions. Hume's collection obtained immediate consents on both sides of the Atlantic and stimulated dozens of translations[28]. The original Humean vision of freedom, trade, exchange, interest, taxes, public debt, and development of nations significantly increased the themes of a participatory and varied debate, and inspired the works of illustrious economics theorists, above all Anne-Robert-Jacques Turgot and Adam Smith, with whom Hume entertained a lasting friendship[29]. In particular, many of Hume's arguments anticipated those of Smith in *The Wealth of Nations* (1776)[30], such as the following: the real source of a nation's wealth as not gold or silver or a positive balance of trade, but rather as productive citizenry; the futility of most attempts by politicians to guide or control people's economic choices; the free trade's working to the benefits of cities and nations; the free market's advantages in the

---

27 Hume, *Political Discourses* (Edinburgh: Printed by R. Fleming, for A. Kincaid and A. Donaldson, 1752).
28 With regard to Hume's fortune in eighteenth-century Europe, see James Fieser (ed. by), *Early Responses to Hume's Life and Reputation* (Bristol: Thoemmes Continuum, 2005); Peter Jones (ed. by), *The Reception of David Hume in Europe* (London and New York: Continuum, 2005).
29 On the fruitful friendship with Smith, in particular, see the recent study by Dennis C. Rasmussen, *The Infidel and the Professor: David Hume, Adam Smith, and the Friendship that Shaped Modern Thought* (Princeton and Oxford: Princeton University Press, 2017).
30 Adam Smith, *An Inquiry into the Nature and Causes of the Wealth of Nations* (London: W. Strahan and T. Cadell, 1776).

international sphere. Incidentally, Hume insisted that there was nothing particularly objectionable about luxury. In contrast to those who worried that luxury distracted people from their more important duties, Hume posited that "ages of refinement are both the happiest and most virtuous"[31], and "industry, knowledge, and humanity, are not advantageous in private life alone: They diffuse their beneficial influence on the *public*, and render the government as great and flourishing as they make individuals happy and prosperous"[32].

Hume also dealt with political issues in places other than essays: the third volume of the *Treatise*, in which he focused on the origin of government and political obedience; the first part of *An Enquiry Concerning the Principles of Morals* (1751)[33], in which he reflected on the problem of the origin of justice and property. Moreover, Hume was not only a lover of political speculation, who dealt with politics in his most famous works, but was also an expert in military strategies and techniques; he was a talented diplomat, a moderate member of the British government, and an original interpreter of international affairs and war, which he experienced first-hand on the battlefield. So he spoke of politics in several letters, brief accounts, both theoretical and practical-polemical, and dispatches, that were mostly written while secretary to the British army general, James St. Clair, *chargé d'affaires* at the English embassy in Paris, and under-secretary of state[34]. In all Hume's political writings, the thinkers of his time, throughout

---

31 Hume, *Of Refinement in the Arts* (1760), in *Essays*, p. 269.
32 *Ibid.*, p. 272.
33 Hume, *An Enquiry Concerning the Principles of Morals* (London: Printed for A. Millar, 1751).
34 In the recent volume: Hume, *A Petty Statesman. Writings on War and International Affairs*, ed. by Spartaco Pupo (Milan: Mimesis International, 2019), in the first complete edition, the five writings concerning Hume's involvement in the practice of policy are collected: *A True Account of the Behaviour and Conduct of Archibald Stewart, late Lord Provost of Edinburgh* (1748); *Account of the Descent on the Coast of Brittany and the Causes of its Failure* (1746); *Journal of the British Embassy to the Courts of Vienna and Turin* (1748); *Dispatches of a British Diplomat at Paris* (1764-65); and *Correspondence of an Under-Secretary of State* (1767-68).

Europe, saw the exhortation to motivate the national ruling classes towards human industriousness, inventiveness, and resourcefulness in the direction both of a "free government", as Hume called it very often[35], that nullified the residues of feudalism and initiated the much-desired civilization, the "refinement" in the arts or manners[36], that aimed at the formation of an authentic civic consciousness. It was not an invitation to promote riots or revolutions for unlikely social palingenesis. For Hume, the "spirit of innovation", that almost always animated revolutionaries and political fanatics, was "in itself pernicious, however favourable its particular object may sometimes appear"[37].

Civilisation proposed by Hume was not a process of perfectibility of human nature or a synonym of "progress," such as the typical concept of the French Enlightenment tradition. In an anti-utopian sense, it looked like the development of humankind coinciding with the development of civil society, or, in other terms, a sociopolitical organization that changed its appearance according to the territory in which it was founded, but always constituted by a government aiming to protect individual liberty, free trade, and relations between persons and between nations. Hume, in short, aimed at the cultural renewal of his country, Scotland, which he did not hesitate to define, because of the religious conflicts, the ignorance of population, and the several military occupations that afflicted it, "the rudest, perhaps, of all European Nations; the most necessitous, the most turbulent, and the most unsettled"[38]. In the problematic context opened by the Union of 1707, Hume's goal was to ask questions and provoke extensive debates on these topics, thus complying with his sceptical attitude, without trying to define theoretical postulates or to elaborate systematic theories about commerce in the manner of Smith, Richard Cantillon or James Steuart[39], but opening the subject to public conversation between

---

35 See Hume, *Essays*, pp. 15-18, 48-52, 66, 90-96, 115-125, 265-277, 407-409, 485, 493, 522-529.
36 *Ibid.*, pp. 106-131, 191-215, 246-264, 268-294.
37 Hume, *Of the Coalition of Parties* (1758), in *Essays*, p. 496.
38 Hume, *To Edward Gibbon (Edinburgh, 18 March 1776)*, in *The Letters of David Hume*, vol. 2, p. 310.
39 For a recent research on this topic, see Tony Aspromourgos, *On the*

those who did not have a direct political interest in this or that sphere of reflection. "When Hume – someone has rightly observed – took up political economy, and encouraged his contemporaries to engage in its discussion, he brought Enlightenment fully to Scotland"[40].

Origins of Classical Economics: Distribution and Value from William Petty to Adam Smith (New York: Routledge, 1995).
40 Robertson, *The Case for the Enlightenment. Scotland and Naples 1680-1760* (Cambridge: Cambridge University Press, 2005), p. 324.

3. AT THE ORIGINS OF GOVERNMENT: INTEREST, JUSTICE, AND PROPERTY

The first aspect to be faced in an analysis of Hume's political thought is undoubtedly his conception of the origin of power, which is also, not surprisingly, the first characteristic element of his anti-rationalism.

A superficial reading of the section of the *Treatise* could make seem the discussion with which Hume intends to solve the problem of government unmotivated, that is why the need arises for a political intervention outside the dynamics of the self-organisation of society. The latter, in fact, for Hume, responds to the logic of the organisation, rather than the foundation. Against Thomas Hobbes's paradox of an order that was built starting from its absence, Hume proposes a vision of society that can organise special forces and make sure the outcome of their cooperation in a perspective in which there is no longer any logical and chronological hierarchy according to the "partition of employments"; when every individual works solely for himself, his force is too small to perform any significant work; being employed in providing all his different necessities, he never reaches a perfection in any particular field. As his force and success are not at all times equivalent, the least failure in either of these particulars must be attended with certain ruin.

> Society – Hume writes in the *Treatise* – provides a remedy for these three inconveniencies. By the conjunction of forces, our power is augmented: By the partition of employments, our ability encreases: And by mutual succour we are less expos'd to fortune and accidents. 'Tis by this additional force, ability, and security, that society becomes advantageous.[1]

---

1   Hume, *Treatise*, p. 312.

Although Hume attributes to the society the charge of synchronising individuals, he assigns to political science the role of investigating the set of social dynamics, but with a descriptive method, not a logical or moral one. This is because, unlike logic, whose end is "to explain the principles and operations of our reasoning faculty, and the nature of our ideas", and unlike morals, that regard "our tastes and sentiments", politics considers "men as united in society, and dependent on each other"[2].

This uniqueness of politics clearly denotes the realist, or Machiavellian strategy with which Hume expels from the political sphere any interference of morals and logic; it appears coherently and punctually in several parts of the *Treatise*, whenever he intends to point out that the union of individuals in society is not attributable solely to the pattern of government of human conduct. To give some examples, in the section dedicated to the explanation of the impressions arising from good or evil, pain or pleasure, Hume claims that "men cannot live without society, and cannot be associated without government"[3]; in rejecting the metaphysical thesis of the mind as a pure thinking substance, and giving an alternative theory as a description of what a person actually observes when inspecting the self's idea, Hume characterises the personal identity with the analogy of the self as a "republic", in which "the several members are united by the reciprocal ties of government and subordination, and give rise to other persons, who propagate the same republic in the incessant changes of its parts"[4]. Hume compares the human mind to a political system of interconnected ideas and changing citizens interacting in some ways regulated by its constitution, driven by shared aims and giving rise to further members (thoughts) who ensure the continuation of the republic (personal identity). In a republic, where the changes of this variable object are the changes of members and laws, in the reciprocal ties of government and subordination, the citizens may bring on a new government, and the leaders may allocate positions for the citizens within the privilege system. The republic, which

---

2   *Ibid.*, p. 4.
3   *Ibid.*, p. 259.
4   *Ibid.*, p. 170.

is the person, may change not only its members (perceptions and ideas) but also its laws and constitutions, which are the character and disposition.

What then is the function and genesis of government?

It is precisely with an interrogative that Hume starts his analysis of the origin of government. Since people are attached to interest, that is strictly related to the political obedience, Hume asks how "any disorder can ever arise in society, and what principle there is in human nature so *powerful* as to overcome so strong a passion, or so *violent* as to obscure so clear a knowledge?"[5]. Hume's answer is that although satisfaction of personal interest can only occur within a system of rules, we cannot regulate our actions by this judgment, "but yield to the solicitations of our passions, which always plead in favour of whatever is near and contiguous"; and any general rule can only confirm the deficient character of a human nature tending always to prefer "any trivial advantage, that is present, to the maintenance of order in society, which so much depends on the observance of justice"[6]. It is here that Hume comes to the concern of the importance of what he calls "rules of justice". These are forms of behaviour of public interest that are not necessarily concerned with the interest of each individual interested in a particular case, but rather ways of action which fall under some laws that are valid both inside and outside to nations and subject both sovereigns and citizens. These laws are three:

> *That of the stability of possession, of its transference by consent,* and *of the performance of promises.* 'Tis on the strict observance of these three laws, that the peace and security of human society entirely depend; nor is there any possibility of establishing a good correspondence among men, where these are neglected.[7]

Hume has no doubts about the human need for a government that defends external affairs as well as economic and cultural ones, but he prioritizes the preservation of the institutions that make social life possible. If people are aware that it is this priority that

---

5   *Ibid.*, p. 342. Hume's italics.
6   *Ibid.*, p. 343.
7   *Ibid.*, p. 337. Hume's italics.

constitutes the public interest and that the government protects this interest, then the government can count on a sure source of loyalty.

Rules of justice, for Hume, must be recognised before people can come to link themselves by promise or contract to any form of government. He argues that, though persons can maintain a small uncivilised society without government, it is impossible they should maintain a society of any kind without the observance of the "three fundamental laws"[8], that are antecedent to government, and are by Hume supposed to "impose an obligation before the duty of allegiance to civil magistrates has once been thought of"[9].

Moreover, Hume shows that only the universal application of the same general, although inflexible, rules of justice will secure the establishment of a general order, and that this, and not any particular rational aims, must guide the application of the rules if an order is to be the result. This has led Friedrich A. von Hayek to observe that, for Hume, "any concern with particular ends of either the individuals or the community, or a regard for the merits of particular individuals, would entirely spoil that aim", and that

> this contention is intimately bound up with Hume's belief in the short-sightedness of men, their propensity to prefer immediate advantage to distant gain and their incapacity to be guided by proper appreciation of their true long-run interest unless they bind themselves by general and inflexible rules which in the particular case are applied without regard to consequences.[10]

Indeed, it explains Hume's rejection of those policies aimed to destroy the fundamental rules of justice, such as, for example, the proposal that the government should treat every single citizen according to his natural merit. Personal merit, or benevolence, for Hume, is recommended because – as he explains in *An Enquiry Concerning the Principles of Morals* – it leads to outcomes that are positively evaluated in society[11]. However, since merit is so

---

8   *Ibid.*, p. 347.
9   *Ibid.*
10 Friedrich A. von Hayek, 'The Legal and Political Philosophy of David Hume', Il Politico, 4 (1963), p. 608.
11 See Hume, *An Enquiry Concerning the Principles of Morals* (1751), ed. by Jerome B. Schneewind (Indianapolis-Cambridge: Hackett,

dependent on the particular situation of every single individual, it is impossible to formulate general rules or standards based on it. Consequently, no assignment of properties could rest on merit. The same criticism Hume extends to those patterns of distribution of goods and status based on personal characteristics and virtues. When government adheres to the rules of justice, it refrains from interfering with the natural qualities of individuals, with their virtues, vices, and personal freedoms. Since the most visible expressions of individuality are productivity and exchange, in the broadest sense of these terms, justice is connected to ownership and contractual relations, and in protecting them, the government protects the integrity of individual persons. Hume, by supposing that a person endowed with reason, but unaccustomed with human nature, deliberates what rules of justice or property would best promote public interest, establishing peace and security, concludes that his obvious thought would be to assign the most extensive properties to the most widespread virtue, and give everyone the power of doing good proportioned to his natural disposition. Moreover, he adds:

> In a perfect theocracy, where a being, infinitely intelligent, governs by particular volitions, this rule would certainly have place, and might serve to the wisest purposes: But were mankind to execute such a law; so great is the uncertainty of merit, both from its natural obscurity, and from the self-conceit of each individual, that no determinate rule of conduct would ever result from it; and the total dissolution of society must be the immediate consequence. Fanatics may suppose, *that dominion is founded on grace, and that saints alone inherit the earth*; but the civil magistrate very justly puts these sublime theorists on the same footing with common robbers, and teaches them by the severest discipline, that a rule, which, in speculation, may seem the most advantageous to society, may yet be found, in practice, totally pernicious and destructive.[12]

It is no coincidence that Jerry Z. Muller has included the text of the third section of *An Enquiry Concerning the Principles of Moral*, from which this passage is taken, in his anthological collection

---

1983), pp. 13-18.
12 *Ibid.*, p. 27. Hume's italics.

on modern conservatism, under the label: "Enlightenment Conservatism"[13]. Unlike the French conservatives, such as de Maistre or de Bonald, who took up themes from "eighteenth-century enlightened conservative" and carried them to extremes, Hume was among the first authors to criticise, by his arguments concerning interest, justice, property, and origin of power, all those "overly rationalistic" theories of political obligation[14].

Indeed, it is the abstract reason, for Hume, that suggests a distribution of material goods as an ideal, but it is the practical experience which confirms that it would destroy the stability of property: there could never be agreement among men on a standard of merit, or on a method of applying such a measure in a particular case, and so a rule, based on merit, could not be implemented impartially. With the same clarity, Hume recognises the moral, but not political, justification for an egalitarian distribution as an instrument of utility, with these words:

> It must also be confessed, that, wherever we depart from this equality, we rob the poor of more satisfaction than we add to the rich, and that the slight gratification of a frivolous vanity, in one individual, frequently costs more than bread to many families, and even provinces.[15]

But, as regards the practicability of what appears to be a rationally valid concept, Hume shows his scepticism when he considers the "ideas of *perfect* equality" as "*impracticable*", "extremely *pernicious to* human society", false hopes, simply because persons have "different degrees of art, care, and industry" which "will immediately break that equality"[16], and there are always more wants than there are goods to satisfy them, and the natural characteristics of human beings, such as expanding desires and limited generosity, prevent the working of what would otherwise be the best arrangement. It is impossible, for Hume, to prevent

---

13   Jerry Z. Muller, *Conservatism: An Anthology of Social and Political Thought from David Hume to the Present* (Princeton: Princeton University Press, 1997), pp. 36-45.
14   *Ibid.*, p. 134.
15   Hume, *An Enquiry Concerning the Principles of Morals*, p. 27.
16   *Ibid.*, p. 28. Hume's italics.

inequalities re-emerging because men's unequal talents will allow some to acquire wealth at the expense of others. Therefore, from a political-practical point of view, "perfect equality of possessions, destroying all subordination, weakens extremely the authority of magistracy, and must reduce all power nearly to a level, as well as property"[17].

Some of these arguments are partially taken from the section of the *Treatise* concerning the origin of justice, namely *"the manner, in which the rules of justice are establish'd by the artifice of men"*[18]; but they are summarised in the following passage of the second *Enquiry*, in which Hume resolutely opposes the Levellers, which were a crucial component of a radical movement during the civil wars in seventeenth-century England:

> The levellers, who claimed an equal distribution of property, were a kind of political fanatics, which arose from the religious species, and more openly avowed their pretensions; as carrying a more plausible appearance, of being practicable in themselves, as well as useful to human society.[19]

Moreover, in *The History of England* (1754-62)[20], to confirm Hume's coherence deriving from historical knowledge, in mentioning the Levellers, who "insisted on an equal distribution of power and property, and disclaimed all dependance and subordination", he remarks: "Every man had framed the model of a republic; and, however new it was, or fantastical, he was eager in recommending it to his fellow citizens, or even imposing it by force upon them"[21].

---

17 *Ibid.*
18 Hume, *Treatise*, p. 311. Hume's italics.
19 Hume, *An Enquiry Concerning the Principles of Morals*, p. 27. On the Levellers, see Andrew Sharp (ed. by), *The English Levellers* (Cambridge: Cambridge University Press, 2002); Rachel Foxley, *The Levellers: Radical Political Thought in the English Revolution* (Manchester: Manchester University Press, 2013).
20 Hume, *The History of England* (Edinburgh: Hamilton, Balfour and Neil, 1754, London: Millar, 1762).
21 Hume, *The History of England from Invasion of Julius Caesar to the Revolution in 1688* (1754-62), ed. by William B. Todd (Indianapolis: Liberty Fund, 1983), vol. VI, p. 3.

For Hume, therefore, it is a question not of rationalistically devising abstract principles on which to base the origin of government, but rather of regulating the distance that separates personal interest from the general in the people's needs to live together peacefully. Moreover, it is a question that only the government can solve. When people have experimented that though the rules of justice be sufficient to maintain any society, they cannot observe those rules in large societies; so "they establish government, as a new invention to attain their ends, and preserve the old, or procure new advantages, by a more strict execution of justice"[22].

Therefore, interest is a decisive element in the spontaneous regulation of human relationships. From the conception of human interest there derives Hume's criticism regarding the process of legitimation of the government, based on the idea, quite in vogue in Hume's time, that the political constitution owes its legitimacy to a contract stipulated by free and rational individuals, in need of an order different from the natural one, that transforms them from living beings into citizens. Concerning this doctrine, known as "contractarianism", Hume places himself so critically as to be rightly defined as "the most formidable anti-contractarian in the middle of the eighteenth century"[23].

The concept of interest, in Hume, has a double meaning extensively analysed by scholars who have dealt with them: that of "mainsprings of human behaviour", which in Humean "psychology of imagination" serves, together with passion, as the basis for the "ego's pursuit of satisfaction and self-esteem"[24], and that of "constitutional interest", which is "the duty of the political philosopher to assist in maintaining the balance of the constitution

---

22 Hume, *Treatise*, p. 348.
23 Patrick Riley, *Social Contract Theory and its Critics*, in Mark Goldie and Robert Wolker (ed. by), *The Cambridge History of Eighteenth-Century Political* (Cambridge: Cambridge University Press, 2006), p. 355.
24 John G. A. Pocock, *The Machiavellian Moment: Florentine Political Thought and the Atlantic Republican Tradition* (Princeton: Princeton University Press, 1975), p. 487.

by maintaining a balance of argument"[25]. The policy of interest, in short, is that which realistically takes note of the fact that principles such as virtue and public spirit – Hume argues – can also be noble and carried forward by parties that are inspired by them, but since these principles "are too disinterested and too difficult to support, it is requisite to govern men by other passions, and animate them with a spirit of avarice and industry, art and luxury"; the "harmony of the whole is still supported; and the natural bent of the mind being more complied with, individuals, as well as the public, find their account in the observance of those maxims"[26].

Against the rationalist dogmatism of consensual foundation, Hume shows that the obligation of subjection to the government does not derive from any "promise" by the subjects. Referring to contractarianism's useless claims, in the *Treatise*, he states:

> Those political writers, who have had recourse to a promise, or original contract, as the source of our allegiance to government, intended to establish a principle, which is perfectly just and reasonable; tho' the reasoning, upon which they endeavour'd to establish it, was fallacious and sophistical. They wou'd prove, that our submission to government admits of exceptions, and that an egregious tyranny in the rulers is sufficient to free the subjects from all ties of allegiance.[27]

Founding the government on a promise, as a principle, does not help, for Hume, understand the functioning of the dynamics of obedience to the government itself:

> I maintain, that tho' the duty of allegiance be at first grafted on the obligation of promises, and be for some time supported by that obligation, yet as soon as the advantages of government are fully known and acknowledg'd, it immediately takes root of itself, and has an original obligation and authority, independent of all contracts.[28]

Thus a government cannot be based on a promise because it

---

25 Geoffrey Marshall, 'David Hume and Political Skepticism', The Philosophical Quarterly, 4 (July 1954), p. 253.
26 Hume, *Of Commerce* (1752), in *Essays*, p. 263.
27 Hume, *Treatise*, p. 352.
28 *Ibid.*, p. 347.

would be enough to return to the weakness of pledge in conveying the actions of individuals over time. In other words, the duty of civil obedience does not arise, as Thomas Hobbes and John Locke imagined, from an original pact that has validated their willingness to live together; the duty of political obedience, therefore, can only result from the incontrovertible fact that society can be maintained only in the presence of an authority. Also, there is no discontinuity between the state of nature and the civil state: man of nature is not the *homo homini lupus* as described by Hobbes, that is the oppression of selfishness which for its survival must fight against his fellowmen. In Hume, selfishness instinctively tends to "sympathy" towards others, which the social "usefulness" as collective interest, and as "the chief source of moral distinctions"[29], makes more and more in need of organisation and development. Sympathy, for Hume, means neither benevolence nor altruism nor solidarity nor friendship, which are feelings that he is careful not to confuse and of which he specifies the respective concepts[30]. By sympathy, Hume indicates the affective communication that often takes the form of imitation of feelings and leads to phenomena of influence and, in some cases, of identification. Sympathy can take on positive connotations that are constructive of the social bond, as well as negative connotations, such as passionate contagion, fanaticism or enthusiasm.

Moreover, according to Hume, obedience to government has no relation to the intentionality and voluntariness of the obedient action, and there is no form of determinism between obedience and command. Interest is a prerequisite of the government and the political obligation towards it: "government is a mere human invention for the interest of society"[31]; and commitment to obey

---

29 *Ibid.*, p. 394.
30 On the topic of sympathy in Hume, see Glenn R. Morrow, 'The Significance of the Doctrine of Sympathy in Hume and Adam Smith', The Philosophical Review, 1 (January 1923), pp. 60-78; Bernard Wand, 'A Note on Sympathy in Hume's Moral Theory', The Philosophical Review, 2 (April 1955), pp. 275-279; Stanley Tweyman (ed. by), *David Hume. Critical Assessments* (London and New York: Routlege, 1995), vol. 4 (*David Hume: Ethics, passions, sympathy, Is and Ought*).
31 Hume, *Treatise*, p. 354.

derives only from the strength of this interest. Just as in practical life individuals are guided by imagination and always act to achieve concrete and personal advantages, so in political life, they submit to the government to safeguard the public interest. Therefore, although this assumption is, for Hume, too subtle for the vulgar, all individuals are aware of duty to obey the government only in consideration of the public interest, and if this were not the case, that is to say, to motivate men formerly to obedience were not the sense of common interest but some abstract principle, Hume asks himself what other solicitation would be able to subjugate the natural ambition of men and force them to submit to the power of the state:

> Imitation and custom – he writes in the *Treatise* – are not sufficient. For the question still recurs, what motive first produces those instances of submission, which we imitate, and that train of actions, which produces the custom? There evidently is no other principle than interest; and if interest first produces obedience to government, the obligation to obedience must cease, whenever the interest ceases, in any great degree, and in a considerable number of instances.[32]

Hence the gradual emergence of a government that has no original or creative function concerning society. It is a political structure that meets the constitutive weakness of human nature and allows persons to better relate to social complexity.

Nor is the foundation of government the theory of divine right, as exploited by the *Tories*, at that time. For Hume, a king is no more nor less dependent upon divine providence than a constable. Therefore, if this fact establishes the king's divine right, it creates the divine right of the constable and a "usurper, or even a robber and a pyrate"[33]; and insofar as the divine right theory carries with it the doctrine of absolute passive obedience, it is necessary to reject it to "defend the rights of injured truth and liberty"[34]. However, Hume does not appeal to such rights in the abstract, but as the conflict over them has received concrete expression in English history. For

---

32 *Ibid.*
33 Hume, *Of the Original Contract* (1748), in *Essays*, p. 467.
34 Hume, *Of Passive Obedience* (1748), in *Essays*, p. 491.

example, he writes that Charles I and James II mistook "the nature of our constitution, and engrossing the whole legislative power, it became necessary to oppose them with some vehemence; and even to deprive the latter formally of that authority, which he had used with such imprudence and indiscretion"[35].

The criterion of usefulness is argued by Hume also in *the second Enquiry*, where he has to solve the problem of the need for positive law and the reduction of natural liberty, since usefulness is the foundation of the duty of obedience, the only one capable of preserving peace and order among men. He writes in that work:

> When a number of political societies are erected, and maintain a great intercourse together, a new set of rules are immediately discovered to be useful in that particular situation; and accordingly take place under the title of laws of nations.[36]

A little further on, Hume focuses on what is meant by usefulness, and adds:

> Usefulness is agreeable, and engages our approbation. This is a matter of fact, confirmed by daily observation. However, useful? For what? For some body's interest, surely. Whose interest then? Not our own only: For our approbation frequently extends farther. It must, therefore, be the interest of those, who are served by the character or action approved of; and these we may conclude, however remote, are not totally indifferent to us.[37]

These assumptions confirm the centrality that, for Hume, the interest in public life has. In practical experience, where individuals act on the impulse of the imagination, they always act in order to attain ephemeral advantages that put the interest of social peace in the hands of the people; so in political life they subject to the government to safeguard the public interest, and their activity is necessarily aimed at preserving an interest, and not at the maintenance of some pact.

---

35 *Ibid.*, p. 492.
36 Hume, *An Enquiry Concerning the Principles of Morals*, p. 35.
37 *Ibid.*, p. 42.

Adam Smith, in *The Theory of Moral Sentiments* (1759)[38], objects to Hume's utilitarianism. According to Smith, the real source of justice does not concern the welfare of society, as Hume claims, but that of individuals: however central the role of justice may be, usefulness is not the primary source of justice. The latter, for Hume, entails nothing more than refraining from harming the life, liberty, or property of others, and it is necessary for the survival of society. However, the real reason that will distance Smith from Hume consists in the first's effort to recover the natural law deduction project of law from the principles of natural love, a project that Hume, on the other hand, completely rejects. More exactly, Hume and Smith both assume that justice, alone among the virtues, is best enforced through a system of rigid rules, "and it is impossible to formulate precise guidelines for how to act courageously or generously or modestly, for instance, but it is both possible and necessary to do so for respecting the life, liberty, and property of others"[39]. Smith rejects every one of Hume's significant propositions, including usefulness, but also scepticism, or relativity of values, theories, and beliefs[40].

In Hume, the virtue of justice is founded entirely on its usefulness; we approve of just conduct because of our sympathy with the public interest. This is why he notoriously labels justice an "artificial virtue" in the *Treatise*[41]: rules respecting property rights are human conventions that we develop as we realise how necessary they are for the maintenance of social order. The political consortium, for Hume, is based on the set of "natural virtues"[42], such as selfishness and benevolence, which characterise man as a living being, and on the "artificial virtues"[43], which are the result of the creative and productive ability of the man

---

38 See Adam Smith, *The Theory of Moral Sentiments* (1759), ed. by Knud Haakonssen (Cambridge: Cambridge University Press, 2002).
39 Rasmussen, *The Infidel and the Professor*, p. 99.
40 See Athol Fitzgibbons, *Adam Smith's System of Liberty, Wealth, and Virtue: The Moral and Political Foundations of the Wealth of Nations* (Oxford: Oxford University Press, 1995), pp. 28-29.
41 Hume, *Treatise*, pp. 307-430.
42 *Ibid.*, pp. 367-377.
43 *Ibid.*, pp. 369-370.

born in a family and forced to keep society alive for need and habit. Government is a response to the need for a justice that principally protects property. With the reduction of the latter to human artifice, Hume deliberately deviates from the Lockean conception of natural law, and leaves room for an idea of justice that ensures the stability in human relations continually presented by "unnatural conjunction"[44] of partiality and scarcity. Conceiving property as a natural right independent of justice, for Hume, would mean supporting it in dependencies of morals, therefore of our passions and actions, which, in turn, would spring from particular judgments. All this, as noted in the *Treatise*, "wou'd produce an infinite confusion in human society", and "the avidity and partiality of men wou'd quickly bring disorder into the world, if not restrain'd by some general and inflexible principles"[45]. Human beings, therefore, for Hume, are not by nature provided with a principle of original justice placed at the foundation of society, but are moved by the nature of the passions to the satisfaction of their desires and interests, which only artificial justice can regulate.

As regards the connections with other thinkers, in conclusion, it should be remembered that while Jeremy Bentham, who was the first systematic exponent of utilitarianism, accepted as essential the Humean principle of usefulness, that he resumed in his *Fragment on Government* (1776) as the standard of right and wrong in the moral and political sphere, and acknowledged Hume as having demolished the notion of original contract[46], John Stuart Mill, in his canonical re-determination of utilitarianism, would never pronounce the name of Hume, and it appears as a historiographical distortion, given the undeniable influence of the Scottish political writer in the history of utilitarian doctrine.

---

44 *Ibid.*, p. 312.
45 *Ibid.*, p. 341.
46 Jeremy Bentham, *A Fragment on Government and An Introduction to the Principles of Morals and Legislation*, ed. by Wilfred Harrison (Oxford: Basil Blackwell, 1948). See, on this topic, Norton, *David Hume: Common-Sense Moralist, Skeptical Metaphysician* (Princeton: Princeton University Press, 1982); Frederick Rosen (ed. by), *Jeremy Bentham* (Aldershot: Ashgate, 2007).

4. A GUIDE FOR HUMANKIND: CUSTOM

Preferring, perhaps, the Aristotelian natural association of men united in society to Locke's liberal individualism, Hume, further confirming his political anti-rationalism, maintains that society is built primarily on the foundations of family institutions. Basing the government on an abstract and metaphysical idea, such as the Lockean "natural law", on which arguments and opinions too distant from the general customs of humanity, means nothing more than to destabilise the government's ability to guarantee utility and social loyalty. Society, for Hume, first came into existence thanks to the natural human inclination to live socially, that over time has become an indispensable "habit" in the best possible management of justice.

Hume embraces the attitude to political "prudence", that is, a typically conservative attitude, in deriving government not from rational or legal arguments, but real human convenience, as partially seen in the previous pages. For him, nothing is more conformable, "both to prudence and morals", than to "quietly" submit to the government "which we find establish'd in the country where we happen to live, without enquiring too curiously into its origin and first establishment"[1]. It follows that the "state of nature" notoriously supposed by contractarian philosophers is nothing, for Hume, but "a mere philosophical fiction, which never had, and never cou'd have any reality", a figment of modern rationalists "not unlike that of the *golden age*, which poets have invented"[2].

In his political essays, Hume regards the notion of an implicit contract to be signed in the state of nature as a wholly fictional

---

1　Hume, *Treatise*, p. 357.
2　*Ibid.*, p. 317. Hume's italics.

idea; and the further purpose of an explicit political pact, together with the view of present political allegiance as suspended upon its continuous renewal, is disdained on the grounds that it was entirely out of accord with the facts and historical experience. For Hume, human society is not the invention of a voluntary agreement aimed at eliminating the disadvantages of pre-social condition. Society represents a variegated set of responses not only to human interests, but also to the human impulses, as the "natural appetite betwixt the sexes" [3] and the oscillation between altruism, which diminishes when it extends through the concentric circles of the subject, family, friends, and strangers, and selfishness, which increases when the needs of society become ever more abstract and remote. Government does not derive from any voluntary consent, since this has never existed or desired, but constitutes a continuous improvement of what already exists in nature. Therefore, political consent is a consequence of established political authority, continually reinforced as those within its orbit come almost insensibly to experience its benefits. So the philosophers who try to justify the existence of an "original contract" should also tell us – Hume ironically observes in an essay of 1748 – "in what records this charter of our liberties is registered"[4].

Hume speaks even more frankly when he addressed the well-known political "preachers" of his time, and the following words seem to confirm it:

> Were you to preach, in most parts of the world, that political connexions are founded altogether on voluntary consent or a mutual promise, the magistrate would soon imprison you, as seditious, for loosening the ties of obedience; if your friends did not before shut you up as delirious, for advancing such absurdities. It is strange, that an act of the mind, which every individual is supposed to have formed, and after he came to the use of reason too, otherwise it could have no authority; that this act, I say, should be so much unknown to all of them, that, over the face of the whole earth, there scarcely remain any traces or memory of it.[5]

---

3   *Ibid.*, p. 312.
4   Hume, *Of the Original Contract*, p. 468. Hume's italics.
5   *Ibid.*, p. 470.

The real origin of political power, for Hume, is not consent, as expected by rationalist philosophies, but *custom* or *habit* (Hume uses the two terms interchangeably), that is "the guide of life", and "determines the mind, in all instances, to suppose the future conformable to the past"[6]. Changing the term used, as often happens, especially in the *Treatise*, but not in meaning, Hume argues that "habit is nothing but one of the principles of nature, and derives all its force from that origin"[7].

A crucial causal link connects custom and belief. The latter – Hume asserts in the *Treatise* – is "an act of the mind arising from custom"[8], and therefore for men these are the basis of their conventional way of thinking and, above all, of acting. Without the belief, which is formed and supported by custom, the "vulgar" or common man would not be able to orient himself in the world. In his tendency to universalise and render the idea of a "human nature" almost timeless, Hume supports the importance of these fundamental principles, on which each individual bases every moment of his existence, and without which he would risk even to extinguish human nature, that is to say man as a living being. It is what in the *Treatise* clearly emerges:

> I must distinguish in the imagination betwixt the principles which are permanent, irresistible, and universal; such as the customary transition from causes to effects, and from effects to causes: And the principles, which are changeable, weak, and irregular [...]. The formers are the foundation of all our thoughts and actions, so that upon their removal human nature must immediately perish and go to ruin. The latter are neither unavoidable to mankind, nor necessary, or so much as useful in the conduct of life; but on the contrary are observ'd only to take place in weak minds, and being opposite to the other principles of custom and reasoning, may easily be subverted by a due contrast and opposition.[9]

Of these principles, belief is considered "a lively idea," that is an idea endowed with its peculiar vivacity, which is always found

---

6   Hume, *Treatise*, p. 411.
7   *Ibid.*, p. 120.
8   *Ibid.*, p. 79.
9   *Ibid.*, p. 148.

"*related to or associated with a present impression*"[10]. As such, belief, at the very moment it is introduced in its treatment, assumes a leading role for Hume:

> Reason can never satisfy us that the existence of any one object does ever imply that of another; so that when we pass from the impression of one to the idea or belief of another, we are not determin'd by reason, but by custom or a principle of association. But belief is somewhat more than a simple idea. 'Tis a particular manner of forming an idea: And as the same idea can only be vary'd by a variation of its degrees of force and vivacity; it follows upon the whole, that belief is a lively idea produc'd by a relation to a present impression, according to the foregoing definition.[11]

Without custom and belief, we would never be able, as Hume also states in *An Enquiry Concerning Human Understanding* (1748)[12], "to adjust means to ends, or employ our natural powers, either to the producing of good, or avoiding of evil"[13]. Custom forms a persons' view of the external world and the system of the common beliefs. Custom produces belief, facilitating various imaginative associations, and all reasoning regarding cause and effect has to do with probabilities, as derived from custom; and belief is more properly an act of the sensitive, rather than the cognitive, part of our nature. Since nothing is ever-present to the mind but its perceptions – all the actions of seeing, hearing, loving, hating, and thinking – fall under this denomination. However, more than belief, it is custom that plays a crucial role in a political key. Our experience of the past proves nothing for our future, unless supposing a resemblance between them; and only custom can allow us to presume that the future will conform to the past.

---

10   *Ibid.*, p. 65. Hume's italics.
11   *Ibid.*, pp. 67-68.
12   The work appeared in April 1748 under the title *Philosophical Essays Concerning Human Understanding. By the Author of the Essays Moral and Political* (London: printed for A. Millar, 1748). Ten years later Hume changed its name to *An Enquiry Concerning Human Understanding*
13   Hume, *An Enquiry Concerning Human Understanding* (1748), ed. by Peter Millican (Oxford: Oxford University Press, 2007), p. 40.

In a middle area between belief and custom, for Hume, education is formed, which is constituted "almost on the same foundation of custom and repetition as our experience or reasonings from causes and effects"[14]; however, since education lacks the element of the naturalness of which custom is supplied, and because it is often also different depending on to places and times, it cannot claim to convince the human mind in the same way as custom does.

Every person, for Hume, is a sort of custom-forming being, and all politics and history take place within a history of custom. In the *Introduction* to the *Treatise*, Hume claims that he is following in the footsteps of thinkers such as Locke, Hutcheson, and Butler, who has "begun to put the science of man on a new footing"[15]. However, what did these authors say about custom? Locke, in the *Essay Concerning Human Understanding* (1689), wrote that our ideas come from our "customs and manner of life"[16], and that "Education, Custom, and the constant din of their Party" are the causes of "the greatest, I had almost said, of all the errors in the World"[17]. Frances Hutcheson made the case against custom with these terms:

> Custom, Education, and Example are so often alleged [...] as the occasion of our relish for beautiful objects, and for our approbation of, or delight in a certain conduct of life in a moral species, that it is necessary [...] to make it appear that there is a natural power of perception, or sense of beauty in objects, antecedent to all custom, education, or example.[18]

According to Joseph Butler, we are capable "of getting a new facility in any kind of Action, and of settled alterations in our

---

14   Hume, *Treatise*, p. 81.
15   *Ibid.*, p. 5.
16   John Locke, *An Essay Concerning Human Understanding Part* (1689), ed. by John W. Yolton (London: Dent and Sons, 1961), vol. 1, pp. 432-3.
17   *Ibid.*, pp. 400-1.
18   Francis Hutcheson, *Philosophical Writings*, ed. by Robert S. Downie (London: Dent, 1994), p. 38.

temper of character" through the "power of habits"[19], and "moral and religious habits" can improve our "virtue and piety"[20].

Hume's conception differs from these standpoints because he above all re-evaluates the importance of custom by freeing it from all its contamination with religion. He asserted in the *Treatise* that custom is the foundation of all our judgments"[21], and that "all reasonings are nothing but the effects of custom"[22]. In the *Abstract* (1740), written to explain the *Treatise*, given its editorial misfortune, he writes: "'Tis not, therefore, reason, which is the guide of life, but custom"[23].

Thus, if human habits and custom create "a *facility* in the performance of any action or the conception of any object; and afterwards a *tendency* or *inclination* towards it"[24], it can be said that they are motivators of our life and behaviour, also in the political sphere. Nothing – Hume, in fact, observes – causes any sentiment to have a more significant influence on us than custom, or turns our imagination more powerfully to any object, and a "constant perseverance in any course of life produces a strong inclination and tendency to continue for the future"[25].

---

19 Joseph Butler, *The Analogy of Religion, Natural and Revealed* (1736), in *The Works of Joseph Butler, late Bishop of Durham* (London: printed and published by J. F. Dove, 1828), pp. 110-11. On Butler, see Austin Duncan-Jones, *Butlers' Moral Philosophy* (Harmondsworth: Penguin, 1952). For an interpretation of Hutcheson's standpoint, see William R. Scott, *Francis Hutcheson: His Life, Teaching, and Position in the History of Philosophy* (New York: Kelley, 1966); Mark Philip Strasser, *Francis Hutcheson's Moral Theory: Its Form and Utility* (Wolfeboro: Longwood Academic, 1990).
20 Butler, p. 116. On the difference with Hume, see John P. Wright, *Butler and Hume on Habit and Moral Character*, in Michael A. Stewart and John P. Wright (ed. by), *Hume and Hume's Connexions* (State College: Penn State University Press, 1994), pp. 105-118.
21 Hume, *Treatise*, p. 100.
22 *Ibid.*, p. 101.
23 Hume, *An Abstract of a Book Lately Published; Entituled, A Treatise of Human Nature, &c. Wherein the Chief Argument of That Book is Farther Illustrated and Explained* (1740), in *A Treatise of Human Nature*, ed. by Peter H. Nidditch (Oxford: Oxford University Press, 1978), p. 652.
24 Hume, *Treatise*, p. 27. Hume's italics.
25 *Ibid.*, p. 91.

This is why Hume finds it utterly unacceptable that politics has an identifiable rational foundation, according to some abstract idea, as Locke suggested. What people do observe are not hypothetical contract at the basis of power, but customs and habits of submitting to sole laws emanated from acknowledged authority, as outcomes of a very long period of trials and errors. In other terms, government is the end, not the beginning, of a long development.

> No compact – Hume writes in *Of the Original Contract* – or agreement, it is evident, was expressly formed for general submission; an idea far beyond the comprehension of savages: Each exertion of authority in the chieftain must have been particular, and called forth by the present exigencies of the case: The sensible utility, resulting from his interposition, made these exertions become daily more frequent; and their frequency gradually produced an habitual, and, if you please to call it so, a voluntary, and therefore precarious, acquiescence in the people.[26]

The breaking of the custom or civil habits, for Hume, is very dangerous. So the revolution, as a clamorous breaking of the civil habits of a people is also perilous. Speaking of the Glorious Revolution, Hume, always in that significant essay, argues:

> Let not the establishment at the *Revolution* deceive us, or make us so much in love with a philosophical origin to government, as to imagine all others monstrous and irregular. Even that event was far from corresponding to these refined ideas. It was only the succession, and that only in the regal part of the government, which was then changed.[27]

This means that there was popular consensus, but only acceptance of a change perpetrated by a few hundred individuals. And this is a refrain of the following traditionalist anti-revolutionary intellectuals.

Many scholars have minimised the political implications of custom in Hume. Some authoritative exceptions are represented

---

26   Hume, *Of the Original Contract*, pp. 468-469.
27   *Ibid.*, p. 472.

by Donald W. Livingston, to whom we will return later, who places the Humean idea of custom in the context of the tradition of political conservatism. He insists on Hume's deference to the world of inherited custom, which intercepts the philosophical core of the conservative intellectual tradition[28]. Annette Baier recognises that Hume is enforcing "community custom"[29] and that law and politics are about "customary rights and obligations"[30] but adds that "clearly the customary rules are not being regarded as sacrosanct by Hume"[31]. Other interpreters engage in a sort of actualisation of Hume's thought in contemporary political philosophy. First Terry Hoy, and then John C. Laursen, try to demonstrate that custom is not inherently conservative because there are, in Hume, some sources of change and progress. By comparing Hume's thought to the American twentieth-century philosopher John Dewey, Hoy sees Dewey's contribution to carry out Hume's project to provide a concern for the settlement of freedom and equality, not envisioned by the Scottish author[32]. Laursen shows that Dewey's assessment of the Humean political philosophy of custom finds implications in a progressive sense[33]. Christopher J. Berry recognises the central role of Hume's interpretation of custom and habit in Hume's thought as "that aspect of his writing that does seem to comport best with conservatism", and he considers it as an argument with which some twentieth-century political theorists create an "alternative to constructivism and technique"[34]. Custom, in Hume, accentuates "not only the issue of the genealogical derivation of peoples, but also the evident existence of a cultural

---

28 Livingston, 'On Hume's Conservatism', Hume Studies, 2 (November 1995), pp. 151-164.
29 Annette Baier, *The Cautious Jealous Virtue: Hume on Justice* (Cambridge: Harvard University Press, 2010), p. 54.
30 *Ibid.*, p. 59.
31 *Ibid.*, p. 92.
32 Terry Hoy, *Toward a Naturalistic Political Theory: Aristotle, Hume, Dewey, Evolutionary Biology, and Deep Ecology* (Westport: Praeger, 2000), pp. 43-67.
33 Laursen, 'David Hume on custom and habit and living with skepticism', Daímon. Revista Internacional de Filosofía, 52 (2011), pp. 87-99.
34 Berry, pp. 128-155.

divide, which was constantly elaborated at a philosophical level"[35] this is a topic, in Hume's political reflection, in which a more respectful connection to the words he himself uses is more helpful. Custom, for Hume, is an outcome of time aimed to give "solidity" to the "right" of the sovereigns, and provokes the inclination towards political action. Thereby, "time and custom give authority to all forms of government" and "that power, which at first was founded only on injustice and violence, becomes in time legal and obligatory"[36]. The Humean relation between time and custom has a direct impact on the legitimacy of the government. Through its gradual action on the minds of men, time leads individuals to reconcile themselves with any reasonable authority. It follows that the so-called "right to authority" is none other than "the constant possession of authority, maintain'd by the laws of society and the interests of mankind"[37].

As Giuseppe Giarrizzo noted, custom is not, for Hume, "a prison from which man aspires to escape, or a chain that he wants to break, but it is the rest to which he anxiously yearns"[38]. We naturally move from the disorder of the license to the order of the custom, and an acceptable policy can only support, however, not hinder this natural movement.

So, the "speculative reasoners"[39] of politics, which almost always correspond, in Hume's terminology, to the political rationalists, should not inquire with excessive curiosity about the government's origin; it would be better for them to submit themselves to the government of his nation and convince themselves that time is the only agent capable of guaranteeing the gradual settlement of the institutions. Rationalists' acritical submission to government, for Hume, would allow them, on the other hand, to understand that violent innovation is the most destructive disaster of the harmony gradually developed in the institutional structures. An

---

35 Silvia Sebastiani, *The Scottish Enlightenment. Race, Gender, and the Limits of Progress* (New York: Palgrave Macmillan, 2013), p. 10.
36 Hume, *Treatise*, p. 362.
37 *Ibid.*, p. 356.
38 Giuseppe Giarrizzo, *David Hume politico e storico* (Turin: Einaudi, 1962), p. 126.
39 Hume, *Essays*, pp. 90, 155, 171, 338.

excessive intellectual curiosity risks both losing that prudential attitude, dispassionately recommended by Hume in politics, and consequently intruding into the caprices of radicalism. Radical change that is produced by the "spirit of innovation", for Hume, is "in itself pernicious, however favourable its particular object may sometimes appear"[40], and rests on the slow and fruitful process of adapting institutions to social usefulness.

Hence the Humean reverence for political continuity, for which every single individual is born in some institutions that embody values and norms of behaviour representing his "time" and his "place", and concerning which he cannot pretend to be a foreigner. Despite the reality of this experience, the rationalist theorists do not hold back from inventing stories of social transformations and formulating hypotheses of abstract civilisations with which to transmit images of human beings conceived as "silk-worms". In *Of the Original Contract*, Hume shows no hesitation about this continuity:

> Did one generation of men – he asserts – go off the stage at once, and another succeed, as is the case with silk-worms and butterflies, the new race, if they had sense enough to choose their government, which surely is never the case with men, might voluntarily, and by general consent, establish their own form of civil polity, without any regard to the laws or precedents, which prevailed among their ancestors.[41]

Since politics is everything but the world of miracles, and above all, it is not the world of human perfectibility, Hume states, in another political essay, that the "sovereigns must take mankind as they find them, and cannot pretend to introduce any violent change in their principles and ways of thinking"[42]; and since, he insists in *Of the Original Contract*, the society of men is in a "perpetual flux", and "one man every hour going out of the world, another coming into it", it is essential that "the new brood should conform themselves to the established constitution, and nearly follow the

---

40 Hume, *Of the Coalition of Parties* (1758), in *Essays*, p. 496.
41 Hume, *Of the Original Contract*, p. 476.
42 Hume, *Of Commerce* (1752), in *Essays*, p. 260.

path which their fathers, treading in the footsteps of theirs, had marked out to them"[43].

The last passage makes Hume the true forerunner of political conservatism, for having anticipated the metaphor used forty years later by Edmund Burke, who is instead considered its initiator, for having seen through the utopian aura of the revolutionary ideologies. In repudiating French Revolution, Burke laid the basis for much of the vigorous conservative political movement that remained to this day: one that was adaptable and forward-thinking, but also aware of the debt people owe to past generations, and their duty to preserve and maintain the institutions they have inherited. For this Burke was "the first conservative"[44], as he is rightly called. It was "proper and indeed inevitable" for every conservative of modern and contemporary times to cite Burke, because, according to one of the most prominent American conservative authors of the twentieth century, Robert A. Nisbet, he was "the prophet – the Marx or the Mill – of conservatism, and it is a mark of his continuing prophetic status that he has been cited and otherwise recognized by conservatives during the last quarter of a century in Britain and America in a degree greater than in any comparable period before" [45].

In the *Reflections on the Revolution in France* (1790), Burke opposed the age of the "sophisters, economists, and calculators"[46], who considered men as insects destined to "become little better than the flies of a summer"[47]. Whoever governs a nation – Burke added under Hume's evident influence – should have firmly in mind that he is nothing more than a temporary owner of power, a tenant of it as

---

43 Hume, *Of the Original Contract*, pp. 476-477.
44 This is the expression used, since the title of the book, by Jesse Norman, *Edmund Burke: The First Conservative* (New York: Basic Books, 2013).
45 Robert A. Nisbet, *Conservatism: Dream and Reality* (1986), new edn. (London and New York: Routledge, 2002), p. 18.
46 Edmund Burke, *Reflections on the Revolution in France* (1790), in *Select Works of Edmund Burke*, ed. by Francis Canavan (Indianapolis: Liberty Fund, 1999), vol. 2, p. 89.
47 *Ibid.*, p. 112.

an entailed inheritance derived to us from our forefathers, and to be transmitted to our posterity; as an estate specially belonging to the people of this kingdom without any reference whatever to any other more general or prior right. By this means our constitution preserves an unity in so great a diversity of its parts. We have an inheritable crown; an inheritable peerage; and an house of commons and a people inheriting privileges, franchises, and liberties, from a long line of ancestors.[48]

These words precede, in Burke's work, the most famous affirmation of social continuity recorded in modern conservative political thought, understood as a "partnership not only between those who are living, but between those who are living, those who are dead, and those who are to be born"[49].

---

48 *Ibid.*, p. 38.
49 *Ibid.*, p. 114.

5. POLITICAL REALISM

Hume denies the existence of any hypothesis of contract at the origin of government. In opposition to the contractarian theories, by Whigs manipulated in order to justify the second English revolution (1688-89), in *Of the Origin of Government* (1777), Hume comes to affirm that he cannot exclude that the government originates "more casually and more imperfectly" and, above all, that probably "the first ascendant of one man over multitudes begun during a state of war", where "the superiority of courage and of genius discovers itself most visibly, where unanimity and concert are most requisite, and where the pernicious effects of disorder are most sensibly felt"[1].

These words open out a significant scenario not only in the Humean treatment of politics but also in the history of modern and contemporary political thought. What we have just read confirms Hume's realistic approach to politics.

Political realism is one of the great guidelines in which the tradition of Western-European political thought is orientated, since from the origin in Greece of political historiography. In this tradition or intellectual family, political thinkers such as Thucydides, Niccolò Machiavelli, Carl Schmitt, Gaetano Mosca, and Max Weber, to mention the most representative interpreters, were united, over the centuries, even in the apparent differences which separated them, from sharing a "realist" attitude, concerning the need to look at the human vicissitudes and affairs of politics with a disenchanted glance, under the guidance of the search for the Machiavellian "actual truth". In fact, the political realism of Machiavelli is understood as the ability "to go straight to the

---

1 Hume, *Of the Origin of Government* (1777), in *Essays*, pp. 39-40.

actual truth of matters rather than to a conception about it"[2]. The qualifying traits of a realist vision of politics are the scepticism towards too sudden changes, the emphasis on the elements of persistence, continuity, and stability, the attitudes of prudence and moderation, the inclination to consider the nature of man unchangeable and the eternal passions that dominate him[3]. These traits seem to be synthesised in Hume's approach.

The real state of nature, for Hume, is not a possible philosophical origin, but is the society itself, composed of institutions that satisfy personal interests and selfish impulses. The contract can also be valid as a simple belief that engages individual wills, but does not possess the absolute meaning assigned to it by natural lawyers. Political history of states clarifies that the origin of government is everything but a contract or pact produced by free human consent, and almost all governments currently existing were founded initially on "usurpation" or "conquest", or on, in one word, war.

In the *Treatise*, Hume clearly states that the genesis of political obligation cannot ignore the recognition that "if we remount to the first origin of every nation, we shall find, that there scarce is any race of kings, or form of a commonwealth, that is not primarily founded on usurpation and rebellion"[4]. It is, therefore, essential to acknowledge the legitimacy of political order as not deriving from its juridical form, which for Hume is a fiction, a product of imagination, but from war, that performs an originating function of power. The following words are emblematic: "I assert the first

---

[2] Niccolò Machiavelli, *The Prince* (1532), ed. by James B. Atkinson (Indianapolis and Cambridge: Hackett, 1976), p. 255.

[3] For a definition and an interpretation of political realism in the history of political thought, see James Burnham, *The Machiavellians: Defenders of Freedom* (London: Putnam, 1943); Sheldon S. Wolin, *Politics and Vision* (Boston: Little Brown and Company, 1960); Michael J. Smith, *Realist Thought form Weber to Kissinger* (Baton Rouge: Lousiana State University, 1986); Joel H. Rosenthal, *Righteous Realists* (Baton Rouge: Lousiana State University, 1991); Jonathan Haslam, *No Virtue Like Necessity: Realist Thought in International Relations since Machiavelli* (New Haven: Yale University Press, 2002); Alessandro Campi and Stefano De Luca, *Il realismo politico. Figure, concetti, prospettive di ricerca* (Soveria Mannelli: Rubbettino, 2014).

[4] Hume, *Treatise*, p. 356.

rudiments of government to arise from quarrels, not among men of the same society, but among those of different societies"[5].

War, not as a civil war or *bellum omnium contra omnes*, but as conquest by one society against another, brings out the need for an original authority, both political and military, which "naturally takes place in that civil government, which succeeds the military"[6]. It necessarily follows that the correct starting point in the analysis of the origins of power lies in the "fact" of civil government, and not in any theoretical hypothesis or conjecture about how civil government is to be justified. The political and military authority, in a system of conquest, appropriation, division, and distribution of physical space, defines the measure and order of the government, which therefore stands out as a need for social organisation on a military basis: military authority instructs men – Hume claims –

> in the advantages of government, and teaches them to have recourse to it, when either by the pillage of war, by commerce, or by any fortuitous inventions, their riches and possessions have become so considerable as to make them forget, on every emergency, the interest they have in the preservation of peace and justice.[7]

Civil government, in other words, follows the military government, even in its repositioning of the authority in one person. This conviction leads Hume to state that "camps are the true mothers of cities; and as war cannot be administered, by reason of the suddenness of every exigency, without some authority in a single person, the same kind of authority naturally takes place in that civil government, which succeeds the military"[8].

To strengthen his conviction about the origin of power from the war and his distance as much from contractarianism as from the theory of the divine right of kings, Hume also gives the example of the American tribes who lived peacefully without any government and submitted to a leader, or a chieftain, in Hume's terms, only in

---

5   *Ibid.*, p. 346.
6   *Ibid.*
7   *Ibid.*
8   *Ibid.*

time of war, which was a proof that the first governments, far from being patriarchal, were monarchists because they were military.

Similar arguments about the central theme of military force, exposed in his first work, are proposed again and coherently by Hume in his political essays, as confirmed by one of the most significant passages taken from *Of the Original Contract*, which is worth reporting here in full:

> Almost all the governments, which exist at present, or of which there remains any record in story, have been founded originally, either on usurpation or conquest, or both, without any pretence of a fair consent, or voluntary subjection of the people. When an artful and bold man is placed at the head of an army or faction, it is often easy for him, by employing, sometimes violence, sometimes false pretences, to establish his dominion over a people a hundred times more numerous than his partisans. He allows no such open communication, that his enemies can know, with certainty, their number or force. He gives them no leisure to assemble together in a body to oppose him. Even all those, who are the instruments of his usurpation, may wish his fall; but their ignorance of each other's intention keeps them in awe, and is the sole cause of his security. By such arts as these, many governments have been established; and this is all the *original contract*, which they have to boast of.[9]

A "state of war", real and not imaginary, in Hume's thinking, has given beginning to the first ascendant of one man over multitudes, because it is in the war that men discover "the superiority of courage and of genius" and perceive the "pernicious effects of disorder"[10].

These assumptions show, definitively, that Hume has no doubt in this respect. He says that it was the long protraction of that state to push the people into submission; and "if the chieftain possessed as much equity as prudence and valour, he became, even during peace, the arbiter of all differences, and could gradually, by a mixture of force and consent, establish his authority"[11]. The perceived benefit made the chieftain loved and respected by the people, and

---

9 Hume, *Of the Original Contract*, p. 471. Hume's italics.
10 Hume, *Of the Origin of Government*, pp. 39-40.
11 *Ibid.*, p. 40.

if his descendant enjoyed the same ability to influence people benevolently, the government arrived at perfection earlier than expected, even by rewards to virtuous citizens and punishments to the disobedient. Originally, every effort of his influence had to be particular and based on the circumstances produced by each case. But subsequently, "submission was no longer a matter of choice in the bulk of the community, but was rigorously exacted by the authority of the supreme magistrate"[12].

In light of these arguments, all praising an unmistakably realistic vision of the government's origin, the interpretations of those scholars, such as David Gauthier, for whom Hume is, in some respects, a contractarian[13], are far from convincing. Hume's arguments confirm the exact opposite.

He thinks that government is created by "force", not by a promise or consent, that it originated immediately out of necessity, and not by choice, and that "administration" is somewhat independent of the optional capability of subjects. The latter do not even imagine their consent may confer authority on the sovereign, but they willingly consent because of their belief in the fact that title derives from the sovereign's long possession. It was the "sensible utility" deriving from the intervention of the sovereign to make frequent and indispensable the exercise of his authority, and it was this necessary repetitiveness that generates a constant acquiescence in the people gradually. The pure reality of facts, and also "reason, history, and experience" show us that "in a settled constitution, their inclinations are often consulted; but during the fury of revolutions, conquests, and public convulsions, military force or political craft usually decides the controversy"[14]. Thus the origin of government is not consent or moral obligation, "conquest or usurpation, that is, in plain terms, force"; and military force, after the end of the ancient governments, is the origin "of almost all the new ones, which were ever established in the world", and "in the few cases, where consent may seem to have taken place, it was

---

12 *Ibid.*
13 See David Gauthier, 'David Hume, Contractarian', Philosophical Review, 1 (1979), pp. 3-38.
14 Hume, *Of the Original Contract*, p. 474.

commonly so irregular, so confined, or so much intermixed either with fraud or violence, that it cannot have any great authority"[15].

Hume's approach generates, in modern times, a devastating effect against the hypothesis of the *state of nature*, as it is formulated in the theories of the social contract, which tried to justify the rebellion against authority based on a philosophical fiction. The contractarian theorists are nothing, for Hume, but "reasoners" who articulate refined systems but who, would

> look abroad into the world, they would meet with nothing that, in the least, corresponds to their ideas, or can warrant so refined and philosophical a system. On the contrary, we find, every where, princes, who claim their subjects as their property, and assert their independent right of sovereignty, from conquest or succession. We find also, every where, subjects, who acknowledge this right in their prince, and suppose themselves born under obligations of obedience to a certain sovereign, as much as under the ties of reverence and duty to certain parents. These connexions are always conceived to be equally independent of our consent, in Persia and China; in France and Spain; and even in Holland and England, wherever the doctrines above-mentioned have not been carefully inculcated. Obedience or subjection becomes so familiar, that most men never make any enquiry about its origin or cause, more than about the principle of gravity, resistance, or the most universal laws of nature. Or if curiosity ever move them; as soon as they learn, that they themselves and their ancestors have, for several ages, or from time immemorial, been subject to such a form of government or such a family; they immediately acquiesce, and acknowledge their obligation to allegiance.[16]

Burke used Hume's same terminology to identify the government (or society) as a device that allows human wills to curb passions with restrictions that, along with freedoms, "vary with times and circumstances, and admit of infinite modifications, they cannot be settled upon any abstract rule; and nothing is so foolish as to discuss them upon that principle"[17].

Hume, as can be seen, rejects any hypothesis about the divine

---

15 *Ibid.*, pp. 473-474.
16 Hume, *Of the Original Contract*, pp. 469-470.
17 Burke, *Reflections on the Revolution in France*, p. 71.

or rationalistic origin of government and natural rights, arguing that all governments are always based on usefulness. Instead of basing the government on abstract and metaphysical principles, such as the Lockean concept of natural law, which destabilises the government's ability to guarantee utility and social loyalty, Hume emphasises the human qualities given as gifts by nature, such as the Aristotelian concept of human nature and attitude to organization family, persuaded that society first came into existence thanks to the natural human inclination to live socially, which over time has become a habit aimed at the best possible management of justice.

In this identification of the state of war as a legitimate origin of power, Hume precedes by two centuries the reflections that Schmitt, one of the most convinced continuators of Machiavellian political realism, develops in the first half of the twentieth century around the foundation of a city that makes "visible" the *nomos* "by which a tribe, a retinue, or a people becomes settled, i.e., by which it becomes historically situated and turns a part of the earth's surface into the force-field of a particular order"[18]. According to Schmitt, conquest, appropriation, and distribution, linked to government, recall the original meaning of the concept of *nomos*, that constitutive historical event which confers legitimacy to power, whose logic is entirely irreducible for the law. Schmitt described the *nomos* as "*a priori* to every legal, economic and social order", whose processes "were applied to and through the *land*"[19]. In Hume, synchronically, government and rules of justice are mutually indispensable and equally necessary.

Lastly, Hume's political realism derives from his critical attitude towards political utopianism. One of his essays that has remained more unexplored, because of the difficulty to classify it in the usual canons of modern historiography, is *Idea of a Perfect Commonwealth*, published for the first time in the collection of *Political Discourses* of 1752, and always added to subsequent

---

18 Carl Schmitt, *The Nomos of the Earth in the International Law of the Jus Publicum Europaeum* (1974), ed. by Gary L. Ulmen (New York: Telos Press, 2006), p. 70.
19 Stephen Legg and Alexander Vasudevan, *Introduction: Geographies of Nomos*, in Legg (ed. by), *Spatiality, Sovereignty and Carl Schmitt* (London and New York: Routledge, 2011), p. 2.

editions of the moral and political writings, up to the last edition of 1777[20]. Here, Hume comes to the culmination of an in-depth research on the object of political science that has characterised one of his first essays: *Whether the British Government Inclines More to Absolute Monarchy; or to a Republic?* (1741), in which he faced the dilemma of defining the contemporary political-institutional situation of Great Britain and tried to envisage some possible theoretical solutions.

In spite of the expectations that its title also creates, *Idea of a Perfect Commonwealth* is everything except the utopian dream of a model government, because of its solid principle from which Hume as an author will never derogate: men do not govern themselves with reason, but with the authority that comes from custom and from the moulding force of time. This overwhelms even the most perfect of speculations about politics. Consequently, the plan or "idea" of a "perfect commonwealth", as Hume calls it, is closely connected not so much to the mere intellectual need to theorise an abstract model of state, but to the search for a possible legal administration that responds effectively to the social and institutional distortions produced by the conflicting, unstable, and uncertain nature of the British mixed constitution. The latter, according to Hume, prevents England from developing as a real "nation", as can be seen from one of his essays of 1748, entitled *Of National Characters*, that was written in response to Montesquieu's *De l'esprit des lois* (1748), to whose climatic theory the Scot opposes the thesis of moral origin of national identities[21]:

> The English government – Hume writes – is a mixture of monarchy, aristocracy, and democracy. The people in authority are composed of gentry and merchants. All sects of religion are to be found among them. And the great liberty and independency, which every man enjoys, allows him to display the manners peculiar to him. Hence the

---

20 Hume, *Essays and Treatises on Several Subjects* (London and Edinburgh: printed for T. Cadell, A. Donaldson, and W. Creech, 1777), 2 vols.
21 A useful analyses of the dialogue between Hume and Montesquieu is Sebastiani, pp. 23-43.

English, of any people in the universe, have the least of a national character; unless this very singularity may pass for such.[22]

This awareness about the fragility of English institutions allows Hume to overcome his usual reluctance towards rationalist generalisations, which derives from his political scepticism, and to elaborate the best possible form of government, although never achievable. It is perhaps the real reason why his scepticism does not degenerate into a "complete nihilism"[23]. Hume offers to his readers the possibility to look at the perfect commonwealth, not as political organisation emerged by any revolution, nor as a proposal for a radical democratization of present or future worlds, but as an intellectual attempt to prevent the advent of tyranny and preserve authority by improving the conditions for the development of freedom in modern society.

Without any kind of normativism in terms of political practice, in this essay, Hume even seems to strengthen his anti-utopianism. In fact, in identifying what for him are the most influential works in the history of political utopianism, namely Plato's *Republic*, Thomas More's *Utopia*, and James Harrington's *Oceana*, Hume argues that to unite all three of these utopian authors was the attitude to design ideal political structures arising from the conception of the mutability of human nature. Plato and More, in particular, started from the theoretical assumption that the egoistic nature of man and the institution of private property could be transformed with the implementation of educational measures. Hume asserts he is in total disagreement, considering the vision of Plato unrealistic and that of More imaginary. He also warns against optimism about educational programmes as a corrective measure of the society's vices that underlie their utopian government projects, which "suppose great reformation in the manners of mankind" and "are plainly imaginary"[24]. Hume concludes that the works of Plato and More are mainly of this whimsical nature, while Harrington's is "the only valuable model of a commonwealth, that has yet been

---

22 Hume, *Of National Characters* (1748), in *Essays*, p. 207.
23 In this regard, see Ryu Susato, *Hume's Sceptical Enlightenment* (Edinburgh: Edinburgh University Press, 2015), pp. 177-180.
24 Hume, *Idea of a Perfect Commonwealth* (1752), p. 514.

offered to the public"²⁵. Despite this appreciation, Hume, however, disapproves of Harrington's claim to pursue social harmony through a commonwealth based on the division of property, agrarian law, and rotation of the judiciary following legal systems aimed at limiting the natural tension between rich and poor.

Hume's arguments on the ideal form of government, and the political projectors, are strictly limited to the theoretical structure of a political organisation, that is to say, beyond any need for education or property reforms. When he asserts that "popular government may be imagined more perfect than absolute monarchy, or even than our present constitution", Hume does not allude to the imagination of certain social habits, to more or less usual manners, but explicitly invites us to beware of the utopian designs centred on the modification of fundamental social structures, starting from that of private property, even if "private property seems to me almost as secure in a civilized European monarchy, as in a republic"²⁶.

---

25 *Ibid.*
26 Hume, *Of Civil Liberty* (1758), in *Essays*, pp. 92-93.

6. AN ADMIRER OF MACHIAVELLI

Some considerations, to better understand the kind of political realism of Hume, must be made on his relationship with Machiavelli, who is notoriously the father of modern political realism. In Humean historiography – not so rich in numerical terms but rather dense for the quality of the proposed critical studies – the interpretative approach of the American scholar Frederik G. Whelan stands out. For Whelan, the Machiavellian part of Hume's thinking denotes a marked sense of the limits of the rationality in social life and a style of political theory, which is part of that tradition of thought, from Isaiah Berlin to Stuart Hampshire, from Judith Shklar to Bernard Williams, which combines ethical commitment and a sense of possibility, contingency, and prudence. This tradition of thought was inaugurated by Machiavelli and continued by Hume[1].

The connections between Machiavelli and Hume were traced, already in the 1960s, by Giuseppe Giarrizzo, who saw them also united by a certain "conservatism"[2]. But the Italian scholar strangely did not analyse in-depth this characterizing element of Hume's political thought. Giarrizzo was followed, after about three decades, by Josef Maček, according to whom Hume shared the views of Machiavelli by emphasising the interests of men and on the history of humanity, in which Hume found an important ethical element, and in this relationship he commended Machiavelli[3]. The

---
1   See Frederick G. Whelan, *Hume and Machiavelli: Political Realism and Liberal Thought* (Lanham: Lexington Books, 2004).
2   Giarrizzo, p. 20.
3   Josef Maček, *Machiavelli e il machiavellismo* (Florence: La Nuova Italia, 1980), p. 301-302. Philippe Saltel, in 'Machiavel himself...: Hume et le "secrétaire de Florence'', Revue Fhilosophique, 1 (2008),

interpretations in the Anglo-American area were decisive. For John G. A. Pocock, the real *trait d'union* between the two authors was their anticlerical ruling[4]; David F. Norton focused on the unmistakable Machiavellian inspiration of some passages from the third book of Hume's *Treatise*, which recall some pieces from the first chapter of *Discourses on the First Decade of Titus Livius* (1531), concerning the sovereign's need to act contrary to the religion and conventional morality[5].

In an attempt to revisit these interpretations, after an in-depth reading of Hume's entire intellectual production, including his numerous letters and the so-called "minor" writings, it was possible to conclude that Hume's knowledge of Machiavelli, who he had already read before the writing of *Treatise* and in Italian language, went beyond the Florentine's principal works, and included less-known writings, such as the *Portrait of French Affairs* (1510), in which the author elevated France to an example of the modern state, insisting on the link between the prosperity of the monarchy and the process of national unification, and *Clizia* (1525), dedicated to the subjective character of beauty.

Machiavelli is never mentioned in Hume's *Treatise*, but is remembered in the second *Enquiry* and in the different editions of his moral and political essays, with several references in the discussion of juridical-political issues and, above all, in the recovery of typically Machiavellian concepts, such as faction, popular militia, and mixed government, which often lead Hume to recognise the importance of the political reflection of an author whom he has no difficulty in placing on the same level as Shaftesbury, Harrington, and Locke.

Hume's intellectual esteem for Machiavelli is not surprising if we look at the very similar way in which both focus on the object of politics: firm opposition to the philosophical lesson on the political "ideal" and unconditional preference for the interpretation of reality against any utopian model, in which

---

    pp. 31-42, speaks about "comparable elaborations" by Hume and Machiavelli about the nature of the political body.
4   Pocock, *The Machiavellian Moment*, pp. 493-7.
5   Norton, *Annotations*, in Hume, *A Treatise of Human Nature*, p. 551-5.

lies the extraordinary originality of the Machiavellian attack on the prevailing moral assumptions of his age. Even for Hume, a perfect political community is a utopic ideal that is typical of those purely imaginary government projects with which we want to envisage significant reforms in the customs of men. This Humean statement that we have already had the opportunity to mention earlier about the works of Plato, More, and Harrington is set out in perfect Machiavellian style. It depends on the original idea of the government as an organization that cannot destroy the order of things according to an abstractly constructed model because of the impossibility to estimate the damages that could occur.

Hume welcomes Machiavelli's proposal of a new method of analysis, as an outcome of a new vision of the world, that is the primacy of phenomenological observation on gnoseological intuitionism, ultimately of empiricism, which thanks to Hume has reached the peak of its success for having undressed it of the Hobbesian matrix of ontological presuppositions, of the Lockian rationalist component, and of the religious elements of which Berkeley had characterised it, and having covered it with a scepticism that ends up emptying the same modern philosophical reason of content.

The realism of Hume entails the consequent aversion to both ideal theorizing and political ideology, based on the abstract principle that politics has to do with the worst things rather than the best, and a ruler should consider the world and the people who inhabit it as they really are, which consciously takes up that actual truth of things on the basis of which Machiavelli disputed against the imaginary representations of " republics and princedoms which have never in fact been seen or known to exist"[6]. It was Machiavelli's intention to reach the affirmation of politics as politics and the recognition of the autonomy of politics from any finalism of either a theological or moral nature.

The Machiavellism of Hume also emerges from his conception of fortune. In the *History of England*, he ascribes political calamities to the immense empire of chance on men and political success to good luck as well as character and talent. If in Machiavelli

---

6   *Ibid.*

fortune refers to the range of unpredictable and ever-changing circumstances in which political leaders are called to make difficult but necessary decisions, in Hume "fortune commonly favours the bold and enterprizing; and nothing inspires us with more boldness than a good opinion of ourselves"[7].

Hume makes the teaching of Machiavelli his own, and Machiavelli appears to him as a "certainly a great genius"[8] capable also of "eternal political truths, which no time nor accidents can vary"[9], but not entirely immune to criticism for some of his fallacious analyses, such as that about the nature of monarchist governments. The judgment of Hume, in this regard, is unequivocal:

> Having confined – he observes in *Of Civil Liberty* – his study to the furious and tyrannical governments of ancient times, or to the little disorderly principalities of Italy, his reasonings especially upon monarchical government, have been found extremely defective; and there scarcely is any maxim in his *Prince*, which subsequent experience has not entirely refuted.[10]

Hume's debt to the Florentine author is revealed above all thanks to the emphasis on power and, against any abstract logical formulation, on concreteness, personal and public interest, ambition of the leaders, need for prudence as a guide of government, and usefulness[11]. The latter by Machiavelli was elevated according to judgments on the things of politics, before which even the "common good" succumbs to become "common" usefulness, consisting in " which consist in the power to enjoy what is our own, openly and undisturbed, in having to feel no anxiety for the

---

7   Hume, *Treatise*, p. 381.
8   Hume, *Of Civil Liberty*, p. 88.
9   Hume, *That Politics may be reduced to a Science* (1741), in *Essays*, p. 21.
10 Hume, *Of Civil Liberty*, p. 88.
11 For an in-depth analysis of the political conntections between Hume and Machiavelli, see my essay *Il Machiavelli di David Hume*, in Piero Innocenti and Marielisa Rossi (ed. by), *Bibliografia delle edizioni di Niccolò Machiavelli: 1506-1914* (Manziana: Vecchiarelli, 2018), pp. 9-25.

honour of wife or child, nor any fear for personal safety"[12]. And it is based on usefulness that, also for Hume, the government is constituted. In fact, in the second *Enquiry* he states:

> The rules of equity or justice depend entirely on the particular state and condition, in which men are placed, and owe their origin and existence to that utility, which results to the public from their strict and regular observance. Reverse, in any considerable circumstance, the condition of men: Produce extreme abundance or extreme necessity: Implant in the human breast perfect moderation and humanity, or perfect rapaciousness and malice: By rendering justice totally *useless*, you thereby totally destroy its essence, and suspend its obligation upon mankind.[13]

To the idea of usefulness, already discussed in previous pages, Hume recurs punctually also in the second *Enquiry*, when he must respond to the most profound questions about the need for positive law and the reduction of natural freedom, since in it he sees the sole foundation of the duty of obedience, the only one capable of preserving peace and order among men, as in this case:

> When a number of political societies are erected, and maintain a great intercourse together, a new set of rules are immediately discovered to be *useful* in that particular situation; and accordingly take place under the title of LAWS of NATIONS. Of this kind are, the sacredness of the person of ambassadors, abstaining from poisoned arms, quarter in war, with others of that kind, which are plainly calculated for the *advantage* of states and kingdoms, in their intercourse with each other.[14]

Moreover, the recognition – from the clear Machiavellian imprint – of the excellent uniformity between the actions of men, in all nations and in all ages, and of the immutability of human nature emerges above all from the first *Enquiry*, in which Hume, among other things, warns the men of his time from certain

---

12 Machiavelli, *Discourses on the First Decade of Titus Livius* (1531), trans. by Ninian H. Thomson (London: Kegan Paul, Trench and Co., 1883), p. 79.
13 Hume, *An Enquiry Concerning the Principles of Morals*, pp. 23-24.
14 *Ibid.*, p. 35. Hume's italics.

idealizations of human nature and the consequent dreams of political redemption with these words:

> Mankind are so much the same, in all times and places, that history informs us of nothing new or strange in this particular. Its chief use is only to discover the constant and universal principles of human nature, by shewing men in all varieties of circumstances and situations, and furnishing us with materials, from which we may form our observations, and become acquainted with the regular springs of human action and behaviour.[15]

The theme of the imperfectness and immutability of human nature, with which the preservation of social relations will be punctually justified, was, in Machiavelli, something rather characteristic, if not almost obsessive, especially when it tends to include the uniformity of the affairs of the government:

> Anyone comparing – Machiavelli claimed in his *Discourses on the First Decade of Titus Livius* – the present with the past will soon perceive that in all cities and in all nations there prevail the same desires and passions as always have prevailed; for which reason it should be an easy matter for him who carefully examines past events, to foresee those which are about to happen in any republic, and to apply such remedies as the ancients have used in like cases; or finding none which have been used by them, to strike out new ones, such as they might have used in similar circumstances.[16]

As for Machiavelli, even for Hume, the disenchanted vision of humanity is a fundamental condition for the good governance of men.

Hume's stance offers other connections with Machiavelli, such as that on the genesis of the idea of *dishonesty*, which brings Hume closer to the well-known anthropological pessimism with which Machiavelli opposed the "sermons" on the ethical ideals of modernity, the emphasis on passions that limit the power of reason, and the understanding of the realist historian as more interested in the facts than in the feelings of guilt or praise.

---

15 Hume, *An Enquiry Concerning Human Understanding*, p. 60.
16 Machiavelli, *Discourses*, p. 140.

However, some disconnections are easily perceived, as in the understanding of commerce in the modern nation. On this topic, Hume's distance from Machiavelli is given by the perspective of the modernist historian who perceives the impracticability of the Machiavellian project of a revival of the glories of the Roman Empire. Modern European monarchies, especially France, for Hume, have become civilised mainly because of the changes made to the modern economy and the innovations introduced by the culture based on civil liberty inaugurated by commerce. The premise of freedom, therefore, is modern commerce, which – as Hume observes – has taken flight in modern European free states, particularly in the Italian city republics, to then be emulated everywhere by European monarchies, of which Machiavelli still knew nothing. Hume assigns a decisive role to the merchant in terms of harmonious civilisation and maintenance of a lasting peace between nations. An open communication between nations, especially among neighbouring ones, always produces peaceful relations and cooperation, just as within the borders of the state, the market creates peaceful relations between the actors of the exchange. The arts and sciences, to develop and prosper, need freedom, and nothing is more favourable to the birth of civilisation than several independent and neighbouring states, connected by trade and politics. In *Of the Rise and Progress of the Arts and Sciences* (1742), Hume claims that the exchange and the mutual knowledge stimulate that spirit of jealous emulation, which is essential in the arts[17]. In the same work, perhaps in an attempt to overcome the Machiavellian idea of a new empire, he produces an interesting theory about the dimensions of the state, from which the problem of freedom depends. Hume writes:

> Extended governments, where a single person has great influence, soon become absolute; but small ones change naturally into commonwealths. A large government is accustomed by degrees to tyranny; because each act of violence is at first performed upon a part, which, being distant from the majority, is not taken notice of, nor excites any violent ferment. [...] In a small government, any act of

---

17 See Hume, *Of the Rise and Progress of the Arts and Sciences* (1742), in *Essays*, pp. 111-137.

oppression is immediately known throughout the whole: The murmurs and discontents, proceeding from it, are easily communicated: And the indignation arises the higher, because the subjects are not apt to apprehend in such states, that the distance is very wide between themselves and their sovereign.[18]

Therefore, the exchange and mutual knowledge, for Hume, stimulate that spirit of emulation so essential to the arts, but there is also a problem concerning the territorial extension. The territorial extent directly corresponds to the degree of difficulty for citizens to control the abuses of government[19].

In a remarkable note of Hume's *Memoranda* (1729-40), which has not yet been explored by scholars, Hume underlined that "there is not a Word of Trade in all Matchiavel, which is strange considering that Florence rose only by Trade"[20]. Perhaps Machiavelli was worried about a huge political growth of Florence's most powerful merchant family, that of the Medici, capable of conquering and maintaining power precisely because of its wealth[21].

Therefore, for Hume, Machiavelli's political science is obsolete because it is based on an outdated vision of pre-commercial policy. The old idea of politics based on the model of imperial Rome, together with the dense literature that accompanied it, appears

---

18 *Ibid.*, pp. 119-120.
19 On this topic, some Italian scholars have observed that, for Hume, from the extension of the state's territory derives a sort of incentive to arbitrary government, which involves huge public expenditures and the cult of pomp typical of absolutism; see Luigi M. Bassani and Alberto Mingardi, *Dalla Polis allo Stato. Introduzione alla Storia del pensiero politico* (Turin: Giappichelli, 2017), p. 126.
20 Mossner, 'Hume's Early Memoranda, 1729-1740: The Complete Text', Journal of the History of Ideas, 4 (October, 1948), p. 508.
21 In the first half of the twentieth century, also Gaetano Mosca became aware of Machiavelli's reluctance to consider trade as an important element of political civilisation. Comparing Machiavelli to Botero, Mosca found Botero more significant for his theories in favor of trade. See Gaetano Mosca, *Il "Principe" di Machiavelli quattro secoli dopo la morte del suo autore* (Rome: Tipografia Il Popolo d'Italia, 1927). As regards Mosca's interpretation of Machiavelli, see Gennaro M. Barbuto, *Machiavelli e i totalitarismi* (Naples: Guida, 2005).

quite chimerical in modern times because of the changes made to the nature of the modern monarchical government.

In conclusion, Hume maybe even "the Scottish Machiavelli", as the editor of *Sister Peg*, the satirical pamphlet written by him in 1760 against William Pitt the Elder recounting the political relations between England (John Bull) and Scotland (Sister Peg), called him[22]. Hume remains an admirer of the Machiavellian realist method, but at the same time, he rejects the content of those Florentine assumptions that result irrelevant in his time. More precisely, Hume considers any attempt to extrapolate uncritically some concept form ancient political culture and use it in modern politics as unnecessary. In the meantime, the world changed, and also contents of political science improved. Therefore, trying to adapt generalizations of ancient political practice to modern situations is an error as well as a risk to stability of government.

---

[22] David R. Raynor, *Introduction* to *Sister Peg: A Pamphlet Hitherto Unknown by David Hume*, ed. by Raynor (Cambridge: Cambridge University Press, 1982), p. 29.

7. GOVERNMENT IS AN OPINION

To affirm, for Hume, that the origin of political power is in no way attributable to some voluntary and rational consensus, does not mean to conceive consensus as a request by the government that its subjects agree with its existence: this would mean passing an obviousness by social agreement, distorting the element of truth also contained in the idea of contract, namely government as founded on something other than mere coercion.

Hume evidently recognises that force, like consensus, cannot guarantee the continued use of authority and power, which is required to ensure order and political stability. Hence Hume's realistic acknowledgement of opinion as a fundamental reason for the government legitimacy.

The theme of opinion is continuously present throughout Hume's political production, reflecting the fact that his research on what constitutes the actual cement of political order leads him to discover that it is not possible to establish the link between governed and sovereigns neither on a hypothetical original contract, nor on the constitutionalist ground or the fundamental laws. A passage of *Of the First Principles of Government* (1741) is indicative of the mysterious, "wonderful" outcome of this research:

> Nothing appears more surprising to those, who consider human affairs with a philosophical eye, than the easiness with which the many are governed by the few; and the implicit submission, with which men resign their own sentiments and passions to those of their rulers. When we enquire by what means this wonder is effected, we shall find, that, as force is always on the side of the governed, the governors have nothing to support them but opinion. It is therefore, on opinion only that government is founded; and this maxim extends

to the most despotic and most military governments, as well as to the most free and most popular.[1]

In undertaking to explain the basis of government power, Hume marvels at the fact that the few with power govern the many rests on the opinion of the governed, who obey because "they believe the government operates in their interest as individuals, that is, the interest they share with all members of the public"[2].

However, a less superficial reading that takes into account all Humean intellectual production, and not only the *Treatise*, allows us to establish that his input to the enhancement of opinion in politics is much more critical and thoughtful. In hindsight Humean treatment of opinion reveals itself as an integral part of the strategy of avoiding the revolution by showing publicly the danger, as well as the historical and philosophical inconsistency, of any attempt to overcome the traditional order and contractual and egalitarian foundation of political power. It is, therefore, worth focusing on this specific and original topic of Hume's political thought.

In Hume's thought, politics takes place within a history of opinions[3]. *Ferment*, *clamour*, *currents*, *tides*, and *streams* are some of the terms used by Hume to describe the functioning of opinion in politics, as the peculiar property of travelling quickly from one individual to another. Fluxes of opinion are of particular interest to Hume in his efforts to defend the world of letters from dangerous political systems.

Where Hume affirms, in the aforementioned essay, that "as force is always on the side of the governed, the governours have nothing to support them but opinion"[4], he indeed supposes that opinion is something more than its conventional meaning, and invests

---

[1] Hume, *Of the First Principles of Government* (1741), in *Essays*, p. 32.
[2] John B. Stewart, *Opinion and Reform in Hume's Political Philosophy* (Princeton: Princeton University Press, 1992), p. 170.
[3] On the role of opinion in Hume's political thought, in addition to Stewart's previously mentioned work, see Whelan, *Order and Artifice in Hume's Political Philosophy* (Princeton: Princeton University Press, 1985); Dario Castiglione, *Dell'opinione. Riflessioni ai margini della teoria politica di David Hume* (Palermo: Mazzone, 1988); Nicholas Phillipson, *Hume* (New York: St. Martin's Press, 1989).
[4] Hume, *Of the First Principles of Government*, p. 32.

the reflection about the genesis of the modern state and authority in general directly. Indeed, after a careful analysis, it cannot be overlooked that Hume's opinion as a foundation of government represents an exciting chapter in the history of modern concepts of public opinion and legitimacy. The same reasons that led Hume to deal with the problems of politics are to be found in his ambition not so much to affect how British society is governed, as to orient public opinion.

Even in the ambiguous meaning of opinion, Hume could not fail to record an evolution. Between the end of the seventeenth and the beginning of the eighteenth centuries, in the philosophical discussions based on the meaning inherited by the ancients who had opposed the *doxa* (belief) to the *episteme* (science), opinion meant the beliefs of the ordinary people associated with superstitions and prejudices. After Hobbes, in the seventh chapter of Book I of *Leviathan* (1651), denied opinion any value in scientific discourse, recognizing only a form of "conditional knowledge, or knowledge of the consequence of words"[5], Voltaire, in the *Dictionnaire Philosophique* (1764), making a difference between opinion and reason, still wrote that opinion is traceable only in backward populations and comes to this conclusion: "Opinion is called the queen of the world; it is so: for when reason opposes it, it is condemned to death. It must rise twenty times from its ashes, to gradually drive away the usurper"[6].

A first, significant conceptual variation was made by Locke, who in *Essay Concerning Human Understanding* (1689) identified a real law of opinion or reputation, which embodied the sovereignty by the collective exercised over its members in the practice of conformism. The latter, for Locke, was more pervasive than divine law:

---

[5] Thomas Hobbes, *Leviathan* (1651), ed. by John C. A. Gaskin (Oxford and New York: Oxford University Press, 1998), p. 43. In this regard, Hobbes adds: "If the definitions be not rightly joined together into syllogisms, then the end or conclusion, is again opinion, namely of the truth of Opinion. Somewhat said, though sometimes in absurd and senseless words, without possibility of being understood" (*Ibid.*).

[6] Voltaire, *A Philosophical Dictionary* (1764), trans. anon. (Boston: Mendum, 1852), vol. 2, p. 179.

The greatest part whereof he shall find to govern themselves chiefly, if not solely, by this law of fashion; and so they do that which keeps them in reputation with their company, little regard the laws of God or the magistrate. The penalties that attend the breach of God's laws some, nay, perhaps most men seldom seriously reflect on; and amongst those that do, many, whilst they break the law, entertain thoughts of future reconciliation and making their peace for such breaches. And as to the punishments due from the laws of the commonwealth, they frequently flatter themselves with the hopes of impunity. But no man escapes the punishment of their censure and dislike who offends against the fashion and opinion of the company he keeps and would recommend himself to.[7]

D'Alembert, in the introductory speech of the *Encyclopaedia*, exalted the philosophy that is opposed to the sophistry of Scholasticism, and began to pose the problem of the foundation of a social dimension of public opinion:

[The theologians] were not content to require a legitimate submission to our mysteries. They tried to elevate their individual opinions into dogmas. And it was these opinions themselves, far more than the dogmas, which they wanted to make secure. They would by this means have inflicted the most terrible blow upon religion, had religion been the work of man.[8]

Hume, who established solid friendships with D'Alembert when he served as ambassador's secretary in Paris, in the 1760s, seems to be influenced by this review of opinion. In his political writings, when he speaks of opinion, he does not refer to the set of irrational, passionate, and violent beliefs, which he calls "superstitions" or "enthusiasm", but to the well-defined product of civilisation and commercial society. Also, this use of *opinion* in the positive context of development of peoples' ways, of refinement of arts and customs, derives from the pioneering political use by Hume of this term, that raises it to a decisive factor regarding the influence of rational convictions on the government of public affairs.

---

7   Locke, *An Essay Concerning Human Understanding*, p. 300.
8   Jean Le Rond d'Alembert, *Preliminary Discourse* to the *Encyclopedia of Diderot* (1751), ed. by Richard N. Schwab (Chicago and London: The University of Chicago Press, 1995), p. 72.

Hume's maxim on opinion as the foundation of government seems to be taken up by the famous *Essay upon the Original and Nature of Government*, dated 1672 and published eight years later, by William Temple, who developed an articulated theory of the role of opinion in politics. For Temple, government cannot stand on force that is on the side of the governed. Therefore, it is on opinion that Temple came to found the government. The strength of opinion, for that author, was the real foundation of the whole government, and the opinion itself was stronger than power or weapons because it could inspire an unsatisfied people to overthrow mercenary armies and even to subvert soldiers. He wrote that "power, arising from strength, is always in those that are governed, who are many: but authority, arising from opinion, is in those that govern, who are few"[9].

But while Temple, who was not "a straightforward champion of the ancients, although he was ranked on that side in the *querelle des anciens et des modernes*"[10], assigned to opinion a passive character as a "law of habit", a mere appendage of custom, which registered the authority (or reputation) of the sovereigns, identifying, in the opposition he created between authority and power, synonymous with force, the same opinion in authority, Hume considers it in its active dimension[11]. From Temple, who is an author that he knows well and cites in his works, Hume recovers the critical reading of non-historical hypotheses of the founding of government in the borders, even if he does not share the excessive emphasis on the natural process of foundation taken up by the Aristotelian tradition of *entelechy*. The argument used by Hume tends to enhance the centrality of opinion in the dynamics of government conservation,

---

9   William Temple, *Essay upon the Original and Nature of Government* (1670), in *The Works of William Temple* (Edinburgh: Printed for G. Hamilton, J. Balfour, A. Kincaid and A. Donaldson, L. Hunter, W. Gordon, J. Yair and C. Wright; Glasgow: A. Stalker, 1754), vol. 2, p. 34.

10 Susato, pp. 60-61.

11 On this topic see Castiglione, *Opinion's Metamorphosis: Hume and the Perception of Public Authority*, in Castiglione and Lesley Sharpe (ed. by), *Shifting the Boundaries, Transformations of the Languages of Public and Private in the Eighteenth Century* (Exeter: University of Exeter Press, 1995), pp. 152-166.

a centrality that has not only a rhetorical value aimed at highlighting the customary and prescriptive nature of power but introduces new elements once again from the perspective of political realism.

Hume distinguishes different types of interrelated opinions, in the sense that they do not operate in isolation but only in a one-to-one relationship between them: "opinion of interest" and "opinion of right". Opinion of interest is, for Hume, the sense of the general advantage which is gathered from government; when this opinion prevails in a state, or among those who have the power in their hands, it gives high security to any government. Opinion of right, for Hume, is of two kinds: "right to power and right to property", and what prevalence opinion of the first kind has over humankind may easily be understood by observing the attachment which all nations have to their ancient government. Antiquity always produces the opinion of right, and whatever damaging sentiments we may entertain of humankind, "they are always found to be prodigal both of blood and treasure in the maintenance of public justice"[12]. With opinions "of interest" Hume indicates both the sureness of the men in the present government and their conviction in the fact that no other government in place of *this* government would satisfy the same benefits; opinions "of right" is referred to the ideas of personal or traditional authority that still maintain a considerable persuasive force about the subjection to power of a given government. A special place in this discussion Hume reserves for the opinions of "right to property", which are a variation of Harrington's materialistic view that "power follows property"[13], as a driving force for social change. In *The Commonwealth of Oceana* (1656), Harrington supposed that this power resides purely in physical possession of a piece of land, and the equal division of property among successors will thus redistribute the related power accordingly. Hume, in contrast to Harrington, states that a gap remains between economic and political power, because political power does not rest directly upon the real balance of property, but

---

12 Hume, *Of the First Principles of Government*, p. 33.
13 James Harrington, *The Commonwealth of Oceana and a System of Politics* (1656), ed. by Pocock (Cambridge: Cambridge University Press, 1992), p. 60.

rather upon the opinion held about it. A government "may endure for several ages, though the balance of power, and the balance of property do not coincide"[14]. Hume rejects the idea of the balance of power founded on that of property, starting from the conviction that power is not always distributed, as Harrington stated, along lines of division of property between individuals and groups, but is built on flexible bases of loyalty and obedience to the government, upon which opinions exercise a direct influence, to a greater extent than property and interest, since it possesses characteristics that are most suited to the levels of subjectivity and objectivity. For Hume, power consists not only of its physical manifestation in the ownership of property, but also of psychological, historical, and cultural elements[15].

Proof of flexibility of opinion, in Hume's treatment, is that these different types of opinions are, in turn, modified by secondary principles such as selfishness, fear, and affection. Governments are based not on just one of these types of opinion; indeed, political power is a complex mechanism both because no single principle ever prevails, and the subjective perception always mediates the interests with which it relates that people have of them. Therefore, it is precisely this flexibility that explains why Hume prefers the concept of opinion to others. In fact, it allows him to overcome the traditional antitheses that characterise the political debate of his time, such as that between monarchy and republic, on which he does not fail to intervene, declaring that, although the republican form of government is to be preferred, Europe's great civilised monarchies guarantee more excellent stability, peace, and justice[16].

Opinion is adaptable to all forms of government. The maxim according to which the government is founded on opinion – Hume claims – "extends to the most despotic and most military

---

14 Hume, Of *the First Principles of Government*, p. 35.
15 See, on this specific topic, James Moore, 'Hume's Political Science and the Classical Republican Tradition', Canadian Journal of Political Science, 4 (1977), p. 816.
16 This is, in summary, the assessment expressed by Pocock, *Virtue, Commerce, and History: Essays on Political Thought and History, Chiefly in the Eighteenth Century* (Cambridge and New York: Cambridge University Press, 1985), pp. 125-141.

governments, as well as to the most free and most popular"[17]; and he immediately adds:

> The soldan of Egypt, or the emperor of Rome, might drive his harmless subjects, like brute beasts, against their sentiments and inclination: But he must, at least, have led his mamalukes, or praetorian bands, like men, by their opinion.[18]

The real reason why the Humean maxim is adaptable to all forms of government, including despotic ones, is that in these latter regimes the sovereign depends on the support of the army and police forces, which he must necessarily drive as men, caring about their opinions, since the sovereign's "power, being founded on opinion, can never subvert other opinions, equally rooted with that of his title to dominion"[19].

This does not mean that Hume does not grasp the differences between the forms of government. He admits that those founded on consensus guarantee a better preservation of civil liberties, and as such are to be preferred. This shows only Hume's attention to those despotic forms of government that existed and that opinion allowed him to explain better than brute force and consensus could do. To affirm that the opinion maxim applies to despotic governments means to establish the impossibility for every kind of political regime to govern against the feelings and inclinations of their subjects. As he states in *Of Commerce*, the best policy for a government is to recognise the presence of opinions within the people of the governed: "It is his best policy to comply with the common bent of mankind, and give it all the improvements of which it is susceptible"[20].

The maintenance of state, in other words, cannot depend only on the action of the government and the passive obedience of people, and the latter is not only a society founded on the division of labour and the circulation and exchange of goods, but it is also the network of different opinions, which are systems of beliefs

---

17   Hume, *Of the First Principles of Government*, p. 32.
18   *Ibid.*, pp. 32-33.
19   Hume, *Of the Origin of Government*, p. 40.
20   Hume, *Of Commerce*, p. 260.

and convictions. An inappropriate elimination of these forms of communication and social subordination would be detrimental to the government in the case of their opposition to it. Government that does not pay attention to the treatment of social opinions risks undermining the structure on which its legitimacy rests. Religion, for example, is "commonly found to be a very intractable principle", but "other principles or prejudices frequently resist all the authority of the civil magistrate; whose power, being founded on opinion, can never subvert other opinions, equally rooted with that of his title to dominion"[21].

Opinion allows Hume to resolve the opposition, also much debated in his time, between authority and freedom, among which – he admits – there is always a perennial struggle, open or secret, to such an extent that "neither of them can ever absolutely prevail in the contest"[22]. In this perpetual struggle, the formation of an opinion plays a leading role in an educational key, where it allows the configuration of a spirit of impartiality capable of mitigating the political bias of political factions, in part dictated by the unconditional trust in utopianism. Hence the importance by Hume assigned to the opinion in terms of the maintenance of that "gentle government", which is, for every aspect, "preferable, and gives the greatest security to the sovereign as well as to the subject"[23]. This is emphasised by Hume for its ability to guarantee the fruitful mediation between power and social stability, in the hope that the more people become accustomed to the discussion of public affairs, the more they will improve in their ability to judge them, and the more difficult it will be for them to seduced by idleness and by clamour and instinct of the vulgar.

Since all governments rest on opinion, "the units of political governance have no existence apart from the opinions and habits of those who live under them"[24]. So opinion comes into play as a foundation of government: the perception of the public interest as

---

21 Hume, *Of the Origin of Government*, p. 40.
22 *Ibid.*
23 Hume, *That Politics may be reduced to a Science*, p. 24.
24 Andrew Sabl, *Hume's Politics. Coordination and Crisis in the "History of England"* (Princeton and Oxford: Princeton University Press, 2012), p. 90.

established on specific rules of justice. People are generally born and live in societies subjected under certain forms of government; the opinions of these subjected individuals about the fact that their government can take care of their public interest and have the right to exercise its authority over them constitute the foundation of government itself.

The maxim of opinion was destined for some success in modern political thought. In particular, it exerted some influence on Burke. In several letters to his electors, Burke admitted that it is opinion that gives legitimacy to the power of Parliament through political parties, and shows that it never necessarily coincides with power. For Burke, opinion, that he often called "general opinion", was mostly a matter of social esteem that helped the transition from a state of nature to civil society, and carried with it an implicit consent to social and economic arrangements. In his political discourses, Burke explained the movement that leads from the general opinion to the formation of a "natural aristocracy", which is not a separate interest in a state. The following passage is quite explanatory:

> To be bred in a place of estimation; to see nothing low and sordid from one's infancy; to be taught to respect one's self; to be habituated to the censorial inspection of the public eye; to look early to public opinion; to stand upon such elevated ground as to be enabled to take a large view of the wide-spread and infinitely diversified combinations of men and affairs in a large society; to have leisure to read, to reflect, to converse [...]. To be led to a guarded and regulated conduct, from a sense that you are considered as an instructor of your fellow-citizens in their highest concerns, and that you act as a reconciler between God and man – to be employed as an administrator of law and justice, and to be thereby amongst the first benefactors to mankind – to be a professor of high science, or of liberal and ingenuous art [...]. These are the circumstances of men, that form what I should call a natural aristocracy, without which there is no nation.[25]

The meaning assigned by Burke to opinion is even more profound concerning, as it does, its direct relationship with government and

---

25 Burke, *Further Reflections on the Revolution in France* (1790), ed. by Daniel E. Ritchie (Indianapolis: Liberty Fund, 1992), pp. 168-169.

public affairs. He holds that the rights of government over people cannot be exercised without regard to the general opinion of those to be governed. In fact, in *A Letter to the Sheriffs of the City of Bristol on the Affairs of America* (1777), Burke writes:

> The general opinion is the vehicle, and organ of legislative omnipotence. Without this, it may be a theory to entertain the mind, but it is nothing in the direction of the affairs [...] In effect, to fellow not to force the publick inclination; to give a direction, a form, a technical dress, and a specifick sanction, to the general sense of the community, is the true end of legislature [...] It was our duty, in all soberness, to conform our government to the character and circumstances of the several people who compose this mighty and strangely diversified mass.[26]

Furthermore, according to some scholars, Hume's idea of opinion is destined to become the inspirational doctrine of the Founding Fathers of the United States of America, and to exercise a decisive influence on the greatest of *The Federalist* theorists, James Madison and Alexander Hamilton[27]. Since Hume demonstrates the abject inability of reason alone to guide philosophy toward truth, then he finds himself compelled to take account of the whole experiential horizon as context, if reason is reliably to direct men toward truth and happiness. From a prudential perspective, which warns against the radical scepticism

---

26 Burke, *A Letter to the Sheriffs of the City of Bristol on the Affairs of America* (1777), in Frederick P. Lock (ed. by), *Edmund Burke* (Oxford: Clarendon Press, 1998), vol. 1 (1730-84), pp. 37-39. For a discussion on Burke's standpoint and the differences with other authors, see Rumold R. Fennessy, *Burke, Paine, and the Rights of Man: A Difference of Political Opinion* (La Haye: M. Nijhoff, 1963). For the role played by opinion and rhetoric in Burke's conception of politics, see Ian W. Hampsher-Monk, 'Rhetoric and Opinion in the Politics of Edmund Burke', History of Political Thought, 3 (Winter 1988), pp. 455-484.

27 See, in particular, Livingston, 'Hume and America', The Kentucky Review, 3 (1983), pp. 15-38; Elisabeth Noelle-Neumann, *The Spiral of Silence: Public Opinion, Our Social Skin* (Chicago: University of Chicago Press, 1984), p. 76; Alan Gibson, *Interpreting the Founding. Guide to the Enduring Debates over the Origins and Foundations of the American Republic* (Lawrence: University Press of Kansas, 2006), pp. 37-52.

and the evocation of the "autonomous Man"[28] after the fashion of generations of immanentising ideologues from 1789 into the present, Hamilton quotes this passage taken from Hume's *Of the Rise and Progress of the Arts and Sciences* (1742):

> To balance a large state or society, whether monarchical or republican, on general laws, is a work of so great difficulty, that no human genius, however comprehensive, is able, by the mere dint of reason and reflection, to effect it. The judgments of many must unite in this work: Experience must guide their labour: Time must bring it to perfection: And the feeling of inconveniencies must correct the mistakes, which they inevitably fall into, in their first trials and experiments.[29]

The sentiments involved in these words, according to some scholars, "signal the sober, realistic, undogmatic yet hopeful outlook of American politics at its inception"[30].

It is also possibly an influence on Jeremy Bentham's idea of "Public Opinion Tribunal", as an organ of protective power, control, and criticism of the administrative and political acts of the sovereigns and their official conduct[31]. In fact, for Bentham, the "public" will have the duty to monitor political power and "compose a tribunal which is more powerful than all the other tribunals together"; moreover,

---

28 On the topic of the autonomous man in Hume, see Livingston's works: *Hume's Philosophy of Common Life* (Chicago: University of Chicago Press, 1984), pp. 20-33; 'Notes and Discussions: A Sellarsian Hume?', Journal of the History of Philosophy, 29 (April 1991), pp. 281-290.

29 Hume, *Of the Rise and Progress of the Arts and Sciences*, p. 124, quoted by John Lay, Alexander Hamilton, and James Madison, *The Federalist*, ed. by Jacob E. Cooke (Middletown: Wesleyan University Press, 1961), p. 594.

30 Ellis Sandoz, *Philosophical and Religious Dimension of the American Founding* (1995), in Mark C. Henrie (ed. by), *Arguing Conservatism. Four Decades of the Intercollegiate Review* (Wilmington: ISI Books, 2008), p. 254.

31 See Jeremy Bentham, *Security Against Misrule* (1822-23), in *The Works of Jeremy Bentham*, ed. by John Bowring (Edinburgh: Tait, 1838-1843), vol. 8. On Bentham's concept of opinion, see Fred Cutler, 'Jeremy Bentham and the Public Opinion Tribunal', The Public Opinion Quarterly, 3 (Autumn, 1999), pp. 321-346.

an individual may pretend to disregard its decrees-to represent them as formed of fluctuating and opposite opinions, which destroy one another; but everyone feels, that though this tribunal may err, it is incorruptible; that it usually tends to become enlightened; that it unites all the wisdom and all the justice of the nation; that it always decides the destiny of public men; and that the punishments which it pronounces are inevitable.[32]

Hume's influence emerging from these words appears to be something more than a mere conjectural hypothesis.

---

32 Bentham, *Essays on Political Tactics* (1789), ed. by Michael James, Cyprian Blamires, and Catherine Pease-Watkin (Oxford: Clarendon Press, 1999), p. 29.

8. FOR INSTITUTIONAL STABILITY

In Hume's political writings is explained the urgency for the formation of good opinions, deriving from the awareness that they are the true actresses of change in a society. When we live with uncertainty about who holds authority or who should hold it, our usual ways of thinking inevitably tend to be influenced more by imagined situations than real conditions, and flights of fantasy dominate our actions.

Since opinions rest upon experience, we can have empirically well-founded opinions about who should do something in society if there is a certain regularity of behaviour. For Hume, such a regularity does not come only from individual wills, but depends on something outside the individual sphere, that is, legitimated and regulated institutions capable of guiding our behaviour and our expectations. If these institutions, once acquired, are abandoned or neglected, we lose the habit and regularity; that is the most important means with which we orient ourselves, among others. Consequently, we cannot know what we can do with an expectation of success and risk losing our primary freedoms. Hence Hume's enormous emphasis on institutional stability.

For Hume, the conduct of a government is stable, and as such foreseeable, only if it publicly follows general rules and deals with matters provided for by law. These are modes of behaviour of public interest, but not necessarily the interest of each individual involved in the particular case, but rather patterns of behaviour falling under rules of justice.

In 1768, the year of the general election, John Wilkes, political agitator and leader of British political radicalism, and the clamour of violent clashes and civil unrests caused in London by the *Wilkes and Liberty!* cries prompted Hume to express all his disappointment towards the frequent riots of the populace, the mutinies which had no connection with any higher order of the state. Wilkes's supporters, "the rascally mob", provided "a vent for a wide range of grievances concerning pay and working conditions among London tradesmen, but, so far as we know, Hume never expressed sympathy for any of these causes"[1]. In fact, in his *Correspondence of an Under-Secretary of State* (1767-68), Hume wrote:

> Here is a people thrown into disorders (not dangerous ones, I hope) merely from the abuse of liberty, chiefly the liberty of the press; without any grievance, I do not only say, real, but even imaginary; and without any of them being able to tell one circumstance of government which they wish to have corrected: they roar liberty, though they have apparently more liberty than any people in the world, a great deal more than they deserve; and perhaps more than any men ought to have.[2]

When Hume says that the English have too much liberty, that appears to be "the unthinking reaction of outraged conservatism", he "means something definite and precise, which he has studied with objectivity and explained in some of his earliest political essays", and it "is the judgement of an impartial spectator with a European and metropolitan point of view"[3]. As a friend of the king's friends, a moderate thinker who in his works proposed a final political check against the violent passions, Hume asserts:

> Licentiousness, or rather the frenzy of liberty, has taken possession of us, and is throwing everything into confusion. How happy do I esteem it, that in all my writings I have always kept at a proper distance from that tempting extreme, and have maintained a due regard to magistracy and established government, suitably to the character of an historian and a philosopher![4]

It should be remembered that the *Wilkes and Liberty!* riots of the late 1760s prompted further reflection on the dangers

---

[1] Harris, p. 421.
[2] Hume, *Correspondence of an Under-Secretary of State* (1767-68), in *A Petty Statesman*, p. 199.
[3] Forbes, *Hume's Philosophical Politics*, p. 187.
[4] Hume, *Correspondence of an Under-Secretary of State*, p. 206.

inherent in a failure to achieve the right constitutional balance between freedom and authority, which was the foundation of the government's stability. The London riots were the third moment of crisis which took place in Hume's lifetime, after a long period of relative political stability in Great Britain, the others having been the Jacobite uprisings (1745) and the Seven Years' War with France (1756-63), episodes that "were both fairly tame by most standards – certainly compared to the upheavals that opened and closed the century, those connected with the Glorious Revolution and the union of 1707, on the one hand, and the American and French Revolutions, on the other"[5].

For *stability of government* the Scotsman understands the stability of political conventions, namely a set of practices, acts, habits, and political strategies to medium and long term. The conventions are supported or reformulated, but not created, by some presumed or actual contract, or by some sovereign command. For Hume, both the promises of the sovereign and the authority expressed by his government are nothing but the result of political conventions, not their cause. Since politics consists in the exercise of a power, the disputes on the agreements that determine it and their proposals to modifying or adapting to new circumstances can be resolved only by appealing to the authority itself, which can judge these disputes, especially those concerning property. Discussions concerning power, however, cannot be requested by any superior judge: they are resolved, for Hume, not by "lawyers and philosophers" but by "the swords of the soldiery"[6].

Thus political stability is more successful when it does not determine future situations, but when it systematically favours those regular activities that can maintain themselves even when the understanding of the persons to whom they are addressed changes radically. It does not mean that conventions must necessarily be understood and actively approved by the governed, but that they perform a large part of their function in being habitually followed as if they were not artificial, but natural, even when they are not.

---

5   Rasmussen, *The Infidel and the Professor*, p. 9.
6   Hume, *Treatise*, pp. 359-360. On this topic, see Sabl, mainly pp. 210-215.

For Hume, who never escapes the historical verification of what he claims, a more exceptional guarantee of stability is offered by modern political societies, compared to the ancient ones, because the measure of their efficiency in terms of good governance no longer derives from the personal qualities of the sovereigns, but from the virtuous institutional organization and the implementation of artificial virtues such as justice. Hume, among other things, rejects the model of democracy of the ancients, which was too unbalanced on the prerogatives of the people and resistant to the corrective measures necessary precisely for the maintenance of government stability.

These arguments suggest that the political concepts, unlike prescriptions or recommendations, are relevant only in crises where the prevailing convention is not clear. In any other case, the political concepts are less crucial than scholars of politics can imagine, and play a much less important role than custom imposes in determining the relations of human interactions. Here is an aspect of Hume's political realism: it is an attitude of prudence concerning the capacity for the realisation of normative theory[7], and the status that it claims. Hume, in the *History*, comes to judge the influence of political academics in France, far less than that of the butchers and carpenters of Paris, whose arguments constituted for him a more significant advantage for common sense[8].

Where there are no stable political conventions or the conquest or revolutions have eradicated the existing ones, political sovereignty becomes the one that Machiavelli described in *The Prince*: a mixture of strength and cunning, personal charisma, and deliberate terror, whatever is useful to convince the governed that the law of that sovereign is relatively enduring. When the prolonged experience and relative satisfaction with the results of the conventions have consolidated the authority of a constitutional order as a whole, thanks to the balance between authority and freedom, sovereignty takes on a peaceful and non-violent form, one that political theorists would rarely emphasise as a matter of

---

[7] On this point, see David Miller, *Philosophy and Ideology in Hume's Political Thought* (Oxford: Clarendon Press, 1981).
[8] See Hume, *The History of England*, vol. 2, p. 360.

great heroism. The kind of heroic and relevant sovereignty for relatively stable regimes is that which is affirmed when some political conventions defining authority and its legitimate limits are widely recognised, but not so much in any standard measure set at a theoretical level as in the concrete capacity to avoid civil war, which for Hume is "the greatest of ills", that "may be apprehended, almost with certainty, upon every vacancy"[9].

This awareness of the need for authority, as a limiting capacity for the excesses of liberty or "licentiousness", accompanies Hume from the beginning to the end of his speculative activity on politics; and he expresses "himself strongly precisely because the continuity of his thought was unbroken: what he had foreseen as likely in his earliest writings had come to pass"[10].

It is not by coincidence that his last political essay ends with these words:

> Authority must be acknowledged essential to its very existence: and in those contests, which so often take place between the one and the other, the latter may, on that account, challenge the preference. Unless perhaps one may say (and it may be said with some reason) that a circumstance, which is essential to the existence of civil society, must always support itself, and needs be guarded with less jealousy, than one that contributes only to its perfection, which the indolence of men is so apt to neglect, or their ignorance to overlook.[11]

Built on the balance between authority and freedom, the stability of government in Hume can be seen from two different perspectives: the stability of those who exercise authority and the stability of those upon whom it is exercised. The conduct of the government is stable, and as such foreseeable, only if it publicly follows specific general rules and if it deals with matters provided for by the law.

Hume has no doubts about the need for a government agenda that defends external as well as economic and cultural affairs, but he gives priority to maintaining the institutional stability that

---

9   Hume, *That Politics may be reduced to a Science*, p. 18.
10 Forbes, *Hume's Philosophical Politics*, p. 192.
11 Hume, *Of the Origin of Government*, p. 41.

makes social life possible. If the society has a clear opinion of the fact that it is a specific priority to constitute the public interest, that it is the government that protects this interest and that every other government would do it, then the government itself can count on a sure loyalty of the governed. It explains Hume's rejection of those patterns of distribution of goods based on personal characteristics and virtues. The government that adheres to the rules of justice refrains from interfering with the natural qualities, virtues, vices, and liberties of the individuals. Since the most visible expression of individuality is the productivity given by exchange, in the broadest sense of this term, justice inevitably connects to negotiating property and relationships, and in protecting them, the government protects the integrity of individual persons.

For Hume, the form of government that most of all assures the preservation of institutional stability is monarchy, for the guarantees that it historically offered against the rise of despotism compared to the modern republics. Asked if it is desirable that the English constitution "inclines more to absolute monarchy; or to a republic", Hume replies in a way that leaves no room for misunderstanding: "Here I would frankly declare, that, though liberty be preferable to slavery, in almost every case; yet I should rather wish to see an absolute monarch than a republic in this island"[12].

Moreover, he adds that

> if we have reason to be more jealous of monarchy, because the danger is more imminent from that quarter; we also have reason to be more jealous of popular government, because that danger is more terrible. This may teach us a lesson of moderation in all our political controversies.[13]

The confirmation of this preference for monarchy, supported by a historical explanation, comes from a letter to his nephew and namesake David Hume, son of his brother John, in which is written verbatim:

---

12 Hume, *Whether the British Government Inclines More to Absolute Monarchy; or to a Republic?* (1741), in *Essays*, p. 52.
13 *Ibid.*, p. 53.

The antient Republics were somewhat ferocious, and torn internally by bloody Factions, but they were still much preferable to the Monarchies or Aristocracies, which seems to have been completely intolerable. Modern Manners have corrected this Abuse, and all the Republics in Europe, without Exception, are so well governd, that one is at a loss to which we shoud give the Preference. [...] One great Advantage of a Commonwealth over our mixt Monarchy is, that it would considerably abridge our Liberty, which is growing to such an Extreme, as to be incompatible with all Government. Such Fools are they, who perpetually cry out liberty, and think to augment it, by shaking off the Monarchy.[14]

---

14 Hume, *To David Hume the Younger (Edinburgh, 8 December 1775)*, in *The Letters of David Hume*, vol. 2, p. 306.

9. FACTIONALISM AND NATIONAL INTEREST

The profound interest in politics, combined with the reluctance to conformism and intellectual fashions, thrusts Hume to face, in a new and original way, the problem of factions in the public and moral life of the society of his time. It is a problem which presents itself as the need not to remove the factions from the political scene, that is an impossible undertaking, since it is, by Hume's admission, a phenomena inherent in the natural human partiality, but to learn to live with them in the most peaceful and possibly useful way for the nation.

The reading of his three essays dedicated to this question, namely *Of Parties in General* and *Of the Parties of Great Britain*, dating back to the first collection of *Essays, Moral and Political* (1741-42), and *Of the Coalition of Parties*, added to the edition of the *Political Discourses* of 1758, together with all the Humean political writings and the whole *History of England*, allows us to demonstrate that Hume's standpoint, contrary to what has been established by some authoritative interpreters interested in diminishing its importance in terms of innovation and ideological impartiality[1], does not consist in a preconceived diffidence towards the factions of type, both political and religious, but in the realistic vision that leads him to classify them.

Hume defines the essential nature of party and criticises its degeneration in sect. The peculiarity of Hume, who on this

---

[1] See, in particular, the interpretation of James Conniff, 'Hume on Political Parties: The Case for Hume as a Whig', Eighteenth-Century Studies, 2 (1978-79), pp. 150-173; Sergio Cotta, 'La nascita dell'idea di partito nel secolo XVIII', Il Mulino, 89 (1959), pp. 445-486; Giovanni Sartori, *Parties and Party Systems. A Framework for Analysis* (Colchester: Ecpr Press, 2005).

topic surpasses Bolingbroke and anticipates Burke, consists in accepting the inevitability of parties and factions, terms that Hume uses interchangeably, without any semantic differentiation, and on the thrust of a single intent: to remedy the perpetual and violent diatribe between political coteries that has always characterised the history of institutions, in order to preserve the supreme national interest, the laboriously achieved British constitutional balance and government stability. According to Hume, the general tendency to factionalism emerges as a guiding force, a powerful *leitmotiv* not only of the modern English people but of the political history of the whole of humanity.

In confirmation of the historical importance he attributed to the political factions, in a letter of 1752 to his friend Adam Smith, Hume reveals that the reason of his project of *The History of England*, starting from the narration of the vicissitudes of the Stuarts, concerns the problem of the genesis of factionalism: it was with the rise of that dynasty that the government of the time, no longer crushed by the cumbersome authority of the Crown, gave proof of its aptitudes, and "the Factions that then arosed, having an Influence on our present Affairs, form the most curious, interesting, & instructive Part of our History"[2]. In *My Own Life*, Hume reiterates that the primary motivation of the project to write the *History* consisted in the narration of the events that marked the rise of the house of the Stuarts, in "an epoch when, I thought, the misrepresentations of faction began chiefly to take place"[3].

Already at the beginning of his intellectual career, that was twenty years before the appearance of the monumental *History*, Hume seems to have quite clear ideas about the origins and kinds of factions. In *Of Parties in General*, he writes:

> Factions may be divided into *personal* and *real*; that is, into factions, founded on personal friendship or animosity among such as compose the contending parties, and into those founded on some real difference of sentiment or interest. The reason of this distinction is obvious; though I must acknowledge, that parties are seldom found

---

[2] Hume, *To Adam Smith (24 September 1752)*, in *The Letters of David Hume*, vol. 1, p. 168.
[3] Hume, *My Own Life*, p. xxxvi.

pure and unmixed, either of the one kind or the other. It is not often seen, that a government divides into factions, where there is no difference in the views of the constituent members, either real or apparent, trivial or material: And in those factions, which are founded on the most real and most material difference, there is always observed a great deal of personal animosity or affection. But notwithstanding this mixture, a party may be denominated either personal or real, according to that principle which is predominant, and is found to have the greatest influence. Personal factions arise most easily in small republics. Every domestic quarrel, there, becomes an affair of state. Love, vanity, emulation, any passion, as well as ambition and resentment, begets public division. The *Neri* and *Bianchi* of *Florence*, the *Fregosi* and *Adorni* of *Genoa*, the *Colonnesi* and *Orsini* of modern *Rome*, were parties of this kind.[4]

Hume looks at factions with the concern to always take into due account the different levels of "reasonableness" and "legitimacy" in the discussion, as well as the importance that those factions have assumed in the concrete historical experience. By attributing to factionalism, as the maximum degeneration of party divisions, a reasonably remote origin concerning the modern history of England, Hume dwells on the strong propensity of men, in all ages and in all the political contexts, to divide themselves into factions. It is the nature of the human mind, which always informs every mind that approaches it, and since an unanimity of sentiments strengthens it, it is also shocked and disturbed by any opposition. Hence the enthusiasm that most people discover in a dispute their impatience for a clash of opinions. It is a principle, however frivolous it may seem, that has arisen from wars and religious divisions[5].

After identifying this primary division that characterises political vicissitudes of men, later on, Hume outlines a further distinction, that is destined to assume a crucial importance in the modern scientific analysis of parties. He specifies that the real factions can be factions of "interest", "principle", and "devotion". While parties of interest respond to the natural selfishness of men, those of principle are inspired by an abstract

---

4 Hume, *Of Parties in General* (1741), in *Essays*, p. 56. Hume's italics.
5 *Ibid.*, pp. 60-61.

ideal of an emotional and passionate origin; parties of devotion, on the other hand, escape both interest and principle, because of their elements of faithfulness or loyalty to persons and families they wish to rule their nation. Hume considers only the former to be justifiable from a rational point of view, the others being true "sects", "hardy plants" that exert an influence in society "farther than that of wise laws"[6], sometimes subversive of government, and in any case generating factionalism and fanaticism, which are socially undesirable marvels as well as incompatible with the authentically free constitutions[7].

Being persuaded that the fragmentation of the political body generated by factionalism is the antechamber of governmental instability, and that the perpetual juxtaposition of the groups almost always, as evidenced by history, leads to tyranny, Hume devotes himself to the analysis, in a comparative key, of merits and demerits of factions which are inspired by principles and those based on interest, while he shows his awareness for personal factions during his reconstruction of the historical genesis of English parties in the period preceding the Glorious Revolution. The main conclusion he reaches is that while the effects of parties of interest are not entirely adverse, since the mutual struggle and compromise to which they came in the attempt to achieve their goals can be useful to the cause of freedom and maintenance of authority, the parties of principle preserve all the characteristics of the revolutionary experience and the Puritan sects: "superstition", "enthusiasm", "zeal", "violent passions"[8], all vices with which these sects impose themselves on those people endowed with reasonableness, meekness, and prudence.

Hume's criticism of the dogmatic orientation of parties is in *Of the Original Contract*, where he dwells on the problem of the imperishable existence of parties of principle, due to the diversity of beliefs about the first principles, the functioning of government,

---

6   *Ibid.*, p. 54.
7   For a detailed analysis of Hume's classification of political parties, which is the first in the history of modern political doctrines, see my essay 'Natura e classificazione dei partiti: la *scoperta* di David Hume', Storia e Politica, 3 (2016), pp. 476-512.
8   See *Essays*, pp. 101-102, p. 466, pp. 577-646.

and the introduction of conflicting convictions regarding political obedience[9]. For Hume, men attached to principles that they consider unquestionable, such as sovereignty by divine right, for the Tories, and consensus on the basis of a hypothetical pact, for the Whigs, rarely compromise for reasons of public utility or defence of the collective interest or for the purpose of introducing standard rules of conduct; instead, they often do everything to obtain the physical and moral destruction of their opponents. Nevertheless, where these parties are based on religious differences, they denote all the qualities of extremist factions, sects, and more biased groups. It is a well-known feature of Hume's philosophy of religion that he allows for the possibility of the occurrence of miracles while at the same time maintaining that there never could be sufficient evidence to establish that a miracle had occurred, and least of all for any such miracle to become the foundation of a religion. Hume states that there is a political equivalent of miracle, in society, unpredictable: the "enthusiasm", a claim to immediate divine inspiration.

Hume so feels the parties' potential danger on the political and social level that he raises it to a primary problem which must be prevented in protection of freedom, even before the established order. Indeed, he thinks that, despite the considerable strengths introduced by modern genius in response to the human spirit of partiality, such as the artificial virtues of justice, tolerance, loyalty to the state, etc., however, the modern world remains full of various kinds of pitfalls in terms of social security. The highest degree of individual freedom that can immediately turn to license and anarchy, where the mass of the uneducated population becomes prey to political fanaticism, is, by far, the most relevant, preceding other full-blown dangers, such as the precarious balance of the mixed constitution, which can prove to be utterly accidental in the case of so much space given to the exaltation of party ideology.

As regards fanaticism, in particular, as the principal ally of factionalism, Hume is aware that the opposition of interests has often led to the rise of antagonistic sects that threatened the delicate balance on which Britain's mixed constitution rested. He sees the

---

9 See Hume, *Of the Original Contract*, p. 466.

Puritan factions as extreme of religious Whigs who promoted an excess of liberty that could ultimately unbalance the constitution, and conversely, he considers the Jacobites as a radical faction of the Tories whose support for monarchy and whose partisanship of the House of Stuart risked tipping the balance toward an excess of authority. Hume refers to Jacobitism, that is, support for Stuart claims, as "the most terrible *ism* of them all"[10]. In particular, for Hume, a body of party ideals that tends to degenerate into the most vulgar extremism, in addition to Jacobitism, is republicanism. Like Bolingbroke, Hume remains faithful to the doctrine of the mixed and balanced monarchy without this preventing him from grasping some premises of the emerging parliamentary system of government, in particular, the growing importance of the municipalities[11].

The question of relations between republicanism and parties remained open: Whigs were favourable to restrictions of real power, and republicans were the left of Whiggism. In this regard, Hume writes:

> The Tories have been so long obliged to talk in the republican stile, that they seem to have made converts of themselves by their hypocrisy, and to have embraced the sentiments, as well as language of their adversaries.[12]

In their anxiety to limit the power and influence of illegitimate legislators – Hume asserts – the Tories went further, embracing the vision of perpetually opposed parties, with all that follows in terms of dangers deriving from the excess of enthusiasm and political zeal.

Hume, in his account concerning the Jacobite uprising of 1745, also writes that "the religious Whigs are a very different set of mortals, and in my opinion are as much worse than the religious

---

10   Hume, *To John Clephane (Edinburgh, 3 September 1757)*, in *The Letters of David Hume*, vol. 1, p. 264.
11   Joaquin Varela Suanzes-Carpegna, 'Estado y Monarquía en Hume', Revista del Centro de Estudios Constitucionales, 22 (1995), pp. 59-90.
12   Hume, *Of the Parties of Great Britain*, p. 72.

Tories"[13]; and in a letter to Smith, he confirms that "faction, next to Fanaticism, is, of all the passions, the most destructive of Morality"[14].

At the most obvious level, faction, for Hume, undermines morality because "members of religious factions perceive actions in defence of their party as selfless and principled, but this simply licenses them to do greater harm with a clear conscience"[15]. Moreover, Hume shows how human beings have an innate tendency toward fanaticism, how fanaticism so often leads to faction, and how faction can ruin a society, threatening it with civil war by impeding people's ability for moral judgment. He attempts to describe the processes through which fanaticism can wreak disorder and chaos in a society. However, concerning the excesses of fanaticism, Hume feels constrained in his means for battling them. In a letter to Henry Home, he expresses his resolve "not to be an Enthusiast, in Philosophy, while [he] was blaming other Enthusiasms"[16].

A parties' animating principle derives from the nature of the English constitution, mostly based on the balance between the authority of the Crown and the liberty represented by Parliament. The party of principle, characterised by the natural inclination of some people to the need for order, is opposed by the party of principle animated by the need to defend liberties as an important political priority. For Hume, the English parties are very much fomented by a difference of interest, without which they could barely ever be violent[17]. It comes naturally to the Crown to reward its supporters with charges and prizes, and often with the same naturalness those who have not received similar rewards, driven

---

13 Hume, *A True Account of the Behaviour and Conduct of Archibald Stewart, late Lord Provost of Edinburgh. In a Letter to a Friend* (1748), in *A Petty Statesman*, p. 91.
14 It is a letter to Adam Smith (1774) regarding Benjamin Franklin's rejection of the stance of Deputy Postmaster-General for the colonies, quoted in Mossner, *The Life of David Hume*, p. 573.
15 Jennifer A. Herdt, *Religion and Faction in Hume's Moral Philosophy* (New York: Cambridge University Press, 1997), p. 205.
16 Mossner, *The Life of David Hume*, p. 112.
17 See Hume, *Of the Parties of Great Britain* (1741), in *Essays*, p. 65.

as they are by disappointment, end up joining the opposition. These opportunistic tendencies are, for Hume, also visible in the leaders of the parties of his time, certainly more inclined to the real giving and distribution of favours and to the evaluations dictated by personal or partisan interest, even when the popular base of the parties they lead, much more open to political idealism, appeals to the importance of principles. It follows that Tories support the Crown authority according to an evaluation both of principle and interest, and recognise the Stuarts as legitimate holders of the Crown itself, while the Whigs, in turn, always for a combination of interests and principles, show themselves as friends of Parliament and supporters of Hanover.

One of the most fundamental aspects of Hume's interpretation of parties is the relationship he identifies, precisely from his perspective as a historian of political institutions, between the parties of his time and those of the previous revolutionary century. While noting a certain degree of continuity between the Cavaliers and the modern Tories and between the Roundheads and the contemporary Whigs, Hume cannot do less than remark on what appears to him to be a reasonably apparent discontinuity: although modern parties share certain principles with their predecessors, they depart from them because of the tendency not to limit themselves to their slavish observance. A party of principle always finds a valid motivation to exaggerate their demands. The Roundheads feared, rightly, certain excesses on the part of the Crown with the restrictions on freedom that could follow them, but beyond their disproportionate reaction, they ended up transposing the remedies proposed as worse than the threat. The fanaticism of the revolutionaries, on the other hand, was a legitimate concern for the supporters of the Crown, but their unconditional support for despotic and foolish kings proved more than imprudent. For this reason, Hume concludes that modern parties inspired solely by principle are the bearers of the seed of civil war, so it becomes indispensable for the much-desired stability of government to ensure that they also receive the right consideration.

In this regard it should be remembered that, in Hume's time, the main challenge to British public life was still the one launched some time before by Bolingbroke, according to which the old "parties of the revolution", on the verge of extinction, should be replaced with new ones political organizations based on the principles of the Court and the Country[18]. The main objective of Bolingbroke was to remove from the political system the real element of interest, that is synonymous with "corruption", and to replace it with a close adhesion to principle. However, if compared to that of Bolingbroke, Hume's vision revealed all its originality, although the two authors will be remembered together as "the most distinguished writers on party in the eighteenth century"[19].

Hume sees his contemporaries as still too tied to old factions. The parties of his time again shared some characteristics of those of the revolutionary era, which were animated versions of the world, centres of biased "inflammation" and always distrusted. Also, on this point, Bolingbroke, according to Hume, was mistaken, because not only were the old parties not wholly dead, but many also remain as the dangers that insinuated themselves in the attempt to make them revive by reordering modern political life based on antiquated and outdated principles. It was, if anything, the need for a political compromise, in which the mutual agreement of the factions in the general interest was increasingly desirable, even at the risk of corruption, as a maximum liberal achievement capable of destroying factions.

It is difficult to identify, in the framework he described, Hume's party sympathies. His critical observations on the emptiness of the concept of social contract seem to bring him closer to the Tories, for the simple fact that Whigs loyal to Locke claimed for themselves the status of contractarian thinkers. Like most of the best-known intellectuals of his time, Hume did not usually indicate the authors with which he agreed or disagreed, and this fact makes it even more difficult to identify his possible political affiliation.

Some scholars have associated Hume to the Whigs because he

---

18 Bolingbroke, *A Dissertation upon Parties* (1733-34), in *Political Writings*, ed. by David Armitage (Cambridge: Cambridge University Press, 1997), pp. 1-191. For more information, see Isaac Kramnick, *Bolingbroke and His Circle. The Politics of Nostalgia in the Age of Walpole* (Ithaca and London: Cornell University Press, 1992).

19 Caroline Robbins, 'Discordant Parties. A Study of the Acceptance of Party by Englishmen', Political Science Quarterly, 4 (1958), p. 523.

"served as Undersecretary of State for Northern Affairs in a Whig government", and, "despite his protestations, Hume even accepted a small pension from a Whig administration"[20]. In truth, Hume had always distanced himself from the so-called liberal party, and when he could, he criticised it harshly. As remembered in *My Own Life*, despite experience having taught him that the "Whig party were in possession of bestowing all places, both in the state and in literature", Hume was "so little inclined to yield to their senseless clamour", always preferring to maintain an independence such as to be able to affirm with living "satisfaction" that he never had "preferred a request to one great man, or even making advances of friendship to any of them"[21].

In one of his several letters, complaining about the intense ostracism reserved for him at home, Hume confirmed that he was anything but a Whig sympathiser:

> I believe, taking the Continent of Europe from Peterburg to Lisbon, & from Bergen to Naples, there is not one that ever heard my Name, who has not heard of it with Advantage, both in point of Morals & Genius. I do not believe there is one Englishman in fifty, who, if he heard I had broke my Neck to night, woud not be rejoic'd with it. Some hate me because I am not a Tory, some because I am not a Whig; some because I am not a Christian; and all because I am a Scotsman.[22]

Aware of the impassable human partiality, Hume is inclined to emphasise the prevention, rather than control, of political factionalism, and to seek its possible pragmatic correspondence, rather than ideological diversity. To prevent the factions from being destructive of the institutions and pervading "free governments", destabilizing even "the legislature itself", which "alone could be able, by the steady application of rewards and punishments, to eradicate them"[23], the only reasonable solution remains the inhibition of sectarianism, extremism, and party dialectics, which

---

20 Conniff, p. 172.
21 Hume, *My Own Life*, p. xxxviii.
22 *Hume, To Gilbert Elliot (Paris, 22 September 1764)*, in *The Letters of David Hume*, vol. I, p. 470.
23 Hume, *Of Parties in General*, pp. 55-56.

are reprehensible elements, typical of the political actions of men. It should not be surprising – writes Hume in the *History* – that

> faction is so productive of vices of all kinds: For, besides that it inflames all the passions, it tends much to remove those great restraints, honour and shame; when men find, that no iniquity can lose them the applause of their own party, and no innocence secure them against the calumnies of the opposite.[24]

In Hume's eyes, the most furious factions are those inspired by religious principles, endowed as they are with a sectarian spirit that is unleashed by ambition and that distinguishes them from philosophical factions, also marked by animosity and ardour typical of sects; indeed – Hume observes – "sects of philosophy, in the ancient world, were more zealous than parties of religion; but in modern times, parties of religion are more furious and enraged than the most cruel factions that ever arose from interest and ambition"[25].

It is worth pointing out that the stance of Hume is not so original: the negative characterisation of factionalism is a relatively widespread intellectual trend in the eighteenth century, especially in the British area. The aforementioned Bolingbroke, in the late thirties of the eighteenth century, reflecting on the political perspectives of England following the failure of the project to create a Country Party and introducing the clear distinction between factions and parties, declared that the latter are still groups of people who join together in the pursuit of particular interests almost never coinciding with those of the community in its entirety:

> For faction – wrote Bolingbroke – is to party what the superlative is to the positive: party is a political evil, and faction is the worst of all parties. The true image of a free people, governed by a Patriot King, is that of a patriarchal family, where the head and all the members unit themselves to one common interest, and they are animated by one common spirit: and where, if any are perverse enough to have another, they will be soon borne down by the

---

24 Hume, *The History of England*, vol. 6, p. 438.
25 Hume, *Of Parties in General*, p. 63.

superiority of those who have the same; and, far from making a division, they will but confirm the union of the little state.[26]

Faction, Bolingbroke also stated, has no regard for the national interest, and it "will bear anything, share in anything, justify anything"[27].

Hume, who, like Bolingbroke, fears a great deal "lingering in opposing interpretations as regards the essential elements of the government", unlike his predecessor aspires to the formation of a coalition of parties that would represent "the most agreeable prospect of future happiness, and ought to be carefully cherished and promoted by every lover of his country"[28].

Hume's analysis is placed by Giovanni Sartori "halfway between Bolingbroke and Burke, though he was closer to the former than to the latter – both in his ideas and in time"[29], having as his objective the overcoming of the "artificial and odious distinctions" of part in political life[30]. In reality, Hume's thinking, compared to Bolingbroke's, appears not only more distant but also more complex.

The Scot, although may seem bizarre, sees in the faction of interest a potential of good that is absent in the interpretations of his time, starting from that of Bolingbroke. Contrary to what is reported by some scholars, according to which Hume does not accept the actual existence of faction[31], what the Scot really criticises is not so much the existence of the faction as such or as a possible degeneration of the political party, but the relentless fanaticism of its followers and the lack of that quality which he frequently calls "calmness" or "moderation", that "might seem a residue of ancient ethics"[32], which a real knowledge of the art of

---

26   Bolingbroke, *The Idea of a Patriot King* (1738), in *Political Writings*, pp. 257-258.
27   Bolingbroke, *Dedication to the Right Honourable Sir Robert Walpole* (1733), in *The Works of the Late Right Honourable Henry St. John, Lord Viscount Bolingbroke* (London: Printed for J. Johnson & Co., 1809), vol. 3, p. 17.
28   Hume, *Of the Coalition of Parties*, p. 494.
29   Sartori, p. 7.
30   *Ibid.*, pp. 7-12.
31   Cotta, pp. 445-486. My own translation.
32   Sabl, p. 79.

government should only promote. Hume's point of view regarding the positivity of the partisan contribution to public life, when not radical and speciously sectarian, seems to approach that of the contemporary Edward Spelman, who Hume indeed reads, given his considerable interest in the classics, as an English translator of Dionysius of Halicarnassus.

Spelman, in 1741, saw in factional activities, especially those opposed to the government, not a danger at all, but a guarantee for the administrated citizens. They guaranteed the control as much on the work of ministers as to the excessive strengthening of their power. After all, according to Spelman, what destroyed liberty was not so much the existence of the parties as the suppression of one of them by the rival:

> Parties, therefore, are not only the Effect, but the Support of Liberty: I do not at all wonder that they are perpetually exclaimed at by Those in Power: They may have, sometimes, Reason to be dissatisfied with the Parties themselves, but have much more to be so with the Heads of them; for these are properly their Rivals.[33]

Sergio Cotta observed that in Hume there are two judgments, "a judgment of value", that is "more acceptable to a thorough reading of all the writings of Hume", and "a judgment of fact of the type: the parties are a historical reality"[34]. Indeed, it is precisely this critical duplicity that gives the character of scientificity to Hume's phenomenological analysis on the political factions.

The Scottish thinker rejects not the factions in themselves, which have always existed in the social and political life of the people, but the extreme ones, described, on several occasions, in his works, as violent, angry, cruel, inveterate, etc. In this work there is no lack of references to the ancient England as inhabited by barbarian peoples in which each state was composed of internal factions and to the uncertain passage from barbarism to civilization due to the scarce concessions among factions. The two centuries preceding

---

33 Edward Spelman, *A Parallel between the Roman and the British Constitution comprehending Polybius' Curious Discourse of the Roman Senate* (London: printed by Mary Cooper, 1747), pp. vi-vii.
34 Cotta, p. 468.

the reign of Henry III – recalls Hume – abounded with factions and revolts of all kinds, and it is not surprising if, at the beginning of the civil war of 1642, when there were two sacred names in the English constitution fighting each other, namely those of King and Parliament, the people "were, in a great measure, cured of that wild fanaticism, by which they had formerly been so much agitated"[35]. This is not to mention the violence between 1679 and 1681, when "the two parties, actuated by mutual rage, but cooped up within the narrow limits of the law, levelled with poisoned daggers the most deadly blows against each other's breast, and buried in their factious divisions all regard to truth, honour, and humanity"[36].

Also in his political essays, Hume emphasises the historical inevitability of political factions, affirming that they are "involved in the very nature of our constitution"[37], that the balance between the republican and monarchical part of our constitution is "so extremely delicate and uncertain, that, when joined to men's passions and prejudices, it is impossible but different opinions must arise concerning it"[38], and that,

> though all reasonable men agree in general to preserve our mixed government; yet, when they come to particulars, some will incline to trust greater powers to the crown, to bestow on it more influence, and to guard against its encroachments with less caution, than others who are terrified at the most distant approaches of tyranny and despotic power.[39]

What Hume strongly recommends is joining the *moderate party*, which also existed at certain times in British history, and is best represented by Henry IV of France, praised by Hume as an "excellent prince", who "was far from being a bigot to his sect" and considered the theological disputes "entirely subordinate to the public good"[40].

As can be seen, Hume does not conceive politics within a

---

35 Hume, *The History of England*, vol. 6, p. 539.
36 *Ibid.*, p. 407.
37 Hume, *Of the Parties of Great Britain*, p. 65.
38 *Ibid.*, p. 64.
39 *Ibid.*, p. 65.
40 Hume, *The History of England*, vol. 4, p. 290.

homogeneous, unitary, and faction-free state, but believes that the parties, when they are moderate and work in harmony in the interest of the nation, must be reasonably defended. In his political essays, he states that "the only dangerous parties are such as entertain opposite views with regard to the essentials of government"[41], and resorting to a happy expression of Cicero he also specifies that he "would only persuade men not to contend, as if they were fighting *pro aris & focis*, and change a good constitution into a bad one, by the violence of their factions"[42].

Opposition to factionalism as a fatal outcome of ideological extremism leads Hume to distance himself from the political thought of his contemporaries. He tends to favour the parties of interest: since those based on principle and devotion contain the seeds of civil war, it is crucial for him that "the modern parties continue to be based at least partly on interest"[43]. Factions of interest are more likely to negotiate their partisan interest with the general interest. Hume, at the same time, invites politicians of his time to take "a lesson of moderation" concerning the parties, into which his country was divided[44].

As much as one can be sympathetic to Hume's appeal for reasonableness against political bias, some critical remarks may be made concerning the admissibility of some positions of the Scotsman.

The first one concerns this preference of the parties of interest, which, if they explicitly pursue the interests of a social or economic class, risk damaging the collective interest when they do not use arguments based on the common good. In this regard it should be pointed out, however, that Hume does not refer to that class interest that will focus the criticisms of the socialist authors of the following century, but it is merely the purpose of every human activity, contrary to what is claimed by contractarian authors, for which this purpose is founded on the maintenance of some pact or a presumed rational and deliberate will. Interest, for Hume, as

---

41 Hume, *Of the Coalition of Parties*, p. 493.
42 Hume, *That Politics may be reduced to a Science*, p. 31.
43 Conniff, p. 162.
44 Hume, *That Politics may be reduced to a Science*, p. 27.

outlined above, is a natural feeling of both personal and public kind, which even marks the origin of government.

The heartfelt exhortation to civil agreement, which is one of the most original features of Hume's political thought, is captured in several places in the *History*, confirming the opinion that only the moderate factions, even if they have an interest, are able to promote processes to improve society and institutions, as opposed to extreme factionalism that actively threatens stability. For example, about the factious divisions between civil and spiritual power in twelfth-century Scotland, Hume notes that the government could abide "by moderation on both sides ", to carry out its legitimate functions, even if imperfectly and irregularly, as happens in "all human institutions"[45]. Moreover, because of the typically human disposition to antisocial action, always exacerbated by a spirit of the faction so strong that even mild temperaments often find it hard to escape, extremist parties have always represented a serious threat to the unity of society, especially when particular interests have come to merge into a single, cohesive political community. However, the bright and explicit arguments about the dangerous consequences of the factious diatribes are traceable in the narration of the events that led to the English civil war, when the qualification of Puritan could apply to three classes of distinguished persons, who acted with views and for different interests. Hume writes in the *History*:

> The political puritans, who maintained the highest principles of civil liberty; the puritans in discipline, who were averse to the ceremonies and episcopal government of the church; and the doctrinal puritans, who rigidly defended the speculative system of the first reformers.[46]

Hume's concern is the tendency of free constitutions, like the British one, to give birth easily degenerate factions in fanaticism, disorder, and anarchy, from which tyranny inevitably arises. Factionalism, therefore, is the main enemy of free constitutions, since it always leads to political fragmentation and the exacerbating

---

45 Hume, *The History of England*, vol. 1, p. 324.
46 *Ibid.*, vol. 5, p. 212.

opposition of particular and group interests to the detriment of public interest.

In his analysis, Hume is always concerned with stigmatizing the action of the parties founded on principles, which are groups of fanatics who do not accept compromises, who radicalise dissent in compliance with abstract political ideals, and extremists which reflect the dogmatic temperament of their members, and tend to sacrifice peace and social order to achieve their goals (*"fiat justitia, ruat caelum"*), as well as to threaten the existence of a political government. The parties founded on principles, inspired by one or more speculative and abstract principles, arose – notes Hume against the hypotheses that would have him sworn enemy of every kind of political education – only relatively recently, and represent "the most extraordinary and unaccountable phenomenon, that has yet appeared in human affairs"[47]. Traces of them can exist in both the Whigs and Tories. This confirms the Humean vision of the principle parties as typically modern formations, due to the ease with which rationalist abstractionism, so distant from common sense and real human interests, has pervaded all sectors of public and social life, especially the political one.

Not surprisingly, Max Weber agreed with Hume that the principle parties are known only in modern times, although, unlike the Scot, he denied that they are irresponsible groups, representing for him, on the contrary, one of the most salient features of modern government[48].

Writing at a time when the tumults over the Hanoverian succession and Jacobite dreams were not yet wholly latent, Hume warned the reader of his political essays of the unfortunate consequences of factious opposition. The dispute over the principles no longer had any meaning, because the historical controversy that had generated the contrast between parties deserved a solution: Whigs were considered the only heirs of revolutionary traditions; Tories proclaimed themselves defenders of the monarchy and insisted

---

47   Hume, *Of Parties in General*, p. 60.
48   See the discussion of this topic in Harvey C. Mansfield, *Statesmanship and Party Government: A Study of Burke and Bolingbroke* (Chicago and London: The University of Chicago Press, 1965), p. 9.

on the primacy of loyalty to the sovereign. With the assumption that "to abolish all distinctions of party may not be practicable, perhaps not desirable, in a free government"[49], Hume anticipated Burke's analysis, albeit with some reservations of the latter about the disputes with which – as noted in his *Speech on Moving His Resolutions for Conciliation with the Colonies* (1775) – parties in free regimes "will be a matter of delay, perplexity, and confusion that never can have an end"[50], which can be coupled with the similar observation made by Hume in a letter to Montesquieu of 1749[51], to recognise the indispensable role of the parties as mediators between people and Parliament, on the one hand, and Parliament and government, on the other.

Burke admitted that "parties must ever exist in a free country" and that "the emulations of such parties, their contradictions, their reciprocal necessities, their hopes, and their fears, must send them all in their turns to him that holds the balance of the state"[52]. The most significant divergence with Hume, towards whose political philosophy Burke also showed interest, apart from the criticism of his academic scepticism and the identification of the limits of the concept proposed by the Scotsman, concerned the judgment on factions born of interest, which for the author of *Reflections on the Revolution in France* (1790) is "the most dangerous of all parties"[53]: their members look to the government only as the most valid guarantee of their investments. In the *Thoughts on the Causes of the Present Discontents* (1770), Burke insisted on the uniqueness of the real party of principle, that is "a body of men united, for promoting by their joint endeavours the national interest, upon some particular principle in which they are all agreed"[54]. This kind

---

49 Hume, *Of the Coalition of Parties*, p. 493.
50 Burke, *Speech on Moving His Resolutions for Conciliation with the Colonies* (1775), in *Select Works of Edmund Burke*, ed. by Ritchie (Indianapolis: Liberty Fund, 1992), vol. 1, p. 226.
51 Hume, *To President de Montesquieu (Londres, 10 Avril 1749)*, in *The Letters of David Hume*, vol. 1, p. 138.
52 Burke, *Speech on Moving His Resolutions*, p. 286.
53 Burke, *Reflections on the Revolution in France*, p. 183.
54 Burke, *Thoughts on the Causes of the Present Discontents* (1770), in *Select Works of Edmund Burke*, ed. Ritchie, vol. 1, p. 86.

of party presents a lasting programme, an ideological line, and an organization, that of broad financial interests to private and public advantages of a family or group of families, which can favour both corruption, that has become the norm of public life in modern society, and the risk of conditioning the voters, when the interest of the great owners translates into political pressure that they can freely exercise on their tenants and employees. To put it in Burke's words: "To love the little platoon we belong to in society, is the first principle (the germ as it were) of public affections. It is the first link in the series by which we proceed towards a love to our country and to mankind"[55].

Beyond this difference, however, Burke's intent was quite similar to Hume's. Both of them wanted a "free constitution" and a mild government, which Hume thought must be defended by a moderate politics and against parties, and Burke believed could be defended only with parties, given their indispensability.

---

55 E. Burke, *Reflections on the Revolution in France*, p. 55.

10. A LESSON OF MODERATION

A public opinion that is independent from political factions can only rest on a policy aimed at satisfying the primary interest, namely that of the British nation, which, for Hume, boasts of excellence not imitable from other European countries of equal wealth and power. One of these excellences is undoubtedly the way to understand, live, and guarantee freedom.

Freedom, for Hume, must be understood as individual, economic, and religious autonomy of person, security of private property, guarantee against arbitrary taxation. The extraordinary level of freedom which English citizens can enjoy derives from three fundamental elements: a mixed constitution, its institutional structure, and a wealth deriving from commerce. The originality of Hume's analysis of freedom in modern political history consists not in the identification of these factors, but in the unveiling of the main errors of interpretation that too often are committed.

Hume shows that there is no evidence of the existence of the much-vaunted ancient constitution of English liberty, in which many people continue to see an inexistent genius of freedom. The bills of rights have always been catalogues of special privileges which are imposed in a despotic manner by monarchs, and satisfy the interests of landowners. Despite these limitations, the concentration of power in the Crown has continuously evolved, reaching suitable proportions throughout Europe, long before the advent of the first Stuart king. Like his European peers, James I did nothing but follow a model of absolutist sovereignty, and his son, Charles I, tried to do the same thing. They found themselves facing unprecedented opposition, which, highlighting the defects of character and the lack of political talent of the sovereign, permanently established dependence on the Parliament that created so many difficulties every time the kings of England tried to play a significant role in Europe, as when they restrained the Spanish ambitions, and afterwards French ones, for the creation of a universal monarchy. The Stuarts, for Hume, were imprudent and unable to manage that explosive mixture of religious fervour and political fanaticism, disguised as mythology of ancient liberties, which in the English Parliament had now become an uncontrollable force. If the imprudence of James II consisted of the ambition to restore the Catholic system in the nation, that of Charles I was to find a compromise with the idea of divine right of the king's power, which proved to be the real cause of his downfall.

According to Hume, the English constitution's rebirth, and the formation of a new "free government", are nor reproducible neither by a revolution nor by an alleged pact or contract. Freedom enjoyed by modern Britons is the result of the power politics of the post-revolutionary years, during which Crown and Parliament have been mutually dependent, limiting and complementing each other in the exercise of their respective powers. For this reason, the novelty of English politics does not consist in that great separation of powers that fills the rhetorical language of the juridical and political theories, and biased historical reconstructions, but it is in a "balance of power"[1] that has been vital for the survival of the English constitution. For Hume, the balance of power originated from the interdependence of Parliament and Crown, and the Crown's influence on the election of some assembly members.

Another distinctive feature of the Humean realistic analysis is the emphasis on the institutional element: in every system characterised by several centres of authority, politics tends to be dominated by formal relations between these centres and by the conventions that govern the exercise of power. It had happened in England, where a semi-republic was born, beginning to politically evaluate the institutional standpoint. Then, the foundations were laid for a genuinely new freedom, no longer depending on the personal qualities or virtues of sovereigns, but on institutional systems. In the essay *That Politics may be reduced to a Science* (1741), Hume

---

1 See Hume, *Essays*, pp. 332-41. For more on this topic, see my *Introduction*, in *A Petty Statesman*, pp. 7-55.

wonders if there is a substantial difference between the various forms of government, and if each of them can prove to be good or bad depending on the administration that characterises it; he argues that if such a difference should consist solely of the personal character of rulers, like Henry IV of France, political disputes would not even open. Moreover, the most important lesson that the modern world has received from the ancient one consisted of the catastrophe that was generated by the ancients with their claim to base the social and political life of the subjects on the individual qualities of the rulers, ignoring that personal virtue, alone, without the support of adequate institutional structures, very soon becomes vice.

According to Hume, the modern world has developed the genius of institutional life, which guarantees to the individuals a more secure and peaceful coexistence. It does not mean that we must always be optimistic about the fact that the modern institutional arrangements are sufficient in themselves to maintain a peaceful social order. History is full of examples of institutional vulnerability.

The political writings in which Hume highlights the features of freedom, constantly confronted with the customs of England, are rich in references to the differences between the ancients and the moderns, about literature, government, institutions, growth of the population, and quality of labour. What emerges is, above all, a knowledge of ancient political history, in particular of the Roman one, which is extraordinary, probably unparalleled in his time and which comes from his reading, directly in Greek and Latin, of the classics, such as Thucydides, Diodorus Siculus, Titus Livius, Polybius, Herodotus, and Xenophon. Comparing ancient society with modern society, Hume denies the "republican novel" on antiquity. First of all, he notes that the economic basis of ancient society was slavery, a bleak institution, which was harmful to the growth of populations and to the economic development of countries[2].

Furthermore, Hume points out how the development of ancient economies were hampered from the lack of production and

---

2   Hume, in *Of the Popolousness of Ancient Nations* (1748), in *Essays*, p. 383, regards the domestic slavery as "more cruel and oppressive than any civil subjection whatsoever".

commerce, which are irreplaceable impulses to the growth of a nation. Hume recognises that as long as the ancient states remained republican cities, they retained some undeniable advantages: their small size, for example, prevented the risk of accumulation of great individual wealth and the creation of a widespread poverty among the citizens; they were able to guarantee the broadest possible participation in political choices, even if this proved to be an intense weakness when institutional structures fell prey to populist extravagance. However, the drawbacks were not lacking, like the one represented by the extreme precariousness of the government, since small communities tended to divide into family factions, and what passed under the name of politics was a bloody struggle between the parties in the field.

As for the art of war, the ancient one was particularly ferocious because it involved all the citizens, who saw everywhere potentially enemy cities to be conquered. The modern army, on the other hand, is not made up of the totality of citizens, but of men enlisted among the poorer classes and subjected to a very rigid discipline.

The real strength of English freedom is its flourishing trade, to which Hume devotes some of the most profound pages of his *Political Discourses*, free from ideological prejudices, and as such are accepted and interpreted throughout Europe as an authoritative confirmation of the validity of a new economic policy. The novelty of the English experiments in the mercantile field, compared to the previous commercial societies, which were none other than the narrow city-states mediating real political powers, lies in the wise conjugation of trade with agriculture; these are, for Hume, complementary, and not competing, sectors in the national economy: trade creates big cities, which in turn produce agriculture thanks to the market and the models of development; the availability of land as potential investment objects of commercial capital is an essential means to promote the development of the nation, thanks to the political and social status conferred on land ownership. For Hume, in fact, the possession of the land, in addition to guaranteeing the necessary social and political qualification, favours the lively social and economic interaction between city and countryside, the real lifeblood of an authentically free society, as well as a rich one: the city always generates new tastes and new occupations for both the mind and arms of men, relieving the tedium of country life.

In this context of civil liberties, the expressed desire of a "coalition of parties" takes on a clear function. It is achievable in an authentically free constitution, which legitimises the healthy and responsible dialectics between parties, and can only flee factionalism to seek a universal and profound understanding, a dynamic harmony between the logic of needs and the reasons of ideals. This – specifies Hume – is achievable only with a policy based on a balance between freedom and authority, so that the former does not turn into licentiousness. The latter is the antechamber of anarchy, in which any proposal of idea of productivity, any trade, initiative, and exchange between people would be impossible. Although Hume develops a theory of government based on which it also governs through the opinion of citizens, nevertheless, he shows himself fully aware that this means running the risk of being confronted with conflicts. This awareness becomes a problem in some passages of his essays, as in this one:

> In all governments, there is a perpetual intestine struggle, open, or secret, between authority and liberty; and neither of them can ever absolutely prevail in the contest. A great sacrifice of liberty must necessarily be made in every government; yet even the authority, which confines liberty, can never, and perhaps ought never, in any constitution, to become quite entire and uncontroulable.[3]

The ideal then would be to promote moderation always and everywhere, which "is of advantage to every establishment: Nothing but zeal can overturn a settled power: And an over-active zeal in friends is apt to beget a like spirit in antagonists"[4].

What for Hume serves both the balance between freedom and authority and the civil coexistence between inhabitants of the same nation is precisely a "lesson of moderation", understood not only as a temperamental trait of those who flee ideological extremism and partisan spirit, but also as a political line to be preferred in the

---

3 Hume, *Of the Origin of Government*, p. 40.
4 Hume, *Of the Coalition of Parties*, p. 500.

government of public affairs, in which Hume even identifies the road to the salvation of humanity. In fact, in *Of Refinement in the Arts* (1760), he writes:

> When the tempers of men are softened as well as their knowledge improved, this humanity appears still more conspicuous, and is the chief characteristic which distinguishes a civilized age from times of barbarity and ignorance. Factions are then less inveterate, revolutions less tragic, authority less severe, and seditions less frequent. Even foreign wars abate of their cruelty; and after the field of battle, where honour and interest steel men against compassion as well as fear, the combatants divest themselves of the brute, and resume the man.[5]

The form of government that most assures political moderation is, according to Hume, once again the monarchy, if only for the higher guarantees that it, compared to the modern republics, has historically offered against the rise of despotism. Therefore, to the question, if the English constitution should result in a popular government or an absolute monarchy, Hume replies in the essay *Whether the British Government Inclines More to Absolute Monarchy; or to a Republic?*:

> Here I would frankly declare, that, though liberty be preferable to slavery, in almost every case; yet I should rather wish to see an absolute monarch than a republic in this island.[6]

Moreover, he adds with equal firmness that "a lesson of moderation in all our political controversies" can only teach us that "popular government" is the danger "more terrible"[7].

The animosity of the Scotsman towards the mob and its licentiousness seems to be dictated by his mistrust towards the radicals, who in his eyes advocate the ideal not of a real freedom, understood as individual, economic, and religious autonomy, and security of private property, but of the license, that is a veritable uncontrolled abuse of freedom quickly generating in uncultured peoples. "From these causes – Hume writes in *Of the Liberty of Press* (1741) – it proceeds, that there is as much liberty, and even,

---

5   Hume, *Of Refinement in the Arts*, p. 274.
6   Hume, *Whether the British Government*, p. 52.
7   *Ibid*.

perhaps, licentiousness in Great Britain, as there were formerly slavery and tyranny in Rome"[8].

Moreover, it is precisely this strong concern for license and disorder that leads him to be wary of the supporters of the republicanism and praise of the democracy of the ancients, which all but a model of constitution to be imitated, as stated in *Of the Original Contract*:

> The republic of Athens was, I believe, the most extensive democracy, that we read of in history: Yet if we make the requisite allowances for the women, the slaves, and the strangers, we shall find, that that establishment was not, at first, made, nor any law ever voted, by a tenth part of those who were bound to pay obedience to it: Not to mention the islands and foreign dominions, which the Athenians claimed as theirs by right of conquest.[9]

Since the opinions for which government can exercise authority are the foundations of the state itself, the primary task that Hume assigns to political science does not consist in the mere speculative analysis and classification of different forms of government, which is often a product of individual preferences, but in the explanation of the formation and transformation of opinions. To do so, it must first of all become aware of the fact that, in view of the supreme purpose of protecting the public interest, a government must be as stable as possible, preferring calmness to tension, moderation to intemperance, and minimizing situations of internal conflict that give rise to factionalism, sectarianism, and fanaticism.

Instead of promoting the tendency of viewing politics "in black and white terms", Hume tries "to lower the temperature of politics and to inculcate moderation by showing that politics always involves questions that are shades of gray"[10]. He believes that, without moderation, which is a unique and specific remedy for the unleashing of political upheavals, as well as an invaluable guide to the careful and thoughtful comparison of the conveniences

---

8 Hume, *Of the Liberty of Press* (1741), in *Essays*, p. 12.
9 Hume, *Of the Original Contract*, p. 473.
10 Scott Yenor, *David Hume's Humanity. The Philosophy of Common Life and its Limits* (New York: Palgrave Macmillan, 2016), p. 94.

deriving from the perpetual changing situations, there would be no prospect of success in political life, and even individual existence would become almost intolerable. Factionalism tends to transform the question of who should assume the positions of government into a problem of balancing the powers of the constitution. It is particularly risky in a mixed constitution such as the British one, where the main factions rest upon different forms of government, monarchy and republic. Hume states:

> There is not a more effectual method of promoting so good an end, than to prevent all unreasonable insult and triumph of the one party over the other, to encourage moderate opinions, to find the proper medium in all disputes, to persuade each that its antagonist may possibly be sometimes in the right, and to keep a balance in the praise and blame, which we bestow on either side.[11]

However, Hume will remain unheard. His contemporaries do not appreciate the prospect of an alliance between parties. Instead of allowing themselves to be enlightened by his idea of political experience as a substantial protection of the national interest, they prefer to give continuity to the heated dialectics of factions that often risk compromising that political and constitutional balance that emerged, and which in Hume provokes an all-out defence. What the political theorists of the second half of the eighteenth century do not accept of his thought is precisely the moderation, the general scepticism towards political enthusiasm and radicalism, concerning which he always distances himself with determination and frankness. He does so, for example, in the essay *That Politics may be reduced to a Science?*, containing a real profession of moderation. Here Hume sustains that he always and everywhere encourages "moderation" rather than "ardour" and "fanaticism" although "perhaps the surest way of producing moderation in every party is to increase our zeal for the public"[12].

Moderation, in Hume's political thought, is almost a natural counterweight to freedom. Together with authority, it is the restrain to be put on licentiousness and libertinism. Freedom, in fact, is no

---

11 Hume, *Of the Coalition of Parties*, p. 494.
12 Hume, *That Politics may be reduced to a Science*, p. 27.

longer the impetuous, anarchic longing of the savage, but it is the delicate and fragile fruit of civilisation; like the latter, freedom is exposed to the ever-present threat of human passions, of which Hume was a great interpreter. As the result of a natural process, the building of English liberty appeared to him to be firmly founded on a broad social basis; but if this basis was corroded by fanaticism, radicalism, and factionalism, the construction, even if stable, would have risked collapsing irreparably. It was not possible, according to Hume, to rely solely on reason as a valid substitute. Custom, in a policy marked by moderation, could have given legitimacy and firmness to any regime, and at the same time, ensure the freedom of people.

11. HUME'S CONSERVATISM: THE HISTORIOGRAPHICAL CERTAINTIES

That David Hume was a political thinker with a definite conservative orientation, is a certainty and has been for a long time now.

Already in the early 1800s, the liberal-socialist John Stuart Mill, who did not hesitate to consider conservatives, in a derogatory way, as "stupid"[1], pointed to Hume as "the profoundest negative thinker on record"[2], and deprecated his romanticism and scepticism with these words:

> Hume possessed powers of a very high order; but regard for truth formed no part of his character. He reasoned with surprising acuteness; but the object of his reasoning was, not to attain truth, but to shew that it is unattainable. His mind, too, was completely enslaved by a taste for literature; not those kinds of literature which teach mankind to know the causes of their happiness and misery, that they may seek the one and avoid the other; but that literature which without regard for truth or utility, seeks only to excite emotion.[3]

In another circumstance, Mill observed that Hume's

---

1 John Stuart Mill, *Considerations on Representative Government* (1861) in *The Collected Works of John Stuart Mill*, ed. by John M. Robson (Toronto: University of Toronto Press, 1963-1991), vol. 19, p. 452: "I did not mean that Conservatives are generally stupid; I meant, that stupid persons are generally Conservative. I believe that to be so obvious and undeniable a fact that I hardly think any hon. Gentleman will question it".
2 Frank Raymond Leavis, *Mill on Bentham and Coleridge* (New York: Harper & Row, 1950), p. 43.
3 Mill, *Review of George Bodie's "History of the British Empire"* (1824), in *The Collected Works of John Stuart Mill*, vol. 6, p. 3.

absolute scepticism in speculation very naturally brought him round to Toryism in practice; for if no faith can be had in the operations of human intellect, and one side of every question is about as likely as another to be true, a man will commonly be inclined to prefer that order of things which, being no more wrong than every other, he has hitherto found compatible with his private comforts.[4]

The allegation of political conservatism as a logical result of scepticism was not new at the time of Mill, but had a long legacy from the history of scepticism, from Sextus Empiricus clear assertion, according to which "attending to what is apparent, we live in accordance with everyday observances, without holding opinions – for we are not able to be utterly inactive"[5], until Leslie Stephen's comment: the translation of Hume's "heretical scepticism into politics is a cynical conservatism", and Hume "evidently inclines to the side of authority as the most favorable to that stagnation which is the natural ideal of a sceptic"[6].

Therefore, stagnation, quietism, and political inertia would be some qualifying traits of scepticism, which in turn would be a substitute of conservatism. However, even before Mill, in the period in which Hume was in the midst of notoriety, thanks to the wide dissemination of his *History*, absolutely one of the most widely read works in the world, among his contemporaries there was who, like Catharine Macaulay, accused him of being "more an advocate than an historian", and in

> the nineteenth century Whig epoch of Macaulay, Froude, Green and Gardiner, Hume's *History of England* was generally denigrated as an old fashioned Tory history, based upon a superficial and tendentious reading of the sources.[7]

---

4 Mill, *Bentham*, in *The Collected Works of John Stuart Mill*, vol. 10, p. 80n.
5 Sextus Empiricus, *The Outlines of Skepticism*, trans. by J. Annas and J. Barnes (Cambridge: Cambridge University Press 2002), p. 9.
6 Leslie Stephen, *History of English Thought in the Eighteenth Century* (London: Smith, Elder & Co., 1876), vol. 2, p. 185.
7 Laird Okie, 'Ideology and Partiality in David Hume's *History of England*', Hume Studies, 1 (April 1985), pp. 1-2. As regards the figure of Hume as a Tory historian, see: Mossner, *Was Hume a Tory Historian? Facts and Reconsiderations*, and Marjorie Grene, *Hume Skeptic or*

Macaulay spoke from above of that "Whig supremacy", as a biographer of Hume called it, which "insisted that he was, at least, a Tory, and the appellation is still customarily employed"[8].

In truth, the publication of the *History*, finally established Hume's reputation as a Tory. More recently, Nicholas Phillipson, with words of less direct meaning, has confirmed that "the Whiggery of George III's reign could probably have survived the effects of his attack on reason, which had destroyed the epistemological foundations on which its theories of natural rights and contract depended", but in what Hume called "the historical age", for Phillipson, "it was much less easy to ignore an assault on Whig historiography which was not only intellectually devastating but was set out in a work which was becoming a bestseller at home and abroad"[9].

It is no coincidence that Macaulay wrote her *History of England* (1763-1782) to subvert the "anti-republican" interpretation given of the Puritan revolution by Hume, who unsuccessfully tried to explain to her the clear difference between the necessary reforms in the political processes and the ideological claims of radical transformation of the world: "I flatter myself – Hume wrote to Macaulay – that we differ less in facts than in our interpretation and construction of them. Perhaps also I have the misfortune to differ from you in some original principles, which it will not be easy to adjust between us"[10].

Macaulay's response confirmed the full weight of the ideological prejudice against Hume the "Tory" and his attachment to *auctoritas*:

    Tory?, in Livingston and Mary Martin (ed. by), *Hume as Philosopher of Society, Politics and History* (Rochester and Woodbridge: Rochester University Press, 1991), pp. 106-117, 118-133.

8 Mossner, *The Life of David Hume*, p. 310.

9 Nicholas Phillipson, *Propriety, Property and Prudence: David Hume and the Defence of the Revolution*, in Phillipson and Quentin Skinner (ed. by), *Political Discourse in Early Modern Britain* (Cambridge: Cambridge University Press, 1992), p. 302.

10 Hume, *To Catherine Macaulay (Paris, 29 March 1764)*, in *New Letters of David Hume*, ed. by Raymond Klibansky and Mossner (Oxford: Oxford University Press, 2011), p. 81.

> Your position, that every government established by custom and authority carry with them obligations to submission and allegiance, does, I am afraid, involve all reformers in unavoidable guilt, since opposition to established error must needs be opposition to authority.[11]

It was also Macaulay, sometime later, for the same reasons that led her to counter the Tory interpretation of Hume's *History*, who published a pamphlet[12] to defend the French Revolution from the heavy criticism of Burke, whose *Reflections* were the "philosophical substance" of political conservatism. She wrote that the "central themes of conservatism over the last two centuries are but widenings of themes enunciated by Burke with specific reference to revolutionary France"[13].

From the end of the nineteenth century onwards, and in continuity with this kind of judgments, Hume's identification with conservatism – understood as an obvious consequence of his scepticism and his political empiricism – became a fact, albeit poorly explored in his conceptualisations and underlying reasons[14]. Many scholars who have dealt with it have confined themselves to superficially detecting Hume's conservatism as a consequence of his scepticism, without to investigate its potential in terms of future development of conservative doctrine.

Just to give some examples from among the most eminent interpreters, for Stephen, undisputed authority in English historical-philosophical criticism, Hume's scepticism was nothing more than a superficial vein, and "to observers at a distance it may appear that his conservatism is really more remarkable than his

---

11 Catharine Macaulay, 'Answer to Mr. Hume's Letter', The European Magazine, and London Review, 4 (1783), p. 331
12 Macaulay, *Observation on the Reflections of the Right Hon. Edmund Burke, on the Revolution in France, in a Letter to the Right Hon. The Earl of Stanhope* (London: C. Dilly, 1790).
13 Nisbet, *Conservatism: Dream and Reality* (1986), with a new introduction by Brad L. Stone (London and New York: Routledge, 2002), p. 19.
14 As regards the reluctance of historians, especially Italian ones, to deal with Hume's conservatism, see Pupo, 'Il conservatorismo politico di David Hume', Rivista di Politica, 2 (2016), pp. 23-41.

destructiveness"[15]. According to William A. Knight, a distinguished Scottish academic, Hume was a conservative political thinker because, like all modern conservatives, "he detested the fanatics of every age (and, rightly enough, condemned them); but he had less sympathy with the struggles of the people after constitutional liberty than with their loyal obedience to existing power"[16]. In the 1900s, the American scholar George H. Sabine, in his attempt to assign Hume a precise position in the history of political doctrines, assimilated the Scot for the first time to Burke, being both opponents of the eighteenth-century political rationalism. Burke, for Sabine, did nothing but receive as an inheritance "the reaction that was to follow upon Hume's destruction of the eternal verities of reason and natural law", and thanks to Hume, "sentiment, tradition, and idealized history stepped in to fill the vacancy left by the removal of self-evident rights"[17].

Hume's thesis as Burke's precursor has found a decent fortune in Anglo-American political historiography, albeit with the superficiality of analysis mentioned above. Harvey C. Mansfield assumed that it was the theory of "prescription" that both dealt with the problem of the establishment of government and the "function of history as an investigation of origins or on the functioning of the original principle"; the government without rational foundation theorised by Burke, for Mansfield, "is compatible only with histories like Hume's *History of England*, whose aim is to parade the follies of such inquiries"[18]. The interpretative line drawn by Mansfield has developed proselytes until relatively recently. Burleigh T. Wilkins, an expert on Burke's political thought, argued that although Hume was an epicurean and Burke a stoic, the former helped to illuminate the "sceptical side" of the latter which, along with that of "certainty", constituted the "two poles of thought" which were always present in conservatism: "The two poles of thought, scepticism and certainly, are always present in Burke; he

---

15 Stephen, p. 9.
16 William A. Knight, *Hume* (Edinburgh: Blackwood and Sons, 1886), pp. 225-226.
17 George H. Sabine *A History of Political Theory* (London: Harrap & C., 1948), p. 511.
18 Mansfield, p. 221.

argues first one cause and then the other with equal fervour. Just as the Scottish philosopher Hume helps illuminate the sceptical side of Burke"[19].

Paul Lucas noted that the historical origin of Burke's reaction to the philosophical and political rationalism of his time, which he pursued in the name of the triad history-change-prescription, was to be sought in the British tradition of empiricist philosophy, of which Hume was the most illustrious exponent[20]. And if the English philosopher Antony Flew admitted candidly that Hume, rather than Burke, should be seen as "the first forefather of the modern conservative intellectual tradition"[21], the Canadian counterpart Neil McArthur saw the Scot as an interpreter of a "precautionary conservatism"[22], whose expressions would be "determined by prudential concerns about the consequences of changes, which often demand that we ignore our own principles about what is ideal or even legitimate"[23]. Francis Snare entitled his chapter on Hume's theory of justice *The Conservative Theory of Justice*, and maintained that Hume provides a conservative's defence of existing forms of government, on the whole, and nothing, in his theory, "no appeal to public interest, no appeal to the other moral sentiments", could be a reason for preferring one particular convention over others; instead "we are just drawn to certain conventions because they stand out, are more striking, stimulate the imagination"[24]. Jeffrey Hart, an authoritative name of the "National Review", an American magazine of conservative orientation, wrote that Hume belonged to a conservative tradition

---

19 Burleigh T. Wilkins, *The Problem of Burke's Political Philosophy* (Oxford: Clarendon Press, 1967), p. 68.
20 Paul Lucas, 'On Edmund Burke's Doctrine of Prescription; or, An Appeal from the New to the Old Lawyers', Historical Journal, 1 (1968), p. 60.
21 Antony Flew, *David Hume: Philosopher of Moral Science* (Oxford: Basil Blackwell, 1986), p. 173.
22 Neil McArthur, *David Hume's Political Theory: Law, Commerce, and the Constitution of Government* (Toronto: University of Toronto Press, 2007), pp. 116-136.
23 *Ibid.*, p. 124.
24 Francis Snare, *Morals, Motivation, and Convention: Hume's Influential Doctrines* (Cambridge: Cambridge University Press, 1991), p. 223.

which cannot be said to be merely compatible with scepticism, but which is sceptical at the root, and conservative precisely because it is sceptical: Hume was too sceptical that he might consider himself one of those radical *philosophes* devoted to materialistic millenarianism; and as a political thinker, among previous writers, had an affinity with Montaigne and Dryden[25].

Enhancing the salient aspects of Hume's political doctrine as a possible source of inspiration for some essential strands of modernist political thought, some authoritative American scholars have conducted in-depth analyses of Hume's presumed conservatism, reaching a surprising result: all the works of the Scottish philosopher denote his undeniable conservative inclination. The first, serious investigation into the theoretical foundations of Hume's political conservatism was carried out by Donald W. Livingston[26]. Considering completely unreliable the interpretations about the alleged liberalism or utilitarianism or positivism which, according to the different critical viewpoints, emerged from the works of Hume, Livingston notes that, in reality, the Scottish thinker stood out in the contemporary political landscape as a pivotal figure in the conservative intellectual movement. First of all, Livingston denies any adhesion of Hume to Whiggism. For him, Hume

> admired the moral character of Charles I and leading royalists more than the characters of Cromwell and the Puritan fanatics. However, he was happy about unintended consequences of the Puritan rebellion, which led to the constitution of liberty of 1689 (the Whig order of "things", namely liberty and the rule of law).[27]

---

25 See Jeffrey Hart, 'David Hume and Skeptical Conservatism', National Review (13 February 1968), pp. 129-32.
26 See Livingston, 'On Hume's Conservatism', pp. 151-164; 'David Hume and the Conservative Tradition', Intercollegiate Review, 22 (Fall 2009), pp. 30-41; *Hume's Philosophy of Common Life* (Chicago: University of Chicago Press, 1984).
27 Livingston, 'On Hume's Conservatism', pp. 151-152. Moreover, as stated by his biographers, Hume disapproved of the Civil War but heartily accepted the Glorious Revolution of 1688-89; he supported both the Union of 1707 and the accession of the House of Hanover in 1711. On this point, see Mossner, *The Life of David Hume*, p. 32.

If, according to Livingston, for its most influential exponents conservatism is essentially a critique of political rationalism, moved by an unconditional trust in "a normal or healthy political society" reposing "in the enjoyment of inherited traditions and practices", and moved by a view of politics as the "art" of the preservation of necessary order, then Hume is for all intents and purposes a conservative political thinker. Having inaugurated a reliable method for overcoming the ideologies that were already underway in his time to revolutionise the habits of men, he can be considered also the initiator of a modern secular conservatism. If conservatism of Burke, who thought and wrote a few decades after Hume, was a "conservatism of the heart", based mostly on political eloquence and oriented "to a romantic, nostalgic view of tradition as a refuge from philosophical reflection", Hume's conservatism was a conservatism of "reflection", with a solid philosophical foundation. Livingston concluded that "conservatism, if it is to have substantial meaning, must be a critical philosophical engagement, and for this project, Hume has more to teach us than Burke"[28].

Livingston's thesis relied on the content of some key passages in the *History*, in which Hume considered the Puritan revolution as a violent intrusion of a false philosophy camouflaged in religious language and politics. The first English revolution (1642-49), which led to the execution of Charles I and the establishment of the military dictatorship of Oliver Cromwell, was the symptom of a spiritual pathology mixed with political ambition: the Puritans, the "Levellers", and the "armed legislators"[29] of the time intended not to implement a simple reform of existing institutions, but a radical transformation of the social order in the name of an ideology proclaimed with the intemperate zeal of a sect, fanatical extravagance, and utopian arguments, all systems of imaginary governments for the organization of the state, in which there should have been no nobility distinction and each citizen would have had the right to equal wealth and power; an illegal violence is as contrary not only to the will of the Parliament but a fundamental

---

28 Livingston, 'David Hume and the Conservative Tradition', pp. 39-40.
29 Hume, *The History of England*, vol. 5, p. 513.

law. Cromwell, for Hume, "purposed by arbitrary power to establish liberty, and, in prosecution of his imagined religious purposes, he thought himself dispensed from all the ordinary rules of morality, by which inferior mortals must allow themselves to be governed"[30]; and the noisy assemblies of the revolutionaries were marked by that "false philosophy" which "seeks to establish foundationalist principles which do not recognize the primordial authority of the inherited customs of common life"[31].

Instead of prudent administrative reforms and interventions, the radical politicians demanded, in the presence of an impotent Crown, the subversion of the ancient constitution and the total transformation of England and the whole world. Indeed, this final judgment of Hume coincides, historically, with the first declaration concerning the conservative rejection of revolutionary politics as motivated by rationalism and ideologism. Burke, but also the French counter-revolutionaries, starting with Joseph de Maistre, used more or less the same words to describe the despotic and bloody regime of Robespierre[32].

But the conservative primacy of Hume, in truth, was the focus, as early as 1954, of the penetrating analysis of Sheldon S. Wolin[33], who was able to draw several cues from the Scot's intellectual production: emphasis on traditionalism, prominence of custom and sentiment, disgust for policy designers, and sensitivity to the complexity of government and politics. Subsequent conservatism, according to Wolin, came to much of the legacy of Hume's empiricism, in which the "useful" was subtly combined with the "factual", even if the revolutionary events led the conservatives to turn, more than to the suitable Humean intellectual conclusions,

---

30 *Ibid.*, p. 514.
31 Livingston, 'On Hume's Conservatism', p. 157.
32 For the identification of the historiographical evidence concerning the influence exerted by Hume's writings on the French counter-revolutionaries, the volume of Laurence L. Bongie, *David Hume: Prophet of the Counter-Revolution* (1965), new edition (Indianapolis: Liberty Fund, 2000) is unsurpassed.
33 Sheldon S. Wolin, 'Hume and Conservatism', The American Political Science Review, 4 (1954), pp. 999-1116. Wolin's conclusion was that the "analytical conservatism" of Hume, in fact, prepared the way for Burke's "metaphysical conservatism".

to the transcendental norms and religious traditionalism. Conservatives draw from irrationalism, romanticism, and religion the new vision of an ancient order which replaced not only the "analytical" Humean conservatism with the "metaphysical" Burkean one, but also Hume's "naturalistic approach" with a philosophy for which the "course" of history was determined by the divine hand that operated from outside of human time and space. It does not mean that the Scot's assumptions, in Wolin's eyes, has remained authentically conservative at the root:

> His conclusions – as he maintained – were conservative for the reason that Hume never probed past a certain point nor carried his scepticism to its ultimate conclusions. He held too much respect for custom and tradition, and for their importance as social cement, to subject them to the kind of devastating critique which Voltaire and his allies were employing in France. With later conservatives he shared a distrust of reform, a hostility toward abstractions, and a scepticism of the claims of reason.[34]

Much later, but with equal authoritativeness, Pierre Manent thought Hume's political conservatism arose from his scepticism about universal human rights, which led Hume the empiricist to investigate collective experience as expressed in moral sentiments, revealing that people distinguish right and wrong in common life. Political investigations aimed to see-through the principles of human nature as they manifest themselves in different societies. That is why – Manent stated – Hume's scepticism leaded to a "conservative practical viewpoint"[35], followed from his judgment that tradition is a source of order in a world shorn of intelligibility. Secure in the inescapable nature of these arguments, the historian of conservatism Muller could affirm that Hume's political thought represented a real turning point in the development of a secularist conservatism[36], which did not leave Burke indifferent, since "for

---

34 Wolin, p. 1015.
35 Pierre Manent, *City of Man* (1994), trans. by Marc A. Le Pain (Princeton: Princeton University Press, 1998), p. 144.
36 Muller, p. 24.

the young Burke, as for Hume, an awareness of the limits of human reasoning led to a principled respect for custom"[37].

For David Resnick, one of the most critical pointers of Humean conservatism was the cautious scepticism deriving from the appreciation of the complex nature of political reality. In particular, Hume called into question the capacity of the ignorant multitude to approach political issues critically, and for this reason, he called for mistrust of the democracy of ancient Athens and of popular power, which for him had several limits. With the conservative defence of private property, which is the core of his political thinking, closely connected to his conception of justice, Hume insisted on the egalitarianism as a form of fanaticism[38]. Certainly, Hume's conservatism was not that "European reactionary" of the end of the eighteenth century, that was traumatised by the French Revolution, but it was historically the first variant of conservatism, which was very much in vogue, both in Europe and in America. Hume – concluded Resnick – freed the conservative theory from nostalgic feudalism and absolute trust in dubious theological premises. He appreciated tradition, but recognised the need for change in terms of adaptation, based on experience, to customs. Hume defended freedom, but invoked its defence to favour, rather than undermine, authority. He opposed the total and radical social transformation derived from abstract metaphysical philosophy and called for gradual pragmatic adjustments and improvements[39]. He was, in short, a modern conservative intellectual.

More recently, Michael L. Frazer, has spoken clearly of "undue conservatism"[40], regarding the moral and political thought of Hume, deriving directly from his particular conception of justice.

---

37 *Ibid.*, p. 63.
38 David Resnick, 'David Hume: A Modern Conservative', The European Legacy, 1 (1996), p. 398.
39 *Ibid.*, p. 401. On the substantial difference between the conservatism of Hume and the post-Enlightenment one, which developed in contrast to the revolutionary ideals of the late eighteenth century, Bongie also insisted in his *David Hume*, p. 128.
40 Michael L. Frazer, *The Enlightenment of Sympathy: Justice and the Moral Sentiments in the Eighteenth Century and Today* (Oxford and New York: Oxford University Press, 2010), p. 12.

The latter is an individual virtue consisting of obedience to existing social conventions, which promote the public interest. Therefore, justice is never the virtue of a "social system"[41] in Hume. This, for Frazer, does not allow the Scottish thinker to capture essential features of what is today ordinarily meant by the term *justice*.

But this also remains a clear proof of conservatism primarily because in Hume *justice* is never intended as *social justice*, that is, it is never synonymous with *egalitarianism*. The egalitarian solution as established in the second *Enquiry* is entirely rejected by Hume, since, far from favouring the interests of society, it would irreparably compromise them.

---

41 *Ibid.*, p. 72.

12. THE IMPOSSIBLE LIBERALISM

Faced with the univocal nature of the interpretations so far briefly illustrated, the readings of those who persisted in denying or circumscribing or minimising Hume's conservatism appear forced and misleading.

One of these distorting points of view is undoubtedly that of John Gray, who argued that Hume's politics contains undoubtedly liberal elements, even though Hume wrote before the term *liberal* came into widespread usage. According to Gray, the reflection upon the history of political thought demonstrates that it was "in the writings of the social philosophers and political economists of the Scottish Enlightenment that we find the first comprehensive statement in systematic form of the principles and foundations of liberalism"[1], and it "is in Hume, indeed, despite his reputation as a conservative theorist, that we find the most powerful defence of the liberal system of limited government"[2].

More or less on the same interpretative line as Gray is the judgement by John B. Stewart, author of liberal orientation, according to whom what is true of conservatives, that is their tendency to reduce ideas to pure manifestations of custom and prejudice, cannot be said of Hume's political thought, which sought to preserve the value of concepts, but transformed their semantics in the direction of scepticism. Stewart's submission is that Hume was not a conservative. He called the Scot "a liberal", using that word "broadly, to refer to those who thought that major reforms were highly desirable in the United Kingdom in

---

1   John Gray, *Liberalism* (Minneapolis: Minnesota University Press, 1986), p. 24.
2   *Ibid.*

the late-eighteenth and early-nineteenth centuries"[3]. For his being an innovator in the economy, Hume went to the top of the list of modern liberal thinkers, as an interpreter of a liberalism devoted to ideological change and to overcome the *status quo*. Hume, for Stewart, not only did not defend, unlike Burke, the hierarchical construction of society[4], but also claimed to free politics from merely constant values, to favour a new process in which public opinion and political institutions tended to reform each other[5]. Ultimately, for Stewart, Hume's scepticism did not necessarily imply political conservatism: the discussion of issues such as the protection of private property, representative government in a state of law, and free-market were indeed evidence of an adherence by Hume to liberalism, for which he also came to elaborate an empirical policy, helping to prepare the English culture for the reforms of the nineteenth century, carried out by politicians who called themselves liberal and identified as conservatives those who used arguments and theories aimed at masking acquired social privileges.

Stewart's standpoint has received some consensus in critical historiography. For example, Russell Hardin stated that Hume wrote "in an age of liberty", and although many scholars think him deeply conservative, he was "strongly in support of liberty in ways and to a degree that are inconsistent with the views of standard conservatism in his time"; so it can be said that Hume shared with conservatives "a sense of history and its role in our beliefs and possibilities", but he did not share with them "their sense of the relations between citizens and government"[6].

Some other less definitive interpretations, with which some scholar have tried to counterbalance the judgment on Hume, are not lacking. According to Dennis C. Rasmussen, for example, Hume's political thought had "its conservative aspects", but the Scot was "too liberal in the broadest sense of the term" because he embraced some ideals as benefits of the rule of law,

---

3   John B. Stewart, p. 6.
4   *Ibid.*, p. 302.
5   *Ibid.*, p. 213.
6   Russell Hardin, *David Hume: Moral and Political Theorist* (Oxford: Oxford University Press, 2007), p. 185.

limited government, freedom of expression, private property, and commerce, which were "the core ideals associated with the liberal tradition"[7]. Although Hume was one of those thinkers, like Smith, Montesquieu, and Voltaire, who cannot accurately be described as a partisan in any forthright sense, however he can be labelled as a "pragmatic liberal", because of his support offered to the constitution resulting from the Glorious Revolution, his embracement of the core ideals of the liberal tradition, and his emphasis on the importance of prudence in applying those ideals[8].

There have been scholars who have even refused to judge the increasing conservatism of Hume. For example, Ryu Susato rejected this argument, assuming that "this is not to deny that there was any intellectual development through his life and writings", but merely to proclaim that there is a "primary concern"[9] that lies in revisiting what Forbes called the "essential continuity of Hume's thought"[10].

The theses summarised above appear rather weakly because not very well supported by direct references to the texts of Hume.

An unequivocal confirmation of Hume's impossible liberalism is his denial of any hypothesis of resistance towards the government, which is perhaps the essential principle of modern liberalism, in which the defence of freedom there has always been related to the right of resistance[11], already starting, one might say, from Locke and his assumption of the people's "Right to resume their original Liberty, and, by the Establishment of a new Legislative (such as they shall think fit) provide for their own Safety and Security, which is the end for which they are"[12]. Things

---

7   Rasmussen, *The Infidel and the Professor*, p. 13.
8   See Rasmussen, *The Pragmatic Enlightenment: Recovering the Liberalism of Hume, Smith, Montesquieu, and Voltaire* (Cambridge: Cambridge University Press, 2014), especially chapters 2 and 4.
9   Susato, p. 25, note 10.
10 Forbes, *Hume's Philosophical Politics*, p. x.
11 See, on this specific topic, David Sidorsky, *The Liberal Tradition in European Thought* (New York: Putnam, 1970); Haakonssen, *Traditions of Liberalism: Essays on John Locke, Adam Smith, and John Stuart Mill* (Sidney: Centre for Independent Studies, 1988).
12 Locke, *Second Treatise of Government: An Essay Concerning the True Original, Extent and End of Civil Government* (1690), ed. by Richard

are very different for Hume: government, if devoid of an "exact obedience", is useless, and a "blind submission is commonly due to magistracy"[13]. Though he admits, in the *Treatise*, that "no nation, that cou'd find any remedy, ever yet suffer'd the cruel ravages of a tyrant, or were blam'd for their resistance"[14], however, he immediately adds that on some occasions "it may be justifiable, both in sound politics and morality, to resist supreme power", but it is "certain" that

> in the ordinary course of human affairs nothing can be more pernicious and criminal; and that besides the convulsions, which always attend revolutions, such a practice tends directly to the subversion of all government, and the causing an universal anarchy and confusion among mankind.[15]

Hume denies the right to resistance responsively and coherently in all his subsequent writings. Assuming that opposition can exist in extraordinary circumstances, the problem would, however, concern the right reason for those who might ask themselves what the need to justify and make it legitimate or even laudable is. In a fairly clarifying essay of 1748, Hume is quite explicit. He speaks of last refuge in desperate cases. The greatest danger for public, violence of rulers, and mischiefs of a civil war are all situations in which "a disposition to rebellion" can force people into many violent measures which they would never have embraced otherwise. However, even in these cases, the right of resistance is not justifiable on the political level, rather than moral. In fact, Hume states in a long and significant passage of the essay *Of the Passive Obedience*:

> Thus the *tyrannicide* or assassination, approved of by ancient maxims, instead of keeping tyrants and usurpers in awe, made them ten times more fierce and unrelenting; and is now justly, upon that account, abolished by the laws of nations, and universally condemned as a base and treacherous method of bringing to justice these disturbers

---

H. Cox (Wheling: Harlan Davidson, 1982), p. 135.
13   Hume, *Treatise*, p. 354.
14   *Ibid.*, p. 353.
15   *Ibid.*, p. 354.

of society. Besides we must consider, that, as obedience is our duty in the common course of things, it ought chiefly to be inculcated; nor can any thing be more preposterous than an anxious care and solicitude in stating all the cases, in which resistance may be allowed. In like manner, though a philosopher reasonably acknowledges, in the course of an argument, that the rules of justice may be dispensed with in cases of urgent necessity; what should we think of a preacher or casuist, who should make it his chief study to find out such cases, and enforce them with all the vehemence of argument and eloquence? Would he not be better employed in inculcating the general doctrine, than in displaying the particular exceptions, which we are, perhaps, but too much inclined, of ourselves, to embrace and to extend?[16]

After these words, any further assessment about a hypothetical legitimation of resistance by Hume would be superfluous. But there is more.

In the *History*, which is a sort of testament to the brutalities of civil war as well as of the tyrannies arising as reactions to failed rebellions, Hume suggests:

If ever, on any occasion, it were laudable to hide truth from the populace, it must be confessed, that the doctrine of resistance affords such an example; and that all speculative reasoners ought to observe, with regard to this principle, the same cautious silence which the laws, in every species of government, have ever prescribed to themselves.[17]

The fairly clear Hume's standpoint led some scholars to speak of a paradoxical rhetoric about his negation of the right of rebellion: on the one hand, freedom of resistance is part of every political society; on the other, no regime can recognise that rightfully. Hume's rhetoric strategy is intended to compel us to reflect upon the more profound tension between freedom and authority, but also to agree, though partially, "with John Stuart Mill's denunciation of Hume as a cynical apologist of the *status quo*"[18]. Whether it is

---

16 Hume, *Of Passive Obedience* (1748), in *Essays*, pp. 490-491. Hume's italics.
17 Hume, *The History of England*, vol. 5, p. 544.
18 Thomas W. Merrill, 'The Rhetoric of Rebellion in Hume's Constitutional Thought', The Review of Politics, 2 (Spring 2005), p. 258.

moderation or conservatism, Hume's "cardinal political virtue"[19] means that his opposition to the right of resistance makes any approach to liberalism impossible.

Although Hume approached the liberals of his time for his defence of property to the bitter end, and his disinterest in religion and any form of obscurantism, his intellectual strategy, for some authors, had all the characteristics of a concealed Whiggish attempt to make it a forerunner of the triumphant nineteenth-century liberalism. However, we know that, as already mentioned, the nineteenth-century liberal authors of the calibre of Mill and Macaulay not only did not see it at all as a companion of their ideals but openly contested his political principles. Add to this the fact that *liberal* and *conservative* are political concepts that began to characterise the political and intellectual debate only in the early nineteenth-century, in relation to the socio-political and economic effects of the French Revolution and the Industrial Revolution, and that both liberalism and conservatism were still unknown to Hume, who died in 1776.

However, what did Hume say about himself? In a letter dated 1756, he said that he felt a Whig for opinions about things and a Tory for prejudices against people:

> With regard to politics – he wrote – and the character of princes and great men, I think I am very moderate. My views of *things* are more conformable to Whig principles; my representations of *persons* to Tory prejudices. Nothing can so much prove that men commonly regard more persons than things, as to find that I am commonly numbered among the Tories.[20]

It was this double attitude to led Hume to praise the morality and leadership of a Charles I instead of those of a Cromwell and the Puritan "fanatics", or of a Wilkes and of the radicals following him, but it was equally valid that he wished to emphasise that he had never been a Whig. In his autobiography he stated unequivocally that, despite the fact that "the Whig party were in possession of

---

19 *Ibid.*, p. 282.
20 Hume, *To John Clephane (1756)*, in *The Letters of David Hume*, vol. 1, p. 237. Hume's italics.

bestowing all places, both in the state and in literature, I was so little inclined to yield to their senseless clamour"[21].

Although Hume could not claim for himself the label of *conservative*, in the modern meaning of the term dating back to 1818, precisely to the first issue of the journal "Le Conservateur" founded by François-René de Chateaubriand[22], however it is quite easy to find in his writings a model that is significantly similar to the structure of thought that shortly afterwards it was possible to call, appropriately, conservative. Nevertheless, often, Hume's juxtaposition with political conservatism were made to pass as a superficial element, irrelevant to the central nucleus of his ideas, that were almost entirely aimed at the creation of a "science of man"[23], and not at the delineation of a possible political orientation. Hume's conservatism, in other words, for some scholars who have dealt with it, especially in Italy, would almost be a dead idea, at times inconsistent, in any case not falling within the circle of his system of thought.

The arguments in support of this thesis are almost always summary, elusive, and often also lacking specific references both to the nature of Hume's conservatism and to the specificities of the tradition of political thought in which it could be placed. In his pioneering study, Giarrizzo went no further than the brief reconstruction of English political events between 1748 and 1762, a period in which Hume's alleged "political conservatism"[24] would have matured; but it was a mere aptitude to prefer, between a world of fanatics and one of superstitious, indeed the latter, a moreover uncertain attitude, always held, "like Humean liberalism itself, on the edge of a contradiction that accompanies oscillating the whole span of his political experience"[25]. In addition to denoting the characters of its contradictory and uncertainty nature, Hume's conservatism, for Giarrizzo, is imbued with a progressivism made explicit not only by the interest in the positions of the Whig authors Adam Smith and John Millar, who took the liberal road,

---

21 Hume, *My Own Life*, p. xxxviii.
22 With regard to this primacy, see Muller, p. 26.
23 Hume, *Treatise*, p. 4.
24 Giarrizzo, *David Hume*, 1962, pp. 96-100.
25 *Ibid.*, pp. 47-48. My own translation.

but also "from the total absence in Hume (nature is too powerful for the reason; however freedom is asserted as the nature and the life) of every sympathy authority in the statist sense"[26]. The fact that conservatism is by Giarrizzo perceived as synonymous with "statism" is symptomatic of the superficiality of the analysis proposed on this specific topic of Hume's political thought by this scholar, according to which, moreover, at the base of the dynamic Humean vision of "progress" of society there would be only liberalism, while conservatism would concern "the political and social structure, the mutual relations between the parties"[27]. Although, therefore, one cannot help but notice his "conservative liberalism"[28], for Giarrizzo, Hume remains a thinker with a "disturbing ambiguity when, disdaining the traits of liberal society, he specularly analyzes its contradiction and crisis"[29].

For another Italian scholar, Lia Formigari, Hume's conservatism can be found both in his vision of history as "great lady of wisdom"[30] and in his indifference to "revolutionary legality", since he considers any revolutionary acting as illegitimate; which not only earned him the reputation of "Tory historian", but also stimulated the "counter-revolutionary use"[31] of the *History of England* by the French conservatives. Formigari's reference is to the work of Laurence L. Bongie, who, by insisting on the intellectual figure of Hume as a possible prophet of the French counter-revolution, demonstrated, on the basis of a considerable number of historical sources, archive materials, and citations in the writings of the

---

26 Giarrizzo, *Introduzione*, in Hume, *Antologia di scritti politici*, ed. by G. Giarrizzo (Bologna: il Mulino, 1978), p. 18. My own translation.
27 Giarrizzo, *David Hume*, p. 48. My own translation.
28 Giarrizzo, *Introduzione*, p. 10. My own translation.
29 *Ibid.*, p. 22.
30 Lia Formigari, *Introduzione*, in Hume, *Politica e scienza dell'uomo*, ed. by Formigari (Rome: Editori Riuniti, 1975), p. 30. My translation. For a complete outline of the cuts operated in the Italian editions of Hume's political writings, and the reasons for the new complete Italian collection edited by me, *Libertà e moderazione. Scritti politici* (Soveria Mannelli: Rubbettino, 2016), see my recent article 'Lost (and Found) in Italian Translation: David Hume as a Political Thinker and Statesman', Eighteenth-Century Scotland, 33 (Spring 2019), pp. 6-9.
31 *Ibid.*, p. 23. My own translation.

major counter-revolutionary theorists, not so much the attempted exploitation of his thought, as much as the extent of Hume's real "impact" on many French conservative authors, including de Maistre and Louis de Bonald. Both before and after 1789, this impact, for Bongie, "was of undeniable importance, greater even for a time than the related influence of Burke, although it represents a contribution to French counter-revolutionary thought which, unlike that of Burke, has been almost totally ignored by historians to this day"[32]. In other words, how Hume had narrated the hapless career of Charles I, and the seventeenth-century English revolution was "of great applicability" in French conservatives' "defence of *ancien régime*"[33]; and Hume's influence, "though in some ways more subtle and diffused, is greater before the turn of the century than even the sensational but somewhat speculative impact of Burke"[34].

Hume's conservatism, in conclusion, is not an irrelevant element which adds to his political thinking. It is an essential characteristic tending to exclude any influence of ideological liberalism, except for economic liberalism, namely the recognition of freedom of economic initiative and of the free market society against all forms of egalitarianism and collectivism. After all, the true Anglo-American conservatism is the political preservation of this kind of freedom. We must ascertain, at this point, the kind of conservatism that inspires Hume's political orientation.

---

32 Bongie, *Preface to the Liberty Fund Edition*, in *David Hume*, pp. xiii-xiv.
33 Bongie, *David Hume*, p. xiii.
34 *Ibid.*, p. 90.

13. A SCEPTICAL CONSERVATISM

From a careful reading of all Hume's writings on politics, and not only of the most well-known ones, it emerges that, although his empiricism may be worth the title of classical liberal thinker, his political thought is authentically conservative.

If one really has to speak of "revolution" in the case of Hume, he cannot but link it to the desired change in the way in which one looks at philosophy without pursuing the pretensions of abstractionism and rationalist innovation and, above all, without ever departing from the real and common sense of things, attachment to tradition, and custom. Otherwise, his conclusions on justice, peace, and security, which he could conquer more with a "passive obedience" to conventional norms, custom, and order stability, which cannot be abolished by revolutionary or subversive acts, would not be explained.

These are the conclusions that led Hume, among other things, to consider the American revolution not precisely as a "revolution", but as an "affirmation" of the conventions developed outside of everyday British habits. His "enlightenment" does not lend itself to being agitated as proof of his alleged rationalism, and not only for its Scottish matrix, already in itself distant from the radical and rationally optimistic declination, typical of the *philosophes*, with regard to the powers of reason, but also for its distinctly conservative vein, deriving from its heated anti-universalism and anti-fanaticism accent, typical, moreover, of the British culture[1].

---

1   On the "conservative Enlightenment", see Pocock, *Clergy and Commerce: The Conservative Enlightenment in England*, in Raffaele Ajello and others (ed. by), *L'età dei Lumi. Studi storici sul Settecento europeo in onore di Franco Venturi* (Naples: Jovene, 1985), pp. 523-562; Vincenzo Ferrone, *I profeti dell'illuminismo: le metamorfosi della*

For his positions, Hume has often eluded definition as an Enlightenment thinker. Peter Gay, for example, wondered "what, after all, does Hume, who was a conservative, have in common with Condorcet, who was a democrat?"[2]. Despite his positive evaluation of civilisation and conversable society, following the example of Parisian salons, Hume's criticism of social contract theory, his respect for convention, stability, custom, continuity, and other positions stand awkwardly alongside the individualistic and rationalistic image of the Enlightenment. To put it in the words of a well-known French scholar confirming that Hume's conservatism is a historiographical truth also in Europe, the "conservative enlightenment" of the Scotsman uses reason as "a merciless sieve" because of the demolition of the "building of the so-called natural right"; this is a philosophical-political stance that makes of Hume an "enlightened conservative (he was a Tory of liberal spirit!) on the political level"[3], that is "a thinker who stubbornly undermined the intellectual supports of his century and precisely of that century of the Enlightenment, of which, on the other hand, he possessed in the highest degree spirit and style"[4].

More recently, about Hume's atypical enlightenment vein, there has been talk of "sceptical enlightenment" as

> the concept representing his distinctive way of supporting what he believes to be the core of modern values (refinement and politeness), while avoiding falling into any kind of dogmatism, including philosophical dogmatism. In doing so, Hume levels his criticism against what has been considered the alleged "Enlightenment" credo of "Reason and Progress", while simultaneously refusing to side with naïve traditionalism.[5]

Therefore, Hume's conservatism, far from being an irrelevant

---

ragione nel tardo Settecento italiano (Rome-Bari: Laterza, 2000), pp. 312-338.
2   Peter Gay, *The Enlightenment: An Interpretation* (London: Weidenfeld & Nicolson 1966-9), vol. 1, p. x.
3   Jean-Jacques Chevallier, *Storia del pensiero politico*, ed. by Nino Tonna (Bologna: il Mulino, 1989), p. 412. My own translation.
4   *Ibid.*, p. 417. My own translation.
5   Susato, p. 21.

element with respect to the organic body of his philosophical, political, and economic ideas, is, on the contrary, the natural outcome, in perfect coherence with that complex of heterodox doctrines hardly sortable in the theoretical schemes of modern era, since they are unsuited to the intellectual fashion of their time and their own alternatives to the most widespread tendencies of theoretical contractarianism and Jacobinism. Moreover, what was referred to conservatism was not only a defence of the *status quo,* or the existing order considered violated by the advent of revolutionary regimes, but a reaction to the rationalist currents that were preparing to dominate much of European thinking, from Hobbes onwards.

Burke's criticisms of the men of theories, Hegel's condemnation of the abstract reason of the French revolutionaries, Metternich's sarcasm of presumptuous men were, in modern times, all testimonies of the conservative refusal of the rationalist claim to elevate reason to supreme arbiter in political questions, and to demolish the traditional order with emphasis on the assumption that the beliefs and institutions accepted by men as natural are inevitably predisposed to suffer the ordeal of rational acceptance. For this aim, conservatism is a political orientation contrary to rationalism and *ideology,* a term that Hume did not yet know, but whose meaning is given by him with "false philosophy", attributing to it the same semantics, with the following expression:

> We may observe a gradation of three opinions, that rise above each other, according as the persons, who form them, acquire new degrees of reason and knowledge. These opinions are that of the vulgar, that of a false philosophy, and that of the true; where we shall find upon enquiry, that the true philosophy approaches nearer to the sentiments of the vulgar, than to those of a mistaken knowledge.[6]

For Hume, the typically modern philosopher reasons in accordance with some abstract speculative principles, detached from the common sense and language, from the pre-philosophical assumptions that cannot be excluded from a public debate which also claims to be universal; false philosophies would like to provide the

---

6 Hume, *Treatise,* p. 147.

unconditional understanding of what is thought to be definitively right, providing abstract paradigms, mere nihilisms shielded under a semblance of objectivity that however escapes the knowledge of the vast majority of persons. Indeed, very few individuals can question the self-referentiality of specific ideological schemes and reopen the road to what for Hume is the "authentic philosophy". Persuaded that the best response to abstruse rationalism is scepticism, Hume sees the "true philosopher" as the one who is willing to humiliate himself, abandon rationalist arrogance, and recognise the indispensable autonomy of custom, as well as that of human feelings: this is the authentic philosophical disposition and can lead to true wisdom. Instead of pompously assuming supreme authority over nature, with the Baconian pretence to dominate it, for Hume, the true philosopher, that is the sceptic thinker and agent, a severe critic of himself and his supposed truths, plays a circumscribed role because he is aware that conscience and rationality do not arise from his rational abilities.

Hume's political conservatism, unlike that of a de Maistre or a de Bonald, does not need to resort to religious tactics aimed at recovering the Holy Scriptures as a manual of the statesman; it is based on a strictly secular analysis of experience and on contempt for that *a priori* so dear to rationalists and, above all, not inspired by any metaphysical traditionalism. The warning of the French counter-revolutionaries that outside of the unity between politics and religion man will never find neither society nor truth nor salvation is totally outside the intentions of Hume, for whom the judgment of fact suffices for which the society is a mere product of human interests whose satisfaction in itself provides the necessary cohesion. The first book of the *Treatise*, which not coincidentally bears the subtitle *Being an Attempt to Introduce the Experimental Method of Reasoning in Moral Subjects*, clearly illustrates Hume's strategy: to reduce the claims of reason with nothing but the use of rational analysis. Reason – Hume states – is a mere tool for the deepening of knowledge, but it acts in a limited area of activity activity. With his words:

> Reason is the discovery of truth or falshood. Truth or falshood consists in an agreement or disagreement either to the *real* relations

of ideas, or to *real* existence and matter of fact. Whatever, therefore, is not susceptible of this agreement or disagreement, is incapable of being true or false, and can never be an object of our reason.[7]

Hume's world is a world in which facts derive from empirical observations, not from reason, which cannot in any way be used to prove or disprove the existence of facts, and human behaviour is mostly governed by custom, that for Hume, as he pointed out in the first *Enquiry* "is the great guide of human life", precisely is "that principle alone, which renders our experience useful to us, and makes us expect, for the future, a similar train of events with those which have appeared in the past"[8]. With this assumption, Hume inflicts a severe blow on that "harmony of reason", which, according to his rationalist contemporaries, animates the totality of nature, to which universal moral imperatives could be deduced. Whatever Stewart says, that Hume's anti-rationalism "is a dogma of orthodox intellectual history"[9], the Humean strategy put in place to demolish the rationalistic assumptions starts from the idea that the external order we attribute to the phenomenal world is not a discovery of reason because it is based on the principles of human nature; therefore, it rests on individual convictions and not on a process of logical validation.

In controversy against the abstractness and unfoundedness of metaphysical knowledge, Hume assigns a purely descriptive task to reason. The true philosopher must neither prescribe human behaviour nor construct abstract theories, as rationalistic metaphysics does, but must only *describe* the faculties of man, just as the geographer describes the configuration of the Earth. Hume, in other words, reduces reason to a mere "discovery of truth or falsehood"[10], which makes it strongly opposed both to the rationalistic extension of the role of reason to the totality of human experience and the claim to reach demonstrative conclusions and permanence in the functioning of life. This is a precise critique

---

7   *Ibid.*, p. 295. Hume's italics.
8   Hume, *An Enquiry Concerning Human Understanding*, p. 32.
9   John B. Stewart, p. 5.
10 Hume, *Treatise*, p. 295.

of the exuberance of reason towards which Hume maintains a consistent sceptical attitude in all his writings.

Equally modest is the role assigned by Hume to reason in the moral sphere: it is "perfectly inert, and can never either prevent or produce any action or affection"[11]. Reason provides neither motivation for action nor final judgments on moral matters. Human activities, in fact, are stimulated *ab initio* by passions, desires, needs, determining feelings, and volitions acting as a response to direct emotional experience, generate behaviour, discover the evolution of the psychic life of man, and they cannot in any way be yoked by reason; and theorizing it would mean admitting that an inert principle is capable of controlling an active one. Hence the famous conclusion by Hume, that is at least unusual for an author who could be defined as an enlightenment one:

> Reason is, and ought only to be the slave of the passions, and can never pretend to any other office than to serve and obey them. As this opinion may appear somewhat extraordinary, it may not be improper to confirm it by some other considerations.[12]

Morality is connected to the behavioural reasons that give rise to action. The assessment of the modes in which a person should act – Hume maintains based on his empiricism – cannot transcend empirical reality, and at most it is possible to evaluate only the most effective means to achieve a given end, since the latter is, in any case, placed beyond the evaluation itself. Therefore, according to Hume, the rules of morality are not necessarily the conclusions of reason. To nourish the moral sense of men are the passions, certainly not the rational calculation.

Hume closes the section of the *Treatise* that argues against moral rationalism by specifying the difference that exists in the moral sphere between *is* and *ought*. He observes that many systems of moral philosophy, proceeding in the logical way of reasoning, at some point make an unremarked transition from premises whose parts are linked only by *is* to conclusions whose pieces are connected by *ought*. This transitions, for Hume, is a deduction

---

11 *Ibid.*, p. 294.
12 *Ibid.*, p. 266.

"altogether inconceivable"[13] because it would "subvert all the vulgar systems of morality, and let us see, that the distinction of vice and virtue is not founded merely on the relations of objects, nor is perceiv'd by reason"[14].

The dominant twentieth-century interpretation has endorsed this putative thesis and has called it "Hume's Law" or "is-ought problem" or "Hume's guillotine"[15]. It states that no ethical or evaluative conclusion whatsoever may be validly inferred from any set of purely factual premises. In other terms, an evaluative statement cannot be derived from purely factual premises, often formulated as: *one can't derive an "ought" from an "is"*. Hume commits himself to a non-propositional view of moral judgment, that can be interpreted as a methodological warning about required procedure in inquiry.

Hume's thesis also provokes considerable consequences in the ethical-political sphere, since it excludes any prescriptive science. The entire construction of natural right, carried out by those thinkers who deduce from the description of human nature a perception of what is right, violates the Hume's law[16]. If it is true that from a description of the world "as it is" cannot derive an *ought*, then the scientific language, not admitting any such bound, obliges us to the clear separation of *facts* from *values*. This precludes the possibility of founding a normative ethics, able to establish with certainty what is good or right to do, and at the same time excludes that in the ethical sphere one can argue on the basis of rational principles. This is a formal warning against the rationalist construction founded on the law of nature.

In Hume's viewfinder, as is easy to guess, there is the theory of

---

13 *Ibid.*, p. 302.
14 *Ibid.*
15 On this specific topic, see Max Black, 'The Gap Between *Is* and *Should*', The Philosophical Review, 2 (1964), p. 165; William D. Hudson, *The Is/Ought Question. A Collection of Papers on the Central Problem in Moral Philosophy* (London: Macmillan, 1969); Charles R. Pidgen, *Hume on Is and Ought* (New York: Palgrave Macmillan, 2010).
16 See Brian Tierney, *The Idea of Natural Rights: Studies on Natural Rights, Natural Law and Church Law 1150-1625* (Atlanta: Scholars Press, 1997).

natural law with all its unquestionable certainties and immutable values, detectable by rational investigation. Subtracting morality from the jurisdiction of reason, Hume can affirm that morality is "felt", and not judged, derived as it is from a moral feeling emerging from "impressions" that can be pleasant or not, good or evil. Morality is, therefore, a product of nature. Relegating reason to a narrow sphere between experience and the world of passions, Hume sets new premises for the enhancement of custom and sentiment, opening the way to political romanticism. In one of his significant political essays, he maintains that nothing is freer than man's imagination, and that the difference between fiction and belief lies in sentiment and passion, without regard to any will and logic. "Men – he concludes – are mightily govern'd by the imagination, and proportion their affections more to the light, under which any object appears to them, than to its real and intrinsic value"[17].

All these considerations have prompted some scholars to rightly observe that "the anti-rationalist conservative tradition begins with Hume" who argued the reason "is inert: if cannot motivate us to action nor provide any fondation for moral and political values"[18].

Hume, perhaps with more significant theoretical and speculative acumen than other subsequent conservative-oriented thinkers, attacks rationalism revealing the dangers and contradictions in its terrain, that is the philosophical one, in his time dominated by the Platonism of Cambridge and by Cartesianism, philosophies that claim to base ethics on pure reason in order to penetrate the ultimate nature of man, God, and universe. The fallacy of rationalist philosophies, for Hume, consists in the failure to assume awareness of the fact that reason cannot ever, in any context, motivate the action. Reason, in itself, does not constitute a motive for the will but plays a merely supporting role, since it informs passions about their object. Since only fools can claim to have achieved absolute certainty in terms of knowledge, we would do well to content ourselves with understanding things as they appear to us, rather than investigating their unknown causes.

---

17 Hume, *Treatise*, pp. 342-343.
18 Nigel Ashford and Stephen Davies (ed. by), *A Dictionary of Conservative and Libertarian Thought* (New York: Routledge, 1991), p. 223.

Moreover, Hume thinks that "so little correspondent is fact and reality to those philosophical notions"[19], as he states in *Of the Original Contract*. To the abstract theories of the rationalists, which are not discernible from the naïve optimism of their philosophic prophecies, Hume prefers a moderate or "mitigated" scepticism for probable sentences, never definitive, and wants to deal with aspects rather than essences. Hume notes in the first *Enquiry* that our mind tends toward dogmatism, but when we are shown the "infermities" of human understanding, we are naturally inspired to "more modesty and reserve"[20]. Hence his first principle, according to which, "in general, there is a degree of doubt, and caution, and modesty, which, in all kinds of scrutiny and decision, ought for ever to accompany a just reasoned"[21]. Further, human imagination tends to ascend to the real limits of the universe, against which tendency Hume offers the principle for which a correct judgment avoids all high enquiries, conforming itself to common life, "and to such subjects as fall under daily practice and experience"[22]. Thus, he advises we should limit our enquiries to such "subjects as are best adapted to the narrow capacity of human understanding"[23]. As an empiricist, Hume believes that all knowledge begins with experience, which he understands as "impressions" left on the mind by the senses, much as marks are left on a chalkboard by the impact of chalk. The mind itself is passive and contributes nothing new to knowledge. On this basis he argues, for example, that he never saw the causal connection between events because the constant conjunction of the events is accompanied by a habitual expectation that some combinations of events somehow belong together. This conclusion makes sense only within a particularly narrow conception of human consciousness, and a more thoroughgoing scepticism would call even this conception into doubt. All human activities, in both the moral and political spheres, for Hume, are driven by vital forces that call for a reason different from that incensed by modern rationalists,

---

19 Hume, *Of the Original Contract*, p. 472.
20 Hume, *An Enquiry Concerning Human Understanding*, p. 161.
21 *Ibid.*, p. 118.
22 *Ibid.*
23 *Ibid.*

a cause which, in the face of concrete situations of experience, leads to the rapid and complete dissolution of the absolutist axioms of natural law to make way for the typical elements of empiricism, utilitarianism, and experimental adaptation. For Hume, not surprisingly, there is a close relationship between the "necessity" in force in physical events and that observable in moral situations: in both cases we have to deal with collections of experiments; therefore the science of ethical-political conduct can only make use of the same method of physical science, and the philosopher of morality and politics can only fix the principles of his science in the same way that the physicist investigates the nature of things by means of the experiments that lead to them.

To the life of the dogmatist, Hume prefers the life of the sceptic. In his essay titled *The Sceptic* (1742), Hume states that while scepticism is often associated with nihilism and paralysis, he suggests that it tends to lead to moderate, balanced disposition, intellectual humility, inner tranquillity, and a passion for ever-further inquiry. Hume's philosophy "affords no remedy" but it asks "if any other philosophy can afford a remedy"[24].

It is precisely an attitude of this kind that he shows in the reflection and experience of politics. Although it sometimes reaches a level that seems to deny any value to mere political speculation[25], Hume's scepticism and political thinking are not mutually exclusive, and his pungent and intense criticism, always objective and never biased, does not attack the political speculation in itself, but rather any imprudent rationalist attempt to translate it into practice, and any utopian design of ideal republics. This specific attitude is what we can call his sceptical conservatism, in the sense of never dogmatic, never prescriptive, never metaphysical, but always prudential, empirical, and pragmatic. It is precisely an attitude of this kind that he shows in the reflection and experience of politics. Moreover, Hume's scepticism is, in hindsight, the basis of his conservatism in politics.

---

24 Hume, *The Sceptic*, p. 170.
25 In *Whether the British Government*, p. 52, Hume says provocatively that "there is no doubt, but a popular government may be imagined more perfect than absolute monarchy, or even than our present constitution".

Historically, scepticism is in itself political conservatism. One classic example of this assumed relationship is found in Mill's assessment, which referred precisely to Hume's thought:

> [Hume's] absolute scepticism in speculation very naturally brought him round to Toryism in practice; for if no faith can be had in the operations of human intellect, and one side of every question is about as likely as another to be true, a man will commonly be inclined to prefer that order of things which, being no more wrong than every other, he has hitherto found compatible with his private comforts.[26]

Sceptics of all historical periods have generally been accused of promoting nihilism or conservatism or political quietism: if they know nothing, and as Pyrrhonists adopt an attitude of suspension of belief or judgment (in Greek, *epoche*), they have no principle to assert in politics, other than the defence of the *status quo*. Some commentators have stated that the political thought of Montaigne, who was the first modern sceptic, the one who introduced the works of Sextus Empiricus into Renaissance culture, was "deeply conservative" or "an almost Burkean form of conservatism"[27], and that his scepticism was "Pyrrhonian conservatism"[28]. Furthermore, the leading experts in the field tend to include scepticism in conservatism, speaking of conservatism "informed by, but not reducible to, scepticism, in particular towards proposals for radical change, towards utopian theories and ideals, and towards liberal and socialist ideas of human nature"[29].

---

26 Mill, *Bentham*, p. 80n.q-q 38.
27 Nannerl O. Keohane, *Philosophy and the State in France: The Renaissance to the Enlightenment* (Princeton: Princeton University Press, 1980), p. 108.
28 Skinner, *The Foundations of Modern Political Thought* (Cambridge: Cambridge University Press, 1978), vol. 2, p. 283; Popkin, *The History of Scepticism from Erasmus to Descartes* (Assen: Van Gorcum, 1960), p. 49; Elaine Limbrick, *La Vie politique et juridique: considérations sceptiques dans les "Essais"*, in *Les Écrivains et la Politique dans le Sud-Ouest de la France autour des années 1580, Actes du Colloque de Bordeaux, 6-7 novembre 1981* (Bordeaux: Presses Universitaires de Bordeaux, 1982), p. 207; Richard D. Hiley, *Philosophy in Question: Essays on a Pyrrhonian Theme* (Chicago: University of Chicago Press, 1988), p. 24.
29 Roger Scruton, *The Palgrave Macmillan Dictionary of Political Thought* (London and New York, Macmillan, 2007), p. 131.

But scepticism is not the only element that makes Hume a true conservative. Like the later political conservatives, Hume has no sympathy for the nascent political science, that was one of the great intellectual adventures of the Enlightenment, which sees it as an ally of progress at all costs. The study of politics, for Hume, is part of the more general project of the "science of man", which he placed at the core of knowledge as an empirical discipline, attentive to the limits of human intellect and founded on the assumption that freedom is regular and reliable. This Humean science of man, replacing itself to ontology and theology, was able to represent the fundamental explanation of the principles of human nature as the sole basis of a complete system of sciences, among which Hume included logic, morals, and politics. All those sciences had "such a dependence on the knowledge of man, what may be expected in the other sciences, whose connexion with human nature is more close and intimate"[30]. More than the mere cataloguing of experience data, in other words, Hume was interested in comparing the various observation experiments and universal principles, and assumed that "we cannot go beyond experience; and any hypothesis, that pretends to discover the ultimate original qualities of human nature, ought at first to be rejected as presumptuous and chimerical"[31]. Therefore, it is the extension to the moral and social sciences of the experimental method that unites all the particular sciences. The total re-foundation of knowledge was thus by Hume planned through a science of man which, against all forms of superstition and dogmatism, and with the intention of giving life to a naturalistic ethic in a descriptive sense, aspired to occupy the place of the old metaphysics and to explore every manifestation of human nature with reasoning, feelings, virtues and vices, social relations, commercial and business relations, principles of law and forms of government. In this epistemological context, a science of politics, for Hume, can only be based on the experience provided by historical investigation and empirical observation of existing society, without attempting to investigate the interactions between institutions and human nature and in order to discover what is the

---

30 Hume, *Treatise*, p. 4.
31 *Ibid.*, p. 5.

exact function of political institutions, that is, the orientation and control of human behaviour[32].

Politics, in other words, far from being the privileged field of interest of the philosopher or the "reasoners" is, above all, the world of the empiricist, sceptic observer, politician, and statesman. One of the proofs of Hume's firm conviction about the necessity of an empiricist approach to politics is in the text of a letter of 1747, written shortly before leaving for a military mission in the guise of intelligence officer. He considered the experience of the war as a kind of experience that, despite being so unusual for a philosopher, may nevertheless constitute the raw material for a more careful and exhaustive preparation for his future writings of history and political economy. As evidence of the impact that the real experience had on his forthcoming reflections, he announced:

> I shall have an opportunity of seeing Courts & Camps, & if I can afterwards be so happy as to attain leizure and other opportunities, this knowledge may even turn to account to me, as a man of letters, which I confess has always been the sole object of my ambition. I have long had an intention, in my riper years, of composing some History; & I question not but some greater experience of the Operations of the Field, & the Intrigues of the Cabinet, will be requisite, in order to enable me to speak with judgement upon these subjects.[33]

Thanks to the empirical impressions he received in the two years spent around the primary economic and political realities of Europe, while secretary of general St. Clair, Hume has been able to devote himself with greater competence to the drafting of essays included in the *Political Discourses* collection, such as *Of Commerce*, *Of Luxury*, *Of Money*, *Of Interest*, *Of the Balance of Trade*, *Of the Balance of Power*, *Of Taxes*, *Of Public Credit*, and others. To mention one of the most typical cases, some of Hume's more generous observations about economic-political topics overcame those doctrines of his time tending to identify

---

32 See Jones (ed. by), *The Science of Man in the Scottish Enlightenment: Hume, Reid, and Their Contemporaries* (Edinburgh: Edinburgh University Press, 1989).

33 Hume, *To James Oswald of Dunnikier (London, 29 January 1747)*, in *The Letters of David Hume*, vol. 1, p. 109.

in the wealth of a nation the primary reason for the misery of the neighbouring ones. Having visited countries such as Germany, Austria, and the Italian peninsula, close to each other, in some cases even bordering, but so distant in terms of wealth, institutional organisation, and population welfare, allowed him to heap heavy criticism on mercantilism. He argued that between the sixteenth and seventeenth centuries, with the urgency to remove every nation from the dominance of foreign merchants, even those of neighbouring countries, the power of the state still derived from exports, necessary to increase national wealth, territorial expansion, and demographic growth, in a system in which economy was subordinated entirely to politics. In his economic-political essays, which not coincidentally attracted the attention of his compatriot Smith, Hume insisted on the importance that a nation exchanges with neighbouring nations, seen as competitors and jealous emulators in a relationship aimed at favouring the development of the arts and sciences, which is always desirable, especially in a free government. Moreover, perhaps from his practical experience of diplomat and under-secretary of state he concluded that political institutions are not merely a reflection of human conduct, but artificial devices aimed at exercising a function and a force independent of a person's character:

> So great is the force of laws, and of particular forms of government, and so little dependence have they on the humours and tempers of men, that consequences almost as general and certain may sometimes be deduced from them, as any which the mathematical sciences afford us.[34]

Then, Hume's conception of politics is that of a descriptive and non-logical science. Hume accepts the reduction of politics to a science, providing that it adheres to the experimental processes, neglects the methods of traditional logic, and is suspicious of the demonstrations based on mere intellectual comprehension, that is useless before the effects of chance and fate. Hume's involvement in the practice of policy was as significant as his theory, and made

---

34 Hume, *That Politics may be reduced to a Science*, p. 16.

his understanding of the world of politics more insightful and applicable to the issues facing the Britain institutions.

This significant elements of Hume's political ideas were destined to influence the development of conservative political thought in the following centuries, starting right from Burke, despite his particular dislike for the Scottish philosopher. Burke does not seem to regard Hume as a companion in his famous support of the established system; instead he became a critic of the philosophical and religious principles of Hume[35]. However, Burke's negative judgment also concerns Hume as a historian. Daniel I. O'Neill assumes that "Burke held a high opinion of Hume's abilities as a historian, if not as a moral philosopher", based on his criticism of Hume's *History*, despite his disagreements with Hume on the Irish Massacre and Marian controversy[36]. O'Neill also demonstrates that Hume's Burkean valuations can be analysed through "The Annual Register", which the politician of Irish origins founded and for which he wrote most of the articles until 1760. O'Neill maintains that there is abundant evidence in the pages of that magazine that "Burke saw Humean scepticism as a mirror image of the descent into moral, political, and social anarchy that necessarily followed from Bolingbroke's rationalism"[37].

Burke's own words can confirm Burke's critical attitude towards Hume's political principles. In *Three Memorials on French Affairs* (1797), Burke spoke about a predominant inclination towards a system of French conspiracy that "appears in all those who have no religion, when otherwise their disposition leads them to be advocates even for despotism", and included Hume, with these words: "Hence Hume, though I cannot say that he does not throw out some expressions of disapprobation on the proceedings of the levellers in the reign of Richard the Second"[38].

However, apart from these distinctions, which also characterise

---

35   Ernest C. Mossner, *The Life of David Hume*, p. 394.
36   *Ibid.*
37   Daniel I. O'Neill, *The Burke-Wollstonecraft Debate: Savagery, Civilization, and Democracy* (University Park: Pennsylvania State University Press 2007), pp. 66-7.
38   Burke, *Three Memorials on French Affairs. Written in the Years 1791, 1792 and 1793* (London: Printed for F. and C. Rivingston, 1797), p. 53.

the personal judgment that Burke had of Hume, unquestionably remains the ability of the Scottish thinker to have interpreted politics conservatively in a clear advance compared to the Irish politician.

Conservatives like Hume, and afterwards like Burke, did not prejudge change, but were opposed to radical, revolutionary, and violent change. Their opposition relied on the thesis that the revolution dangerously upsets an order that was established gradually over time, and the real and only evolutionary change was that made possible by habit, whose power is consistently signalled in Hume's works, especially in political writings, in which it exalted as a power-consolidating force.

> Habit – wrote Hume – soon consolidates what other principles of human nature had imperfectly founded; and men, once accustomed to obedience, never think of departing from that path, in which they and their ancestors have constantly trod, and to which they are confined by so many urgent and visible motives.[39]

Trying to accelerate the gradual process of habit or custom meant, for Hume, to risk provoking real disasters, such as the "total dissolution of government, which gives liberty to the multitude, and makes the determination or choice of a new establishment depend upon a number, which nearly approaches to that of the body of the people"[40], and the loosening of the constraints of civil society due to the alteration of the social order.

A conservative of the twentieth century, Peter Viereck, using words different from those of Hume but with the same meaning, pointed out that conservative political doctrine is not opposed to all innovations but only to those "enlightened" in an abstract sense, "but in practice unworkable and disruptive because they have not evolved from the solid roots of past experience"[41].

---

39 Hume, *Of the Origin of Government*, p. 39.
40 Hume, *Of the Original Contract*, p. 472.
41 Peter Viereck, 'Liberals and Conservatives, 1789-1951', The Antioch Review, 4 (1951), p. 390.

14. CONSERVATIVE BECAUSE REALIST

Hume's political realism is another, irrefutable fact of his conservatism. Political realism is a "cousin" of political conservatism, and in Hume this kinship emerges in all clarity. As some authoritative studies confirm, realism cannot be understood in isolation from conservatism, that constitutes the foundation of realism, and the conservatives are mainly realist in the international politics[1].

In the previous chapter the salient features of Hume's political realism have been described, which here is not the case for resuming, except for a brief clarification on the element that most seems to unite a realist with a conservative, that is the fixity and non-perfectibility of human nature[2].

Being conservative, notoriously, is to stand upon the solid ground of reality by accepting the existing order of things as given and considered good in themselves, from a perspective that allows the rulers to act prudently, when they are really sure that their actions produce results. In other words, the conservative is the true defender of freedom, because he bases his reasoning on the real order of things and nurtures a profound distrust of the human

---

1   On the topic of interconnectedness between realism and conservatism, see Piki Ish-Shalom, 'The Triptych of Realism and Conservatism', International Studies Review, 8 (2006), pp. 441-468; Brian C. Rathbun, 'Does One Right Make a Realist? Conservatism, Neoconservatism, and Isolationism in the Foreign Policy Ideology of American Elites', Political Science Quarterly, 2 (Summer, 2008), pp. 271-299.
2   I dealt with the relationship, if not identification, between political realism and political conservatism in the essay *Il realismo politico nel movimento conservatore angloamericano del Novecento*, in Campi and De Luca, pp. 333-49.

capacity to change the established order through the coercive power of the state. So, the conservative is the protector of the stable reality of the nature of things and of men. Consequently, he is a privileged continuator of Machiavelli, who was the undisputed father of modern political realism, which became, over the following centuries, a counterpart of utopianism.

Hume's conception of nature has a fatal weakness, for which any change introduced into society could only be imperfect, heralded what for later conservatives turn out an indispensable truth, namely the idea of the imperfectness and immutability of human nature, with which the preservation of social relations will be punctually justified.

According to the conservatives, man could not make his will a law without any regard for the "stable nature of things", because they accepted things as useful in themselves[3]. Hume's recognition of the high uniformity between human actions, in all nations and all ages, and of the fixity of human nature which always remains the same in its principles and operations, emerged above all from the first *Enquiry*, as has been said before[4].

Hume warned his contemporaries from those certainties of the philosophes in the overwhelming the progress of society. The belief in progress is, with the words used by the conservative philosopher Michael Oakeshott in *On Being Conservative* (1956), "the most cruel and unprofitable of all beliefs, arousing cupidity without satisfying it, in order to think it inappropriate for a government to be conspicuously 'progressive'"[5]. In contrast to this "progressive belief", Oakeshott invoked Hume's authority to legitimise the "disposition to be conservative", which is appropriate, he said,

---

3   To this topic, the conservative author Richard Weaver dedicated very profound reflections, in *Ideas Have Consequences* (Chicago: University of Chicago Press, 1948).

4   Hume, *An Enquiry Concerning Human Understanding*, ed. Millican, p. 60.

5   Michael Oakeshott, *On Being Conservative* (1956), in *Rationalism in Politics, and Other Essays*, ed. by Timothy Fuller (Indianapolis: Liberty Press, 1991) p. 194.

to men who have something to do and something to think about on their own account, who have a skill to practice or an intellectual fortune to make, to people whose passions do not need to be inflamed, whose desires do not need to be provoked and whose dreams of a better world need no prompting.[6]

Therefore, there is a mutual influence between the conservative intellectual movement emerged in the Anglo-American area, especially in the second half of the twentieth century, and the political realism. The realistic view of human nature inspired the conservative conception of society and politics; conversely, realism found solid roots in conservatism. Burkean conservatism and political realism were animated by a pessimistic conception of man, based on the awareness of his limits and defects. The Burkean consideration of man as a creature of habits, traditions, and customs, who desires stability and order over any other political ideal and human value persisted in the more secular variants of twentieth-century conservatism, in which the description of the human being as an animal of lust, passion, selfishness, and emotion, together with the demonstration that these elements are nothing but integral components of social relations, was very recurrent.

The affinity between realism and conservatism has been evidenced by Hans J. Morgenthau, one of the most influential intellectuals of twentieth-century political realism. His *Scientific Man Versus Power Politics* (1946)[7], in which the historical and intellectual roots of realism are identified, opens with a quote from Burke: "Politicks ought to be adjusted, not to human reasoning, but to human nature; of which the reason is but a part, and by no means the greatest part"[8]. This passage, taken from a minor paper by Burke, *Observations on a Late Publication on the Present State of the Nation*, dating back to 1769, twenty-one years earlier than the famous *Reflections on the Revolution in France*, referred

---

6   *Ibid.*
7   Hans. J. Morgenthau, *Scientific Man Versus Power Politics* (Chicago and London: The University of Chicago Press, 1946).
8   Burke's sentence appears on the back cover of Morgenthau's volume, and is taken from Burke, *Observations on a Late Publication on the Present State of the Nation* (London: Printed for J. Dodsley, 1769), p. 123.

to an overview of human nature and relationships between the state, intermediate social bodies, and individuals. It constituted an irrefutable proof of the influence exerted by the father of Anglo-American conservatism on the realist Morgenthau.

In truth, it is not the only circumstance in which Morgenthau recognised the intellectual debt towards Burke. The authentic realist – Morgenthau asserted in the last chapter of his book – is neither the scientist who draws his conclusions from postulates or empirical premises nor the theorist who acts on the social world by means of abstract concepts. The realist is the "statesman", the one who "recognises in the contingencies of the social world the concretizations of eternal laws"[9]. According to Morgenthau, nobody in the history of political ideas has ever traced the profile of the statesman better than Burke, who in his *Speech on the Petition of the Unitarians* (1792) had written:

> A statesman differs from a professor in an university: the latter has only the general view of society; the former, the statesman, has a number of circumstances to combine with those general ideas, and to take into his consideration. Circumstances are infinite, are infinitely combined, are variable and transient: he who does not take them into consideration is not erroneous, but stark mad; *dat operam ut cum ratione insaniat*; he is metaphysically mad. A statesman, never losing sight of principles, is to be guided by circumstances; and judging contrary to the exigencies of the moment, he may ruin his country forever.[10]

This quote facilitated Morgenthau's conclusions on the subject in question, which, moreover, offered him the main alternative argument to the social engineering of socialist politics[11].

The distinctive characteristic of a practical statesmen is the

---

9   Morgenthau, p. 220.
10 Burke, *Speech on a motion for leave to bring in a Bill to Repeal and alter certain acts respecting religious opinions, upon the occasion of a petition of the Unitarian Society, May 11 1792*, in *The Works of the Right Honourable Edmund Burke in Twelve Volumes* (London: John C. Nimmo, 1899), vol. 7, p. 41.
11 Morgenthau, p. 221: "As the scientist creates a new nature out of his knowledge of the forces of nature, so the statesman creates a new society out of his knowledge of the nature of man".

ability to understand empathically, as different from the mere possibility of comprehend, the character of a situation in its uniqueness. Capacity for judgment, sense of time, immediate understanding of the relationship between means and results – explained Isaiah Berlin – depend on empirical factors such as experience, observation, and above all that "sense of reality", which consists of a conscious integration of a large number of apparently irrelevant or imperceptible elements present in that situation; elements that form some kind of design that in itself "suggests" or "invites" the appropriate action. The art of government implies a kind of knowledge that Berlin called "practical wisdom", which statesman needs if is to succeed in "understanding the societies of their own or other times", and which allows him, "faced with a critical situation and forced to choose between alternative courses", to "judge the situation, assess it so that he can answer objectors" and give reasons "for rejecting alternative solutions", without "demonstrate the truth of what he is saying by reference to theories or system of knowledge"[12]. This kind of knowledge, in other words, allows those who govern to guess what in certain circumstances is feasible and what is not possible without referring to some teachable general formula, for political action must take care of the complexity of the real situation. This consideration remembers somewhat the description of politics given by Oakeshott in *Political Education* (1951), as a "pursuit of intimations" of a "tradition of behaviour"[13].

George F. Kennan, another important exponent of twentieth-century political realism, considered himself an expatriate from his time, an intellectual more suited to the eighteenth century, a conservative, in the European meaning of the term, who desired a world of fixed hierarchies, in which the statesmen, namely the political decision-makers, acted on behalf of real subjects, polls or tendencies, and popular claims[14].

---

12 Isaiah Berlin, *The Sense of Reality: Studies in Ideas and Their History* (1996), ed. by Henry Hardy (Princeton and Oxford: Princeton University Press, 2019), pp. 41-42.
13 Oakeshott, *Political Education* (1951), in *Rationalism in Politics and Other Essays* (London: Methuen,1962), p. 125.
14 See Lee Congdon, *George Kennan: A Writing Life* (Wilmington: ISI

Concerning the inverse relationship, that of the influence of political realism on the intellectual journey of conservatives, an analysis of the theoretical components of the variegate conservative political-cultural movement cannot escape that realistic arguments about the nature of man and his "community" constitute an irreplaceable ideal foundation. In the writings of some of its most representative exponents of the twentieth century, from Richard M. Weaver to Eric Voegelin, from Russell A. Kirk to Roger Scruton, conservatism is presented essentially as a realistic approach to politics.

Weaver showed that the conservative is a realist who believes that there is a structure of reality independent of his will and desires[15]. Realism was the background to the philosophical themes of the latest works by Weaver, in which he denounced the evils of contemporary society as united by a cultural and ideological reluctance to conceive the ontological order as real[16]. Voegelin, from an anti-Gnostic perspective, always distinguished between *truth* and *idolatry*, *real problems* and *existential problems* (or *representation*) as some of the fundamental characteristics of political modernity[17]. Kirk demonstrated that conservatism, because of its realistic vision of society and politics, is nothing but a psychological inclination, a character attitude that is the opposite of ideological abstraction. Kirk suggested that conservatism is the most realistic vision of politics because it is an affirmation of normality towards society, an appreciation of the wisdom of past generations and the eternal values ascertained through the study of history and a reconciliation of authority with the changing circumstances of human life[18].

Books, 2008).

15 Richard M. Weaver, 'Conservatism and Libertarianism: The Common Ground', The Individualist, 4 (May 1960), pp. 1-8,

16 See Weaver, *Visions of Order: The Cultural Crisis of Our Time* (Baton Rouge: Louisiana State University Press, 1964); Weaver, *Life Without Prejudice and Other Essays* (Chicago: University of Chicago Press, Chicago 1965).

17 See Eric Voegelin, *The New Science of Politics* (Chicago: The University of Chicago Press, 1952).

18 See Russell A. Kirk, *A Program for Conservatives* (Chicago: Regnery, 1962), p. 4.

Scruton considered political realism as an inclination and capacity for seeing things as they are actually, rather than as they should be, and to recognise that the primary purposes of all those people acting in the political sphere are power and self-gratification[19]. Scruton regarded the conservative as a realist who prefers the stable, real, and lasting facts of ordinary life as concrete antidotes to social ills. For this reason he concluded that it is realism that allows the conservatives in politics to be anti-socialist without being liberal[20].

According all these conservative intellectuals, conservatism is an affirmation of normality in relation to society, which is sheltered from claims of radical transformation of the social order and of those abstract ideas useful only for the construction of imaginary political systems, without any relation to the objective truth. As a methodological aptitude for distrust concerning the abstractly conceived ideals which do not spring from the guts of society, conservatism is closely connected with realism.

Conservatism, especially in its Anglo-American declination, represents, already starting from Hume, more than a parallel cultural world, with accidentally common postulates. Political realism is a necessary option of political conservatism.

---

19 See Scruton, *The Palgrave Macmillan Dictionary of Political Thought*, p. 582.
20 See Scruton, 'How to be a Non-Liberal, Anti-Socialist Conservative', The Intercollegiate Review, 2 (Spring 1993), pp.19-20.

15. A CONSERVATIVE AMONG THE CONSERVATIVES

Hume's inscription in the conservative tradition is due to the ongoing of some of the most successful political philosophers, sociologist, and historians of the twenty-century Anglo-American area, the self-avowed *conservatives* Robert A. Nisbet, Russell A. Kirk, Giuseppe Prezzolini, Michael Oakeshott, and Roger Scruton.

Through volumes such as *The Quest for Community* (1953)[1], *The Sociological Tradition* (1966)[2], and *Conservatism: Dream and Reality* (1986)[3], Nisbet contributed decisively to the construction of an identity of conservatism as a political doctrine, even before as a lifestyle. He gave conservatism of the twentieth century an ideological dignity that allowed him to obtain some success in the last quarter of the century, continuing to move in the wake of the European counter-revolutionary tradition and overcoming the prejudices that had always been in vogue against the conservatives of all ages, labelled as "stupid", as has been said with reference to the contemptuous judgment of Mill, but also "compleat reactionaries", "medievalist", and "nostalgic"[4].

Nisbet's main purpose was to endow conservatism with accurate definition. Far from considering conservatism as nothing more than a particular temperament or a psychological

---

1 Nisbet, *The Quest for Community: A Study in the Ethics of Order and Freedom* (New York: Oxford University Press, 1953).
2 Nisbet, *The Sociological Tradition* (New York: Basic Books, 1966).
3 Nisbet, *Conservatism: Dream and Reality* (Minneapolis: University of Minnesota Press, 1986). Here I quote from the successive edition (2002).
4 See Henrie, *Understanding Traditionalist Conservatism*, in Peter Berkowitz (ed. by), *Varieties of Conservatism in America* (Stanford: Hoover Institution Press, 2004), pp. 3-30.

inclination against political innovation and social changing, Nisbet demonstrated that conservatism is, instead, a "structure of thought", a "style", as well as "a set of political dispositions toward state and property"[5], a "genuine ideology", one of the "three major political ideologies" of the past two centuries, "the other two being liberalism and socialism"[6]. In defining what he called an "anatomy" or "dogmatics" of the conservative ideology, Nisbet aimed at the elements of conservatism which seemed to him characteristic when seen against the background of other ideologies:

> It may be true – he wrote – to call conservatism the "politics of liberty" or "the search for political virtue" […], but we are not greatly advantaged, it seems to me, when, rightly or wrongly, liberalism and socialism might with equal warrant so describe themselves. I have sought therefore the themes which are at once distinctive in conservatism and which have had demonstrable continuity over the last 200 years.[7]

Nisbet explained the conservative commitment to history and tradition, religion and morality, property and liberty.

Already in the 1950s, he warned Western culture not to underestimate the greatest social and political problem of our time, namely the quest for community, which is a phenomenon that, over the centuries, has been accompanied by the exorbitant development of the "total state", that nowadays directs the life of every man, in both the public and the private sphere. The "monistic state" that was legitimized by the modern theorists of the social contract, such as Hobbes and Rousseau, has swept the social intermediate bodies, from family to neighbourhood, from corporation to village, from church to association of mutual aid, and has grown the individual in the absolute social void. Authentic liberty, for Nisbet, is not generated in the monistic system of the "omnicompetent" state, but arises spontaneously in the pluralistic

---

5   Nisbet, *Introduction* to *Tradition and Revolt* (New Brunswick and London: Transaction, 1999), p. 4.
6   Nisbet, *Conservatism: Dream and Reality*, p. 15.
7   *Ibid.*, p. 17.

society, where a variety of intermediate social groups holds real roles, functions, responsibility, and sufficient autonomy to offer the individual a sense of protection, purpose, identity, and belonging. Thanks to its continuous weakening of the communities, the modern bureaucratic state, from the height of its vertical power, has replaced the variety of traditional horizontal authorities.

In this framework of reflections, Nisbet recalled Hume's political thought. He caught the historical importance of Hume's political realism. By emphasising Hume's controversy against the origin of the state by an imaginary contract as the sole institution entitled to exercise absolute power over the life of men, replacing the plurality of traditional authorities, Nisbet agreed with the Scottish's characterisation of the asocial natural condition as a "*philosophical* fiction"[8] and echoed his account on the origins of government from warfare. Citing just Hume, in *Cloaking the State's Dagger* (1984), Nisbet observed:

> Euphemisms for the state drawn from kinship, religion, nature, reason, mechanics, biology, the people, and other essentially nonpolitical sources have been ascendant for so long in Western history that it is downright difficult to keep in mind that the state's origin and essential function is, as philosopher David Hume pointed out in the 18th century, in and of force – above all, military force. What procreation is to kinship and propitiation of gods is to religion, monopolization of power is to the state.[9]

According to Nisbet, Hume did well to say that the origin of government lied in the military force and that there has never been a political order, "from ancient Egypt to contemporary Israel, that has not originated in war", and that does not owe its sovereignty to what the Romans called *imperium*, or the absolute military command[10]. Thus the seed of the political government was not the "war of every man against every man" envisioned by Hobbes in the asocial condition. No such condition ever existed. It was the

---

8 Hume, *An Enquiry Concerning the Principles of Morals*, p. 24. Hume's italics.
9 Nisbet, 'Cloaking the State's Dagger', Reason, October (1984), p. 42.
10 *Ibid.*, pp. 42-43.

war based on particular kinds of political and moral ideals the true origin of the state, whose essence always consists in its exclusive possession of sovereignty, as absolute and unconditional power on all individuals, associations, and possessions in a given territory. And to this assumption, concludes Nisbet, twentieth century conservatives can only oppose, just as Hume did in the eighteenth century.

The reception of Hume by Nisbet is strategically relevant. He observed that Hume's "force", as established by him in the *Treatise* concerning the chieftain who became "the arbiter of all differences, and could gradually, by a mixture of force and consent, establish his authority established authority", was focused initially upon the function and authority of family and kindred. As Nisbet putted it in another text, "everywhere the state, as we first encounter it in the history, is simply the institutionalization, and projection to wider areas of function and authority, of the command-tie that in the beginning binds only the warrior-leader and his men"[11]. In other terms, for Hume, as for Nisbet, the warring state and the family grow and vanish inversely.

Nisbet also praised Hume for his "social pluralism". In his denunciation of the loss of community, Nisbet showed a particular predilection for the sociological vision of Scottish moralists, especially Hume, Ferguson, and Smith. Each of those thinkers was representative of that strand of pluralism which also included Montesquieu, who was the first to speak of "intermediate" groups, and which directly led "via Tocqueville's reading of Montesquieu" and "via Madison's reading of Montesquieu and Hume, to the social pluralism of the American Constitution"[12]. In particular, Nisbet linked Hume as social pluralist to Locke, Burke, and Tocqueville, for their suggestions in opposition to the visions of monists such as Plato, Rousseau, and Marx. In *The Making of Modern Society* (1986), Nisbet stated:

---

11   Nisbet, *Foreword* to Joseph R. Peden and Fred Glahe (ed. by), *The American Family and the State* (San Francisco: Pacific Research Institute, 1986) p. xxi.
12   Stone, *Robert Nisbet: Communitarian Traditionalist* (Wilmington: ISI Books, 2002), p. 113.

In almost sole opposition to these visions are the ideas of Locke, Hume, the Founding Fathers, Burke, Tocqueville and their intellectual descendents who relish the plural, differentiated, particularistic and decentralized state in which the freedom of individuals is buttressed by the autonomy of all groups and associations which mass.[13]

Hume and other social pluralists, for Nisbet, found in the intermediate bodies between individual and state a barrier against the degeneration of monarchy into despotism, and conceived the history of civil society as a transition from small, homogeneous, and pluralistic communities to large nations. Human nature, according to them, is uniform, but our passions and interests are directed by different institutions and circumstances, and the small communities live by the submission of the individual to the good of the whole. Therefore, according to Nisbet, rather than trying to eliminate social differences, we need to encourage them, so that no single group can dominate the others. The community of belonging is the main source of identity and sense of security for the individual man. The destruction of community, in the modern era, coincides with the obligation imposed by political absolutism to adhere to the "national community", that for Nisbet is but an oxymoron. Restabilising lively communities presumes some degree of political decentralisation, that is, allowing groups and associations to have real functions. Politically, this meant, on the Madisonian model, distribution of political power in such a manner that power is both fragmented and self-checking; culturally, it meant social pluralism, which, more concretely, referred to the differentiated presence of communities subjected to a regime, so to speak, of institutionalized tolerance.

Kirk was a well-known American historian who had the final merit of having given "scholarly and timely pedigree to conservatism in England and the United States, demonstrating the key role of Burke in both countries"[14]. Today, Kirk is regarded as

---

13 Nisbet, *The Making of Modem Society* (New York: NYU Press, 1986), pp. 28-29.
14 Nisbet, *Conservatism*, p. 106. For an introduction to the conservative political thought of Kirk, see: James E. Person, *Russell Kirk: A Critical Biography of a Conservative Mind* (Lanham: Madison Books, 1999);

the author most responsible for the revival of conservative thought in the latter half of the twentieth century. His conservative thinking was well-established with his main work, *The Conservative Mind*, published in 1953, and remained constant until his death in 1994[15]. For Kirk, conservatism is "a state of mind, a type of character, a way of looking at the civil social order"[16], sustained by "a body of sentiments, rather than by a system of ideological dogmata", and based on some general principles, such as belief there exists "an enduring moral order"[17], "imperfectability", close linking between freedom and property, defence of "voluntary community", opposition to "involuntary collectivism"[18], and adhesion to "custom, convention, and continuity"[19]. The latter is, for Kirk, "the means of linking generation to generation; it matters as much for society as it does for the individual; without it, life is meaningless"[20]. Moreover, conservatives believe in the principle of "prescription", that is, of permanent things "established by immemorial usage, so that the mind of man runneth not to the contrary"[21], and in the principle of "prudence". Liberals and radicals, for Kirk, are imprudent: "for they dash at their objectives without giving much heed to the risk of new abuses worse than the evils they hope to sweep away"[22].

Kirk sees Hume as the initiator of sceptical empiricism, as one of the few "men of letters" who, in the period between the revolution of 1688 and the Jacobin execution of Louis XVI and Marie Antoinette of 1793, dominated the western political scene, together with the Locke of the theory of social contract, the Montesquieu of the doctrine of social order, and the Burke of

---

    Wesley W. McDonald, *Russell Kirk and the Age of Ideology* (Columbia and London: University of Missouri Press, 2004).
15   John M. Pafford, *Russell Kirk* (New York and London: Bloomsbury, 2013).
16   Kirk, *The Politics of Prudence* (Wilmington: ISI Books, 1993), p. 16.
17   *Ibid.*, p. 17.
18   *Ibid.*, p. 22.
19   *Ibid.*, p. 18.
20   *Ibid.*
21   *Ibid.*, p. 19.
22   *Ibid.*, p. 20.

the demolition of abstract natural rights. All these authors – Kirk observed keenly – "did not play the comic role in politics, even though this or that notion of theirs may seem absurd by hindsight. These are the giants on whose shoulders we moderns stand"[23]. Kirk's praise, though surprising for Hume's scepticism towards ethical virtue, which is in contrast with the Catholic faith of this conservative American traditionalist, is all in this statement:

> We may be waxed by Hume's complacency, thinking him Mr. Know-All; but we would be intellectually poorer, were we deprived of his realistic analysis of human motives and his understanding of the foundations of the civil social order.[24]

What Kirk most appreciated in Hume, considering it very useful to the cause of political conservatism, was the conception of the role of the "prescriptive order" in maintaining society. In fact, with Hume, Kirk himself shared the belief in the principles of "prescription", that is of natural, slow, prudential change, and opposed to the radical "transformation" of society on the basis of abstract theoretical systems, of the imperfectness of man and his nature, "rejecting the mechanistic model of society that was so fashionable in the eighteenth century" among those who believed it could be "improved as an engineer might work with a machine, except at its mortal peril"[25].

Within the framework of the origins of the American nation and its culture, reconstructed in *The Roots of the American Order* (1974), Kirk also indicated among the noble fathers of the United States of America, together with Montesquieu, Blackstone, and Burke, just David Hume, to whom he dedicated a whole paragraph, entitled *Skeptical Realism: Hume*, in that book. Kirk remembered Hamilton's description of Hume as "a writer equally

---

23 Kirk, *Men of Letters as Statists: Locke, Montesquieu, Hume, Burke*, in *Literature Criticism from 1400 to 1800*, ed. by Person (Detroit: Gale Research, 1989), p. xiii.
24 *Ibid.*, p. xviii.
25 Forrest McDonald, *Russell Kirk: The American Cicero*, in Person (ed. by), *The Unbought Grace of Life: Essays in Honor of Russell Kirk* (Peru: Sherwood Sugden, 1994), p. 17.

solid and judicious", John Adams's letter to Jefferson, in 1813, in which Hume's *History of England* was described as the work that "had destroyed the best effects of the Revolution of 1688", and "Hume's Tory doctrines" as the students at the University of Virginia considered that historical work. Kirk welcomed the Hume's formidable assault on the theory of the social contract, the disgust for religious, political, and philosophical fanaticism, and the disliking for "revolutionary minds and revolutionary slogans"[26]. Moreover, Kirk was particularly fascinated by Hume's interpretation of custom as a "prescriptive wisdom", embodied in tradition, without which we would remain completely unaware of any fact, and in the presence of which "Reason" (term expressly written by Kirk with an initial capital letter) appears as an extravagance of the wandering ideology in the world of metaphysical abstraction, wholly detached from the concreteness of past experiences of order. What we learn in this world, we learn through custom and repeated experiences, rather than through "pure Reason", and

> the ways of society are not the ways of reason, but of the customary experience of the species, beginning with small family-groups and growing upward into the state. It is perilous to meddle, on principles of pure rationality, with valuable social institutions that thus are natural developments, not logical schemes.[27]

Moreover, Kirk underlined the bad judgment Hume had of Rousseau, which emerged in all its clarity from Hume's *A Concise and Genuine Account of the Dispute between Mr. Hume and Mr. Rousseau* (1766)[28]. Kirk acutely understood the absolute

---

26 Kirk, *The Roots of American Order* (La Salle: Open Court, 1974), p. 365.
27 *Ibid.*, p. 361.
28 Hume, *A Concise and Genuine Account of the Dispute between Mr. Hume and Mr. Rousseau with the Letters that Passed between them during their Controversy. As also, the Letters of the Hon. Mr. Walpole, and Mr. D'Alembert, Relative to this Extraordinary Affair* (London: T. Becket and P. A. de Hondt, 1766). See, on this topic, Robert Zaretsky and John T. Scott, *The Philosophers' Quarrel: Rousseau, Hume and the Limits of Human Understanding* (New Haven: Yale University Press,

irreconcilability between a radical thinker, such as Rousseau, and a conservative one, as was Hume. In fact, he wrote: "Hume had treated Rousseau with invariable kindness, but the Frenchman's eccentricities eventually led the canny Scot to conclude that Rousseau was little better than a madman – one of those gloomy, hair-brained enthusiasts"[29]. Kirk evidently and wisely identifies the genuine conservative attitude of Hume in the profound reasons for his quarrel with Rousseau, who is the most Jacobean philosopher of his time. In fact, at the origin of the dispute there were opposing styles and philosophical views of the world and politics: Hume's language was dispassionate, Rousseau's emotional; Hume was a combination of reason and scepticism, Rousseau a creature of feeling and certainty; Hume was the diplomat, the political thinker and statesman who reflects on the national identities and the meaning of Europe, Rousseau the fugitive, naturalist, and forerunner (through the myth of the good savage) of that veneration of the "other" that often hides a profound self-hatred; Hume was a realist who theorises about the origin of the state by force, war, conquest, and obedience of the subject as passive obedience based on custom, Rousseau, a theorist of the social contract; Hume accepted the connection between pride and appetite for luxury, while Rousseau viewed leisure as the mother of laxity and vanity, depriving the state of all its citizens by making them slaves to one another[30].

According to Kirk, it was an act of arrogance to say, following the example of the Jacobins indifferent to the effects of the "uprooting" of institutions, that human beings could build and preserve civilisation without the benefits of prescriptive wisdom and historical experience. Finally, in Kirk's words,

> with his dislike of all things vulgar, David Hume probably would have been uncomfortable in the twentieth century. And yet our era is

---

2009).
29 Kirk, *The Roots of American Order*, p. 362.
30 For a picture of these substantial differences that make Hume and Rousseau two political thinkers at the antipodes, see my introductory essay to the Italian edition of the dispute: Hume, *Contro Rousseau*, ed. by Pupo (Milan: Bietti, 2017), pp. 7-64.

of Hume's making, in part. In France, d'Alembert and Turgot were Hume's intimates: the great rationalizer and the great centralizer, the advocates of radical social reform and democracy, who reaped the whirlwind – curious friends for the champion of customary ways and Stuart causes.[31]

Although, therefore, Hume's conservatism was a secular conservatism, based on a moral and social order of human nature and ordinary life, rather than on certain metaphysical models, the role the Scot assigned to custom had, for Kirk, a decisive influence on Burke's conservatism, according to which pure reason is not able to direct the behaviour of people to good without the aid of custom. The latter, on the one hand, guarantees continuity with the past, bringing historical experience to support human action in the present and, on the other, exercises control over the drives of reformists and radicals who act on the basis of the progressive assumption for which the current generation is culturally and socially better equipped, compared to the past ones, to the governance of society.

Custom, so idealised by Hume and Kirk, is one of the most important "articles of the conservative creed"[32], because it allows people to live in peace; and those who oppose it, such as the revolutionaries, who "have effaced old customs, derided old conventions, and broken the continuity of social institutions"[33], very soon will "discover the necessity of establishing fresh customs, conventions, and continuity"[34].

Kirk saw Hume as a thinker who, in connection with the ancient Greek sceptics and medieval nominalists, liked to empty the "inflated balloons" of modern rationalism and its principal exponent, Locke, whose thesis the Scot demolished above all in *Enquiry Concerning Human Understanding*, a work that Kirk knew very well having also edited the American reprint, in 1956[35].

---

31 Kirk, *The Roots of American Order*, p. 366.
32 Kirk, *The Politics of Prudence*, p. 16.
33 *Ibid.*, p. 18.
34 *Ibid.*
35 Hume, *An Enquiry Concerning Human Understanding*, introduction by Russell A. Kirk (Chicago: Gateway, 1956).

It was in this work, not surprisingly, that Hume drastically reduced the claims of pure Reason to become the authoritative guide of human action, and lowered morality to mere obedience to the rules of approval and disapproval. In *The Conservative Mind*, Kirk wrote that "Hume demolished the eighteenth-century intellectuals, who took Reason for the guide to the whole nature of man; they were the a priori reasoners, on the model of Locke"[36].

Kirk's editorial initiative about Hume's first *Enquiry*, among other things, united him with another twentieth-century conservative and anti-rationalist intellectual, the Italian Giuseppe Prezzolini, who was the author, back in 1910, of the Italian translation (in the series of "Classics of modern philosophy", edited by Benedetto Croce and Giovanni Gentile) of *Enquiries Concerning Human Understanding and Principles of Morals*[37]. With his translation Prezzolini introduced Hume's thought to the audience of Italian readers in the early twentieth century.

According to Prezzolini, Hume intended "to establish a kind of geography of the spirit, where the treacherous snakes and the propellant seas in which certainty is shipwreck are marked", and had to "accentuate his anti-liberal views and to correct some too lively judgments on Lord Bolingbroke or Swift or Catholics"[38]. In a subsequent work entitled *Manifesto dei conservatori (1972)*, in which he is concerned with clarifying the semantic of the word *conservation*, Prezzolini argued that an authentic conservative always has "a dose of little respect for the findings of human ingenuity" and a reason to "beware of the news and the risks of rapid and rationalistic upheavals", and be "always at the bottom a pessimist"[39]. The true conservative, as Prezzolini, following the example of the Humean idea of *continuity*, put it, is neither a reactionary nor a nostalgic one, but one who wants to "continue

---

36 Kirk, *The Conservative Mind: From Burke to Eliot* (1953), new edn. (Washington: Regnery 2001), p. 477.
37 Hume, *Ricerche sull'intelletto umano e sui principii della morale*, ed. by Giuseppe Prezzolini (Bari: Laterza, 1910).
38 Prezzolini, *Prefazione*, in Hume, *Ricerche sull'intelletto umano e sui principii della morale*, p. IX. My own translation.
39 Prezzolini, *Manifesto dei conservatori* (Milan: Rusconi, 1972), pp. 114-115. My own translation.

maintaining"[40], who gives new answers to new problems, inspired by permanent principles, who renew the eternal forgotten laws stupidly and hypocritically hidden, powerlessly neglected, daily violated, and is persuaded to be, if not the man of tomorrow, certainly the man of the day after tomorrow[41].

Oakeshott, who was the most influential English conservative philosopher in the nineteenth-century[42], for his part, considered Hume in his dual aptitude: as an interpreter of the "authority" in modern politics and as the chief interpreter of "modern political scepticism"[43], based on the assumption that political perfection is a mere illusion and that the maintenance of social order and peace between individuals does not impose any substantial event uniformity[44].

In *The Vocabulary of a Modern European State* (1975), Oakeshott explored the terminology which relates to the office of rule and its "authority". The latter, in modern political thought, denotes a formal consideration in which a statement or an action is understood not in terms of what it prescribes, but "in relation to an office, a practice or a procedure, or a rule recognised as such"[45]. Oakeshott gave Hume credit for having revealed authority in the

---

40 *Ibid.*, p. 47.
41 *Ibid.*, pp. 47-61.
42 About Oakeshott's political thought in general, see: William H. Greenleaf, *Oakeshott's Philosophical Politics* (London: Longmans, 1966); Paul Franco, *Michael Oakeshott. An Introduction* (New Haven and London: Yale University Press, 2004); Suvi Soininen, *From a "Necessary Evil" to the Art of the Contingency. Michael Oakeshott's Conception of Political Activity* (Exeter: Imprint Academic, 2005).
43 On Oakeshott's political scepticism, see Steven A. Gerencser, *The Skeptic's Oakeshott* (New York: St. Martin's Press, 2000); Roy Tseng, *The Sceptical Idealist. Michael Oakeshott as a Critical of the Enlightenment* (Exeter: Imprint Academic, 2003), pp. 213-274; Aryeh Botwinick, *Oakeshott's Skepticism* (Princeton and Oxford: Princeton University Press, 2011).
44 Some affinities between Hume and Oakeshott have been identified, about a decade ago, by Berry, pp. 133-134, with regard to their common anti-rationalism.
45 Oakeshott, *The Vocabulary of a Modern European State* (1975), in *The Vocabulary of a Modern European State*, ed. by Luke O' Sullivan (Exeter: Imprint Academic, 2008), p. 235.

eighteenth century as the matter of prime concern, more interesting than any other. This attention – Oakeshott argued – is clearly notable in Hume, who recognises it as one of the considerations which distinguish him from the classical republicans whose concerns lay elsewhere:

> When Hume – Oakeshott added taking inspiration from Humean maxim on *opinion* – says that, whatever their relationship with the rest of their subjects, the Sultan of Egypt or the emperor of Rome "at least led his mamelukes or pretorian guard by their opinion" he did not mean belief in their authority; he meant belief that the game was worth the candle.[46]

The political scepticism, of which Oakeshott considered himself an exponent, consists in the healthy attitude to look at the reality of things, slowing down the impulse to utopianism. In a series of essays dating back to the 1950s, Oakeshott developed a highly articulated critique of political rationalism, formed on two substantial arguments based on his scepticism. The first consisted in the refusal of "total change", which

> is always more extensive than the change designed; and the whole of what is entailed can neither be foreseen nor circumscribed. Thus, whenever there is innovation there is the certainty that the change will be greater than was intended, that there will be loss as well as gain and that the loss and the gain will not be equally distributed among the people affected; there is the chance that the benefits derived will be greater than those which were designed; and there is the risk that they will be off-set by changes for the worse.[47]

The second argument against political rationalism is based on the recognition of the limits of reason and therefore of the unattainability of political "perfection", that is a "form of the moral life will offer to a society advantages similar to those of a religion which has taken to itself a theology (though not necessarily a popular theology) but without losing its character as

---

46 *Ibid.*, p. 246, note 5.
47 Oakeshott, *On Being Conservative*, p. 411.

a way of living"⁴⁸, to which Oakeshott opposed the concreteness of contingency, anti-revolutionary gradualism, and respect for custom. Oakeshott saw men operating and thinking with a hereditary and complex reason, in a specific context and, taking up again what is one of the cardinal principles of Hume's thought, according to their unchanging nature.

According to Oakeshott, there exists in the cultural and political world a sole intellectual figure capable of enclosing in itself all the qualities that conservatives consider inadequate: the "rationalist". The rationalist is "the enemy of authority, of prejudice, of the merely traditional, customary or habitual"⁴⁹; his mental approach is at once sceptical and optimistic: sceptical because there is no opinion, habit, conviction so deeply rooted as to question it and judge it by what it calls its "reason"; optimistic because the rationalist never doubts the power of his reason to determine the value of a thing, the truth of an opinion or the ownership of an action. Moreover, it is strengthened by the "belief in a "reason" common to all mankind, a common power of rational consideration, which is the ground and inspiration of argument"; but besides this, which "gives the rationalist a touch of intellectual equalitarianism, he is something also of an individualist, finding it difficult to believe that anyone who can think honestly and dearly will think differently from himself"⁵⁰.

Moreover, for Oakeshott, the rationalist orientation contrasts with the conservative disposition to favour "the familiar to the unknown, to prefer the tried to the untried, fact to mystery, the actual to the possible, the limited to the unbounded, the near to the distant, the sufficient to the superabundant, the convenient to the perfect, present laughter to utopian bliss"⁵¹.

These two provisions reflect the following conceptions of knowledge: that of the rationalist, who is the interpreter of a technical knowledge that proceeds by formulations of rules; that

---

48 Oakeshott, *The Tower of Babel* (1962), in *Rationalism in Politics*, p. 478.
49 Oakeshott, *Rationalism in Politics* (1962), in *Rationalism in Politics*, p. 1.
50 *Ibid.*, pp. 1-2.
51 Oakeshott, *On Being Conservative*, p. 196.

of the conservative, who adopts a practical knowledge, which escapes the formulation in certain and indisputable rules.

While technical knowledge can only be learned in theory, the practice is acquired through experience, as the apprentice does, and since it requires time and refinement, it falls into what Oakeshott called "traditional knowledge"[52]. The practice is identified with a series of considerations, customs, uses, rituals, canons, maxims, principles, rules, and procedures that denote precise obligations with respect to human actions. The same conservative disposition in politics is not the "ability" in recognizing and preserving these imprints, similar to that acquired in the use of an instrument, with which one becomes familiar in time and which from the rationalist is rejected as the opposite of knowledge:

> Now, as I understand it, Rationalism is the assertion that what I have called practical knowledge is not knowledge at all, the assertion that, properly speaking, there is no knowledge which is not technical knowledge. The Rationalist holds that the only element of knowledge involved in any human activity is technical knowledge, and that what I have called practical knowledge is really only a sort of nescience which would be negligible if it were not positively mischievous. The sovereignty of "reason", for the Rationalist, means the sovereignty of technique.[53]

We must remember here another affinity between the conservatism of Oakeshott and that of Hume. In *The Politics of Faith and the Politics of Scepticism* (1996), Oakeshott opposed to the rationalistic "politics of faith" represented in modern times by Francis Bacon, for which the search for "perfection" was a supreme human activity, legitimised to the "transformation" of individuals and society in an imaginary road to redemption, the "politics of scepticism"[54], embodied by Montaigne and Hume. The sceptical disposition, in politics, is more opened to the contingencies of the human condition manifested in history, and its remembrance

---

52 Oakeshott, *Rationalism in Politics*, pp. 2-9.
53 *Ibid.*, p. 11.
54 Oakeshott, *The Politics of Faith and the Politics of Scepticism*, ed. by Fuller (New Haven and London: Yale University Press, 1996).

function suggests sobriety when the others are exuberant. In the politics of faith, observed Oakeshott,

> political decision and enterprise may be understood as a response to an inspired perception of what *the* common good is, or it may be understood as the conclusions which follow a rational argument; what it can never be understood as is a temporary expedient or just doing something to keep things going[55];

conversely,

> the politics of scepticism (regarded as an abstract style of politics) may be said to have its roots either in the radical belief that human perfection is an illusion, or in the less radical belief that we know too little about the condition of human perfection for it to be wise to concentrate our energies in a single direction by associating its pursuit with the activity of governing. [...] To pursue perfection in one direction only [...] is to invite disappointment and (what might be worse than the mortification of non-arrival) misery on the way.[56]

In other words, Oakeshott preferred a pragmatic and sceptical conservatism, not perfectly embedded in the Anglo-Saxon tradition[57]. With this motivation, among other things, Irving Kristol, editor of the conservative review "Encounter", refused to publish the Oakeshott's essay entitled *On Being Conservative*. Kristol, while admitting to "loving every line" of Oakeshott's piece, to admiring it "immensely", claimed that its "irredeemably secular" character repelled him[58]. Actually, rejecting the figure of Burke as a projection of a conservatism mainly based on metaphysical beliefs, Oakeshott defended the authentic conservative "disposition", invoking the function of a government that is not the imposition of a given conception of common good,

---

55 *Ibid.*, p. 27. Oakeshott's italics.
56 *Ibid.*, p. 31.
57 On Oakeshott's kind of conservatism, see Corey Abel (ed. by), *The Meanings of Michael Oakeshott's Conservatism* (Exeter: Imprint Academic, 2010).
58 Irving Kristol, *Neocoservatism: The Autobiography of an Idea* (New York: The Free Press, 1995), p. 373.

but a limited and specific activity which supplies and preserves the rules of general conduct.

But it was not only in the political essays that Oakeshott's kindness for Hume's conservatism emerged. Already in his first work, *Experience and its Modes* (1933), demonstrating how much Hume's thought was a constant reference in his intellectual production, Oakeshott indicated in the Scottish author's empiricism the model to be followed for the purpose of authentic definition of that "practical knowledge" which constituted the ultimate foundation of a conservative political action. According to Hume – Oakeshott wrote in that text – the practical knowledge was not a conclusion of reason, but one of intuition, not of reflection but of instinct; and when Oakeshott resorted to the very expression of "practical knowledge" he did so to "indicate the disparity between practical experience and philosophy, and not to assert the impossibility of practical knowledge" as a collection of immediate insights, "easily distinguished from what we take to be knowledge"[59]. Hume understood earlier than many others that if "an attempt is made to force the entry of practical thought into the world of philosophy, nothing but error and confusion can follow"[60].

Based on the thought that belongs to a given form of experience to criticise another one means, for Hume, to simply fall into the *ignoratio elenchi*, which is the mistake made – pointed out Oakeshott – "in the name of common sense, but also in the names of religion and morality"[61], when an argument is presented that is in itself valid but in support of something other than what it was originally intended to demonstrate. It is no coincidence that Oakeshott cited a significant passage from the first Hume's *Enquiry*, perhaps the most appreciated by conservatives of Hume's texts, in which the Scotsman stated: "There is no method of reasoning more common, and yet none more blameable, than, in philosophical disputes, to endeavour the refutation of any hypothesis, by a pretence of its

---

59 Oakeshott, *Experience and Its Modes* (Cambridge: Cambridge University Press, 1995), pp. 252-253.
60 *Ibid.*, pp. 319-320.
61 *Ibid.*, p. 320.

dangerous consequences to religion and morality"[62]. This is – concluded Oakeshott – "meaningless alike either to accept or to reject a philosophical proposition for a practical reason"[63].

It was therefore in Hume's scepticism that the Oakeshott's conservative orientation found its most significant historical precedent. Timothy Fuller noticed this when he spoke of Hume and Oakeshott as political sceptics that "do not live and die by the prevailing sentiments and longings, the political rages, of their time and place"; and neither they are "reactionaries who long far an imagined past which is, after all, over and done with"[64]. Their political reflections, for Fuller, are "un-deludes as to the dominant political terrain of their time", and they "think beyond the confines of their time without believing they can leap out of their time into some other"[65].

Here is the case to add that in a review of one of the foundational texts of 900's conservatism, *The Conservative Mind* by Kirk, Oakeshott openly declared that "on account of his speculative moderation and his clear recognition of politics as a specific activity, it would perhaps have been more fortunate if the modern conservative had paid more attention to Hume and less to Burke"[66]. By this, Oakeshott meant that Hume's "sceptical conservatism" was different from Burke's "cosmic conservatism", which Oakeshott blamed for not having clarified that "there is indeed no inconstancy in being conservative in politics and "radical" in everything else"[67]. It was a peculiarity that Oakeshott himself resumed later in his *On Being Conservative*, where the name of Hume was inserted among the modern thinkers with an unequivocal conservative disposition. Here, in fact, Oakeshott reiterated that "it is not at all inconsistent to be conservative in respect of government and radical in respect of almost every other

---

62 Hume, *An Enquiry Concerning Human Understanding*, p. 70.
63 Oakeshott, *Experience and Its Modes*, p. 320.
64 Fuller, *The Relation of Philosophy to Conservatism in the Thought of Michael Oakeshott*, in Abel, p. 116.
65 Ibid.
66 Oakeshott, *Review of Russell Kirk's "The Conservative Mind"* (1954), in *The Vocabulary of a Modern European State*, p. 83.
67 Ibid.

activity", and that "there is more to be learnt about this disposition from Montaigne, Pascal, Hobbes and Hume than from Burke or Bentham"[68].

Hume's political thought, ultimately, for Oakeshott, was the clear demonstration of how political conservatism is not at all extraneous to people inclined to "adventure", "initiative", who tend to rationalise their affections in terms of progress without thereby claiming the belief in "progressivism" is the cruellest of all beliefs, arousing cupidity without satisfying it, in order to think it inappropriate for a government to be "progressive". Conservative disposition is appropriate to persons who have a skill to practise to make, and whose passions do not need to be inflamed, and whose desires do not need to be provoked. The Humean sceptic model of thought, in other words, followed in support of Oakeshott's in-depth description of being conservative. The true conservative, he said,

> might even be prepared to suffer a legally established ecclesiastical order; but it would not be because they believed it to represent some unassailable religious truth, but merely because it restrained the indecent competition of sects and (as Hume said) moderated "the plague of a too diligent clergy".[69]

The quotation was taken by Oakeshott from the third book of *The History of England*, where Hume spoke of "ecclesiastics" as persons endowed with the particular vocation to be "attached to their doctrines" and to "find benefit or consolation from their spiritual ministry and assistance", whose "skill in the profession, as well as their address in governing the minds of the people, must receive daily encrease, from their encreasing practice, study, and attention"[70]. With reference to the repercussions of this same vocation on the level of political experience, Hume affirmed that an "interested diligence of the clergy is what every wise legislator will study to prevent; because in every religion, except the true, it is highly pernicious, and it has even a natural tendency to pervert

---

68   Oakeshott, *On Being Conservative*, p. 435.
69   *Ibid.*
70   Hume, *The History of England*, vol. 3, p. 135.

the true, by infusing into it a strong mixture of superstition, folly, and delusion"[71].

As noted, Hume is essential for Oakeshott's description of being conservative.

Another authoritative conservative thinker who took Hume's conservatism seriously was Roger Scruton, who died a few weeks ago. Scruton was one of the greatest interpreters of contemporary political conservatism[72], who dedicated several works[73] to the semantics of conservatism, as a "social and political outlook that embodies a desire to conserve existing things, held to be either good in themselves, or better than the likely alternatives, or at least safe, familiar, and the objects of trust and affection"[74].

According to Scruton, conservatism expresses a reaction against both the abstract thinking of liberalism and the goal-directed politics of the socialist movement; in other words, it consists in a refusal of theoretical arguments, theories, and programmers, in favour of a quiet and pragmatic politics whose principal concern is to maintain the ship of state afloat on the sea of destiny, defending prejudice, custom, and tradition, against system, planning, and rationalism. Conservatism, for Scruton, regards the individual, his freedom, and his happiness, as the products of social order. It places duty before right, emphasises the sovereignty and corporate personality as the preconditions of legal order, rather than on the individual and his right. It puts politics, culture, and morality before economic order and the distribution of power, rejects economic determinism, and sees politics not as the pursuit of some

---

71 *Ibid.*, pp. 135-136.
72 For an introduction to the conservative thought of Scruton, see Mark Dooley, *Roger Scruton: The Philosopher on Dover Beach* (London and New York: Continuum 2009); by the same author see also *The Roger Scruton Reader* (London: Bloomsbury Academic, 2011).
73 Scruton (ed. by), *Conservative Thinkers: Essays from "The Salisbury Review"* (London and Lexington: The Claridge Press, 1989); *How to be a Conservative* (London: Bloomsbury Continuum, 2014); *Conservatism: Ideas in Profile* (London: Profile Books, 2017); *Conservatism: An Invitation to the Great Tradition* (New York: St-Martin's Press, 2018).
74 Scruton, *Conservatism*, in *The Palgrave Macmillan Dictionary of Political Thought*, p. 131.

ultimate goal, but an attempt to reconcile conflicting interest and to establish peace and order throughout society[75].

Scruton has looked at the central ideas of conservatism over the centuries and has traced the origins and development of the conservative ideology in the thoughts of several philosophers, and not only did he contemplate Hume among them, but he even claimed that the beginnings of British intellectual conservatism are to be found in the works of two educated writers "who belonged, explicitly or implicitly, to the Tory camp": the Scottish philosopher David Hume and the English critic and poet Samuel Johnson. Both regarded liberty as the goal of civilised order, and neither believed in the liberal idea of the social contract. Hume, for Scruton, was a Tory in the meaning that did not imply his subscription to the Anglican Church's doctrine or the English king's divine right. He was – Scruton stated in one of his previous philosophical works – "nevertheless a staunch and articulate Tory, a man seemingly at peace with the world"[76]; he was "almost certainly an atheist and believed in the established church and the established monarchy precisely because they were established, embodying in their structure and history the solutions to social conflicts and the tacit instructions for carrying on"[77].

In Hume's political philosophy Scruton saw "the essence of Toryism throughout the modern era"[78] that was possible to make out because of the following positions: strict criticism of the theories of the social contract; acknowledgement of the importance of popular consent in securing political order; conception of political science as deduced from the study of human nature; reaction to the Enlightenment project of founding our political obligations in the exercise of reason; defence of private rights and proprieties; emphasis on the utility of custom in guiding us along the path of peaceful coexistence; acceptance of "established order, founded on customs that are followed and accepted", as preferable to the ideas of those would liberate us from our inherited sense of

---

75 Scruton, *Introduction*, in *Conservative Thinkers*, pp. 7-13.
76 Scruton, *A Short History of Modern Philosophy From Descartes to Wittgenstein* (London and New York: Routledge, 1995), p. 115.
77 Scruton, *Conservatism: Ideas in Profile*, pp. 21-22.
78 *Ibid.*, p. 24.

obligation[79]. The Humean thought – Scruton concluded – "was to become pivotal in the aftermath of the French Revolution, when Burke set out to provide it with a philosophy"[80].

In another circumstance, Scruton classified Hume's intellectual figure among those "British conservative thinkers" who emphasised a traditionalist vision of social order as arousing spontaneously, and not through a rational plan. In fact, he wrote:

> We should not be surprised therefore if British conservative thinkers – notably Hume, Smith, Burke and Oakeshott – have tended to see no tension between a defence of the free market and a traditionalist vision of social order. For they have put their faith in the spontaneous limits placed on the market by the moral consensus of the community and have seen both the market and the constraints as the work of the same invisible hand.[81]

Scruton also regarded Hume as the initiator of a conservative tradition of community thinking, reaching up to de Maistre and Tocqueville, that is concerned about the protection of small communities in the interest of the values and loyalties that constitute the sum of their social capital, starting with belonging and autonomy from the state. In fact, in his original work dedicated to conservative environmentalism, we read the following passage:

> Since its origins in the writings of Hume, Smith and Burke intellectual conservatism has emphasized the importance of small associations, autonomous institutions and the various trusts and colleges that lie beyond the reach of the state. The emphasis was shared by de Maistre and Hegel on the Continent and made pivotal to his analysis of American democracy by Tocqueville. What those thinkers had in mind was civil association: gatherings of people that exist for the sake of membership – sometimes, but by no means always, with a common purpose – conducting their affairs without interference from the state, and usually without the desire for political prominence. Such associations form the stuff of civil society, and conservatives emphasize them precisely because they are the

---

79 *Ibid.*, pp. 22-24.
80 *Ibid.*, p. 24.
81 Scruton, *How to be a Conservative*, p. 57.

guarantee that society will renew itself without being led and controlled by the state.[82]

A volume edited by Scruton, entitled *Conservative Thinkers: Essays from the Salisbury Review* (1988), contains several essays, each concerned with a writer who is alleged to exhibit the conservative disposition. Among these, a brief study by Paul Heim on Hume identifies the main elements of Humean political conservatism: the emphasis on the "givenness of experience", the stress upon "human habits", and the vision of human nature. These elements, presented with adequate vocabulary, make Hume "a pre-conservative conservative, a conservative setting out his position during an era when the impact of the French Revolution, with its social upheaval based upon optimistic views of human nature, was yet to be felt"[83].

In conclusion, we can only reiterate what we have tried to demonstrate since the first chapters, namely that Hume was undoubtedly a conservative thinker. The intellectual affinity and psychological approach to the problems of society and politics, and above all the interest objectively shown for Hume by the most influential conservative intellectuals, must undoubtedly be brought back to a common conservative inspiration. The only element that divides them, and it is not a trivial factor, was that event of radical transformation of the society that was the French Revolution. It cannot be said with certainty what Hume would have thought and spoke about it, but if the simple, however famous, revolt of Wilkes was enough to make Hume worry about radicalism and political extremism, one can be reasonably sure that in the face of the Revolution he would have written things more or less similar to those that Burke left to posterity. Perhaps with less traditionalist and spiritualist emphasis, but with the same, if not higher, philosophical and conceptual strength, the strength of the most influential philosopher ever to write in English.

---

[82] Scruton, *How to Think Seriously* About the Planet: The Case for an Environmental Conservatism (Oxford and New York: Oxford University Press, 2012), pp. 27-28.

[83] Paul Helm, *David Hume*, in *Conservative Thinkers*, p. 74.

BIBLIOGRAPHY

I
WORKS BY HUME

A Treatise of Human Nature: Being an Attempt to introduce the experimental Method of Reasoning into Moral Subjects (London: Printed for John Noon, 1739), vols 1-2;
A Treatise of Human Nature: Being an Attempt to introduce the experimental Method of Reasoning into Moral Subjects (London: Printed for Thomas Longman, 1740), vol. 3.
Essays, Moral and Political (Edinburgh: printed by Robert Fleming and Alexander Alison, 1741-42).
Philosophical Essays Concerning Human Understanding. By the Author of the Essays Moral and Political (London: printed for A. Millar, 1748).
An Enquiry Concerning the Principles of Morals (London: printed for A. Millar, 1751).
Political Discourses (Edinburgh: printed by R. Fleming, for A. Kincaid and A. Donaldson, 1752).
The History of the Proceedings in the Case of Margaret, commonly called Peg, only lawful sister of John Bull (1760), in *Sister Peg: A Pamphlet Hitherto Unknown by David Hume* (Cambridge: Cambridge University Press, 1982), ed. D. R. Raynor.
The History of England (Edinburgh: Hamilton, Balfour and Neil, 1754, London: Millar, 1762).
A Concise and Genuine Account of the Dispute between Mr. Hume and Mr. Rousseau with the Letters that Passed between them during their Controversy. As also, the Letters of the Hon. Mr. Walpole, and Mr. D'Alembert, Relative to this Extraordinary Affair (London: T. Becket and P. A. de Hondt, 1766).

Essays and Treatises on Several Subjects (London and Edinburgh: printed for T. Cadell, A. Donaldson, and W. Creech, 1777).
Ricerche sull'intelletto umano e sui principii della morale (Bari: Laterza, 1910), ed. G. Prezzolini.
The Letters of David Hume, 2 vols (Oxford: Clarendon, 1932), ed. J. Y. T. Greig.
An Enquiry Concerning Human Understanding (Chicago: Gateway, 1956), intr. R. A. Kirk.
A Collection of Critical Essays (Garden City: Doubleday, 1966), ed. V. C. Chappell.
Politica e scienza dell'uomo (Rome: Editori Riuniti, 1975), ed. L. Formigari.
A Treatise of Human Nature (Oxford: Oxford University Press, 1978), ed. P. H. Nidditch.
Antologia di scritti politici (Bologna: il Mulino, 1978), ed. G. Giarrizzo.
An Enquiry Concerning the Principles of Morals (Indianapolis-Cambridge: Hackett, 1983) ed. J. B. Schneewind.
The History of England from the Invasion of Julius Caesar to the Revolution in 1688, 6 vols (Indianapolis: Liberty Fund, 1983) ed. W. B. Todd.
Essays Moral, Political, and Literary (Indianapolis: Liberty Fund, 1987), ed. E. F. Miller.
A Treatise of Human Nature (Oxford: Clarendon Press, 2007), vol. 1, ed. D. F. Norton, M. J. Norton.
An Enquiry Concerning Human Understanding (Oxford: Oxford University Press, 2007), ed. P. Millican.
New Letters of David Hume (Oxford: Oxford University Press, 2011) ed. R. Klibansky, E. C. Mossner.
Libertà e moderazione. Scritti politici (Soveria Mannelli: Rubbettino, 2016), ed. S. Pupo.
Contro Rousseau (Milan: Bietti, 2017), ed. S. Pupo.
A Petty Statesman. Writings on War and International Affairs (Milan: Mimesis International, 2019), ed. S. Pupo.

II
OTHER WORKS

Ajello, Raffaele, and others, *L'età dei Lumi. Studi storici sul Settecento europeo in onore di Franco Venturi* (Naples: Jovene, 1985).

Alembert, Jean Le Rond d', *Preliminary Discourse* to the *Encyclopedia of Diderot* (Chicago and London: The University of Chicago Press, 1995) ed. R. N. Schwab.

Ashford, Nigel, and S. Davies, *A Dictionary of Conservative and Libertarian Thought* (New York: Routledge, 1991).

Aspromourgos, Tony, *On the Origins of Classical Economics: Distribution and Value from William Petty to Adam Smith* (New York: Routledge, 1995).

Baier, Annette, *The Cautious Jealous Virtue: Hume on Justice* (Cambridge: Harvard University Press, 2010).

Bailey, Alan, *Sextus Empiricus and Pyrrhonean Scepticism* (Oxford: Clarendon Press, 2002).

Barbuto, Gennaro M., *Machiavelli e i totalitarismi* (Naples: Guida, 2005).

Bassani, Luigi M., and A. Mingardi, *Dalla Polis allo Stato. Introduzione alla Storia del pensiero politico* (Turin: Giappichelli, 2017).

Bayle, Pierre, *The Historical and Critical Dictionary* (London: J. J. and P. Knapton, 1734).

Bentham, Jeremy, *The Works of Jeremy Bentham*, (Edinburgh: Tait, 1838-1843), ed. J. Bowring.

Bentham, Jeremy, *A Fragment on Government and An Introduction to the Principles of Morals and Legislation* (Oxford: Basil Blackwell, 1948), ed. W. Harrison.

Bentham, Jeremy, *Essays on Political Tactics* (Oxford: Clarendon Press, 1999), ed. M. James, C. Blamires, C. Pease-Watkin.

Berkowitz, Peter, *Varieties of Conservatism in America* (Stanford: Hoover Institution Press, 2004).

Berlin, Isaiah, *The Sense of Reality: Studies in Ideas and Their History* (Princeton and Oxford: Princeton University Press, 2019), ed. H. Hardy.

Berry, Cristopher J., *David Hume* (New York-London: Continuum, 2009).
Black, Max, 'The Gap Between *Is* and *Should*', *The Philosophical Review*, 2 (1964), 165-181.
Bolingbroke, *The Works of the Late Right Honourable Henry St. John, Lord Viscount Bolingbroke* (London: printed for J. Johnson & Co., 1809).
Bolingbroke, *Political Writings* (Cambridge: Cambridge University Press, 1997) ed. D. Armitage.
Bongie, Laurence L., *David Hume: Prophet of the Counter-Revolution* (Indianapolis: Liberty Fund, 2000).
Botwinick, Arye, *Oakeshott's Skepticism* (Princeton and Oxford: Princeton University Press, 2011).
Brewer, John, *Party Ideology and Popular Politics at the Accession of George Third* (New York: Cambridge University Press, 1976).
Burke, Edmund, *Observations on a Late Publication on the Present State of the Nation* (London: Printed for J. Dodsley, 1769).
Burke, Edmund, *Three Memorials on French Affairs. Written in the Years 1791, 1792 and 1793* (London: Printed for F. and C. Rivingston, 1797).
Burke, Edmund, *The Works of the Right Honourable Edmund Burke in Twelve Volumes* (London: John C. Nimmo, 1899).
Burke, Edmund, *Select Works of Edmund Burke* (Indianapolis: Liberty Fund, 1992), ed. D. E. Ritchie.
Burke, Edmund, *Select Works of Edmund Burke* (Indianapolis: Liberty Fund, 1999), ed. F. Canavan.
Burke, Peter, *Montaigne* (Oxford: Oxford University Press, 1981).
Burnham, James, *The Machiavellians: Defenders of Freedom* (London, Putnam, 1943).
Butler, Joseph, *The Works of Joseph Butler, late Bishop of Durham* (London: printed and published by J. F. Dove, 1828).
Campi, Alessandro, and S. De Luca, *Il realismo politico. Figure, concetti, prospettive di ricerca* (Soveria Mannelli: Rubbettino, 2014).
Castiglione, Dario, *Dell'opinione. Riflessioni ai margini della teoria politica di David Hume* (Palermo: Mazzone, 1988).

Castiglione, Dario, and L. Sharpe, *Shifting the Boundaries, Transformations of the Languages of Public and Private in the Eighteenth Century* (Exeter: University of Exeter Press, 1995).

Chevallier, Jean-Jacques, *Storia del pensiero politico* (Bologna: il Mulino, 1989), ed. Nino Tonna.

Congdon, Lee, *George Kennan: A Writing Life* (Wilmington: ISI Books, 2008).

Conniff, James, 'Hume on Political Parties: The Case for Hume as a Whig', *Eighteenth-Century Studies*, 2 (1978-79), 150-173.

Corey, Abel, *The Meanings of Michael Oakeshott's Conservatism* (Exeter: Imprint Academic, 2010).

Cotta, Sergio, 'La nascita dell'idea di partito nel secolo XVIII', *Il Mulino*, 89 (1959) pp. 445-486.

Cutler, Fred, 'Jeremy Bentham and the Public Opinion Tribunal', *The Public Opinion Quarterly*, 3 (Autumn, 1999), 321-346.

Dooley, Mark, *Roger Scruton: The Philosopher on Dover Beach* (London and New York: Continuum 2009).

Dooley, Mark, *The Roger Scruton Reader* (London: Bloomsbury Academic, 2011).

Dow, Alexander, and S. Dow, *A History of Scottish Economic Thought* (London and New York: Routledge, 2006).

Duncan-Jones, Austin, *Butlers' Moral Philosophy* (Harmondsworth: Penguin, 1952).

Emerson, Roger L., *Essays on David Hume, Medical Men and the Scottish Enlightenment* (Burlington: Ashgate, 2009).

Fennessy, Rumold R., *Burke, Paine, and the Rights of Man: A Difference of Political Opinion* (La Haye: M. Nijhoff, 1963).

Fieser, James, *Early Responses to Hume's Life and Reputation* (Bristol: Thoemmes Continuum, 2005).

Fitzgibbons, Athol, *Adam Smith's System of Liberty, Wealth, and Virtue: The Moral and Political Foundations of the Wealth of Nations* (Oxford: Oxford University Press, 1995).

Flew, Antony, *David Hume: Philosopher of Moral Science* (Oxford: Basil Blackwell, 1986).

Floridi, Luciano, *Sextus Empiricus: The Transmission and Recovery of Pyrrhonism* (Oxford and New York: Oxford University Press, 2002).

Forbes Duncan, *Hume's Philosophical Politics* (Cambridge: Cambridge University Press, 1975).
Foxley, Rachel, *The Levellers: Radical Political Thought in the English Revolution* (Manchester: Manchester University Press, 2013).
Franco, Paul, *Michael Oakeshott. An Introduction* (New Haven and London: Yale University Press, 2004).
Frazer, Michael L., *The Enlightenment of Sympathy: Justice and the Moral Sentiments in the Eighteenth Century and Today* (Oxford and New York: Oxford University Press, 2010).
Gauthier, David, 'David Hume, Contractarian', *Philosophical Review*, 1 (1979), 3-38.
Gay, Peter, *The Enlightenment: An Interpretation* (London: Weidenfeld & Nicolson 1966-9).
Giarratana, Corrado, *Contra Hume. The Eighteenth-Century Debate on Hume's Work on Religion* (Rome: Bonanno, 2017).
Giarrizzo, Giuseppe, *David Hume politico e storico* (Turin: Einaudi, 1962).
Gibson, Alan, *Interpreting the Founding. Guide to the Enduring Debates over the Origins and Foundations of the American Republic* (Lawrence: University Press of Kansas, 2006).
Goldie, Mark, and R. Wolker, *The Cambridge History of Eighteenth-Century Political* (Cambridge: Cambridge University Press, 2006).
Gray, John, *Liberalism* (Minneapolis: Minnesota University Press, 1986).
Greenleaf, William H., *Oakeshott's Philosophical Politics* (London: Longmans, 1966).
Hampsher-Monk, Ian W., 'Rhetoric and Opinion in the Politics of Edmund Burke', *History of Political Thought*, 3 (Winter 1988), 455-484.
Hardin, Russell, *David Hume: Moral and Political Theorist* (Oxford: Oxford University Press, 2007).
Harrington, James, *The Commonwealth of Oceana and a System of Politics*, (Cambridge: Cambridge University Press, 1992), ed. J. G. A. Pocock.
Harris, James A., *Hume. An Intellectual Biography* (New York: Cambridge University Press, 2015).

Hart, Jeffrey, 'David Hume and Skeptical Conservatism', *National Review* (13 February 1968), 129-132.

Haslam, Jonathan, *No Virtue Like Necessity: Realist Thought in International Relations since Machiavelli* (New Haven: Yale University Press, 2002).

Hayek, Friedrich A. von, 'The Legal and Political Philosophy of David Hume', *Il Politico*, 4 (1963), 691-704.

Henrie, Mark C., *Arguing Conservatism. Four Decades of the Intercollegiate Review* (Wilmington: ISI Books, 2008).

Herdt, Jennifer A., *Religion and Faction in Hume's Moral Philosophy* (New York: Cambridge University Press, 1997).

Hiley, Richard D., *Philosophy in Question: Essays on a Pyrrhonian Theme* (Chicago: University of Chicago Press, 1988).

Hobbes, Thomas, *Leviathan* (Oxford and New York: Oxford University Press, 1998), ed. J. C. A. Gaskin.

Hoy, Terry, *Toward a Naturalistic Political Theory: Aristotle, Hume, Dewey, Evolutionary Biology, and Deep Ecology* (Westport: Praeger, 2000).

Hudson, William D., *The Is/Ought Question. A Collection of Papers on the Central Problem in Moral Philosophy* (London: Macmillan, 1969).

Hutcheson, Francis, *Philosophical Writings* (London: Dent, 1994), ed. R. S. Downie.

Ish-Shalom, Piki, 'The Triptych of Realism and Conservatism', *International Studies Review*, 8 (2006), 441-468.

Jones, Peter, *The Science of Man in the Scottish Enlightenment: Hume, Reid, and Their Contemporaries* (Edinburgh: Edinburgh University Press, 1989).

Jones, Peter, *The Reception of David Hume in Europe* (London and New York: Continuum, 2005).

Kahn, Victoria A., *Rhetoric, Prudence, and Skepticism in the Renaissance* (Ithaca: Cornell University Press 1985).

Keohane, Nannerl O., *Philosophy and the State in France: The Renaissance to the Enlightenment* (Princeton: Princeton University Press, 1980).

Kirk, Russell A., *A Program for Conservatives* (Chicago: Regnery, 1962).

Kirk, Russell A., *The Roots of American Order* (La Salle: Open Court, 1974).
Kirk, Russell A., *Men of Letters as Statists: Locke, Montesquieu, Hume, Burke*, in *Literature Criticism from 1400 to 1800* (Detroit: Gale Research, 1989), ed. by James E. Person.
Kirk, Russell A., *The Politics of Prudence* (Wilmington: ISI Books, 1993).
Kirk, Russell A., *The Conservative Mind: From Burke to Eliot* (Washington: Regnery 2001).
Knight, William A., *Hume* (Edinburgh: Blackwood and Sons, 1886).
Knud Haakonssen, *Traditions of Liberalism: Essays on John Locke, Adam Smith, and John Stuart Mill* (Sidney: Centre for Independent Studies, 1988).
Kramnick, Isaac, *Bolingbroke and His Circle. The Politics of Nostalgia in the Age of Walpole* (Ithaca and London: Cornell University Press, 1992).
Kristol, Irving, *Neocoservatism: The Autobiography of an Idea* (New York: The Free Press, 1995).
Laursen, John C., *The Politics of Skepticism in the Ancients, Montaigne, Hume, and Kant* (Leiden: Brill, 1992).
Laursen, John C., 'David Hume on custom and habit and living with skepticism', *Daímon Revista Internacional de Filosofía*, 52 (2011), 87-99.
Lay, John, and A. Hamilton and J. Madison, *The Federalist* (Middletown: Wesleyan University Press, 1961), ed. J. E. Cooke.
Leavis, Frank Raymond, *Mill on Bentham and Coleridge* (New York: Harper & Row, 1950).
Legg Stephen, *Spatiality, Sovereignity and Carl Schmitt* (London and New York: Routledge, 2011).
Limbrick, Elaine, *La Vie politique et juridique: considérations sceptiques dans les "Essais"*, in *Les Écrivains et la Politique dans le Sud-Ouest de la France autour des années 1580, Actes du Colloque de Bordeaux, 6-7 novembre 1981* (Bordeaux: Presses Universitaires de Bordeaux, 1982).
Livingston, Donald W., 'Hume and America', *The Kentucky Review*, 3 (1983), 15-38.

Livingston, Donald W., 'Notes and Discussions: A Sellarsian Hume?', *Journal of the History of Philosophy*, 29 (April 1991), 281-290.

Livingston, Donald W., *Hume's Philosophy of Common Life* (Chicago: University of Chicago Press, 1984).

Livingston, Donald W., 'On Hume's Conservatism', *Hume Studies*, 2 (November 1995), 151-164.

Livingston, Donald W., *Philosophical Melancholy and Delirium: Hume's Pathology of Philosophy* (Chicago: University of Chicago Press, 1998).

Livingston, Donald W., 'David Hume and the Conservative Tradition', *Intercollegiate Review*, 22 (Fall 2009), 30-41.

Livingston, Donald W., and M. Martin, *Hume as Philosopher of Society, Politics and History* (Rochester and Woodbridge: Rochester University Press, 1991).

Lock, Frederick P., *Edmund Burke* (Oxford: Clarendon Press, 1998).

Locke, John, *An Essay Concerning Human Understanding Part* (London: Dent and Sons, 1961), ed. J. W. Yolton.

Locke, John, *Second Treatise of Government: An Essay Concerning the True Original, Extent and End of Civil Government* (Wheling: Harlan Davidson, 1982), ed. R. H. Cox.

Lucas, Paul, 'On Edmund Burke's Doctrine of Prescription; or, An Appeal from the New to the Old Lawyers', *Historical Journal*, 1 (1968), 35-63.

Macaulay, Catharine, 'Answer to Mr. Hume's Letter', *The European Magazine, and London Review*, 4 (1783), 37-39.

Macaulay, Catharine, *Observation on the Reflections of the Right Hon. Edmund Burke, on the Revolution in France, in a Letter to the Right Hon. The Earl of Stanhope* (London: C. Dilly, 1790).

Maček, Josef, *Machiavelli e il machiavellismo* (Florence: La Nuova Italia, 1980).

Machiavelli, Niccolò, *Discourses on the First Decade of Titus Livius* (London: Kegan Paul, Trench and Co., 1883).

Machiavelli, Niccolò, *The Prince* (Indianapolis and Cambridge: Hackett, 1976), ed. J. B. Atkinson.

Macinnes, Allan I., *Union and Empire: The Making of the United Kingdom in 1707* (Cambridge: Cambridge University Press, 2007).

MacIntosh, John J., and H. A. Meynell, *Faith, Skepticism, and Personal Identity: A Festschrift for Terence Penelham* (Alberta: University of Calgary Press, 1994).
Maia Neto, José R., G. Paganini and J. C. Laursen, *Skepticism in the Modern Age. Building on the Work of Richard Popkin* (Leiden-Boston: Brill 2009).
Manent, Pierre, *City of Man* (Princeton: Princeton University Press, 1998).
Mansfield, Harvey C., *Statesmanship and Party Government: A Study of Burke and Bolingbroke* (Chicago and London: The University of Chicago Press, 1965).
Marshall, Geoffrey, 'David Hume and Political Skepticism', *The Philosophical Quarterly*, 4 (July 1954), 247-257.
McArthur, Neil, *David Hume's Political Theory: Law, Commerce, and the Constitution of Government* (Toronto: University of Toronto Press, 2007).
McDonald, Wesley W., *Russell Kirk and the Age of Ideology* (Columbia and London: University of Missouri Press, 2004).
Michaud, Yves, 'How to Become a Moderate Skeptic: Hume's Way Out of Pyrrhonism', *Hume Studies*, 11 (1985), 33-46.
Mill, John Stuart, *The Collected Works of John Stuart Mill* (Toronto: University of Toronto Press, 1963-1991), ed. J. M. Robson.
Miller, David, *Philosophy and Ideology in Hume's Political Thought* (Oxford: Clarendon Press, 1981).
Montaigne, Michel de, *On Cannibals*, in *Essays*, ed. by John M. Cohen (New York: Penguin, 1993).
Moore, James, 'Hume's Political Science and the Classical Republican Tradition', *Canadian Journal of Political Science*, 4 (1977) 809-839.
Morgenthau, Hans. J., *Scientific Man Versus Power Politics* (Chicago and London: The University of Chicago Press, 1946).
Morice, George P., *David Hume: Bicentenary Papers* (Edinburgh: Edinburgh University Press, 1977).
Morrow, Glenn R., 'The Significance of the Doctrine of Sympathy in Hume and Adam Smith', *The Philosophical Review*, 1 (January 1923), 60-78.
Mosca, Gaetano, *Il "Principe" di Machiavelli quattro secoli dopo*

la morte del suo autore (Rome: Tipografia Il Popolo d'Italia, 1927).

Mossner, Ernest C., 'Hume's Early Memoranda, 1729-1740: The Complete Text', *Journal of the History of Ideas*, 4 (October, 1948), 492-518.

Mossner, Ernest C., *The Life of David Hume* (Oxford: Clarendon Press, 1980).

Muller, Jerry Z., *Conservatism: An Anthology of Social and Political Thought from David Hume to the Present* (Princeton: Princeton University Press, 1997).

Nisbet, Robert A., *The Quest for Community: A Study in the Ethics of Order and Freedom* (New York: Oxford University Press, 1953).

Nisbet, Robert A., *The Sociological Tradition* (New York: Basic Books, 1966).

Nisbet, Robert A., 'Cloaking the State's Dagger', *Reason*, October (1984), 42-48.

Nisbet, Robert A., *The Making of Modem Society* (New York: NYU Press, 1986).

Nisbet, Robert A., *Tradition and Revolt* (New Brunswick and London: Transaction, 1999).

Nisbet, Robert A., *Conservatism: Dream and Reality* (London and New York: Routledge, 2002).

Noelle-Neumann, Elisabeth, *The Spiral of Silence: Public Opinion, Our Social Skin* (Chicago: University of Chicago Press, 1984).

Norman, Jesse, *Edmund Burke: The First Conservative* (New York: Basic Books, 2013).

Norton, David F., *David Hume: Common-Sense Moralist, Skeptical Metaphysician* (Princeton: Princeton University Press, 1982).

O'Neill, Daniel I., *The Burke-Wollstonecraft Debate: Savagery, Civilization, and Democracy* (University Park: Pennsylvania State University Press 2007).

Oakeshott, Michael, *Rationalism in Politics and Other Essays* (London: Methuen, 1962).

Oakeshott, Michael, *Rationalism in Politics, and Other Essays* (Indianapolis: Liberty Press, 1991), ed. T. Fuller.

Oakeshott, Michael, *Experience and Its Modes* (Cambridge: Cambridge University Press, 1995).

Oakeshott, Michael, *The Politics of Faith and the Politics of Scepticism* (New Haven and London: Yale University Press, 1996) ed. T. Fuller.
Oakeshott, Michael, *The Vocabulary of a Modern European State* (Exeter: Imprint Academic, 2008), ed. L. O' Sullivan.
Okie, Laird, 'Ideology and Partiality in David Hume's *History of England*', *Hume Studies*, 1 (April 1985), 1-32.
Pafford, John M., *Russell Kirk* (New York and London: Bloomsbury, 2013).
Peden, Joseph R., and F. Glahe, *The American Family and the State* (San Francisco: Pacific Research Institute, 1986).
Person, James E., *The Unbought Grace of Life: Essays in Honor of Russell Kirk* (Peru: Sherwood Sugden, 1994).
Person, James E., *Russell Kirk: A Critical Biography of a Conservative Mind* (Lanham: Madison Books, 1999).
Phillipson, Nicholas, *Hume* (New York: St. Martin's Press, 1989).
Phillipson, Nicholas, and Q. Skinner, *Political Discourse in Early Modern Britain* (Cambridge: Cambridge University Press, 1992).
Pidgen, Charles R., *Hume on Is and Ought* (New York: Palgrave Macmillan, 2010).
Pocock, John G. A., *The Machiavellian Moment: Florentine Political Thought and the Atlantic Republican Tradition* (Princeton and Oxford: Princeton University Press, 1975).
Pocock, John G. A., *Virtue, Commerce, and History: Essays on Political Thought and History, Chiefly in the Eighteenth Century* (Cambridge and New York: Cambridge University Press, 1985).
Popkin, Richard H., *The History of Scepticism from Erasmus to Descartes* (Assen: Van Gorcum, 1960).
Popkin, Richard H., *The High Road to Pyrrhonism* (San Diego: Austin Hill Press, 1980).
Popkin, Richard H., *The History of Scepticism: From Savonarola to Bayle* (Oxford-New York: Oxford University Press, 2003).
Prezzolini, Giuseppe, *Manifesto dei conservatori* (Milan: Rusconi, 1972).
Pupo Spartaco, 'Oikophobic Prejudice Against Nation in the Contemporary Political Thought: The Italian Case', *Notizie di Politeia*, 118 (2015), 3-22.

Pupo, Spartaco, 'Natura e classificazione dei partiti: la *scoperta* di David Hume', *Storia e Politica*, 3 (2016), pp. 476-512.
Pupo, Spartaco, 'Il conservatorismo politico di David Hume', *Rivista di Politica*, 2 (2016), pp. 23-41.
Pupo, Spartaco, *Il Machiavelli di David Hume*, in Piero Innocenti and Marielisa Rossi, *Bibliografia delle edizioni di Niccolò Machiavelli: 1506-1914* (Manziana: Vecchiarelli, 2018), pp. 9-25.
Pupo, Spartaco, 'Lost (and Found) in Italian Translation: David Hume as a Political Thinker and Statesman', in *Eighteenth-Century Scotland*, 33 (Spring 2019), 6-9.
Rasmussen, Dennis C., *The Pragmatic Enlightenment: Recovering the Liberalism of Hume, Smith, Montesquieu, and Voltaire* (Cambridge: Cambridge University Press, 2014).
Rasmussen, Dennis C., *The Infidel and the Professor: David Hume, Adam Smith, and the Friendship that Shaped Modern Thought* (Princeton and Oxford: Princeton University Press, 2017).
Rathbun, Brian C., 'Does One Right Make a Realist? Conservatism, Neoconservatism, and Isolationism in the Foreign Policy Ideology of American Elites', *Political Science Quarterly*, 2 (Summer, 2008), 271-299.
Raynor, David R., *Sister Peg: A Pamphlet Hitherto Unknown by David Hume* (Cambridge: Cambridge University Press, 1982).
Resnick, David, 'David Hume: A Modern Conservative', *The European Legacy*, 1 (1996), 397-402.
Robbins, Caroline, 'Discordant Parties. A Study of the Acceptance of Party by Englishmen', *Political Science Quarterly*, 4 (1958), 505-529.
Robertson, John, *A Union for Empire. Political Thought and the British Union of 1707* (Cambridge: Cambridge University Press, 1995).
Robertson, John, *The Case for the Enlightenment. Scotland and Naples 1680-1760* (Cambridge: Cambridge University Press, 2005).
Rosen, Frederick, *Jeremy Bentham* (Aldershot: Ashgate, 2007).
Rosenthal, Joel H., *Righteous Realists* (Baton Rouge: Lousiana State University, 1991).

Sabine, George H., *A History of Political Theory* (London: Harrap & C., 1948).
Sabl, Andrew, *Hume's Politics. Coordination and Crisis in the "History of England"* (Princeton and Oxford: Princeton University Press, 2012).
Saltel, Philippe, 'Machiavel himself…: Hume et le «secrétaire de Florence', *Revue Fhilosophique*, 1 (2008), 31-42.
Sartori, Giovanni, *Parties and Party Systems. A Framework for Analysis* (Colchester: Ecpr Press, 2005).
Schmitt, Carl, *The Nomos of the Earth in the International Law of the Jus Publicum Europaeum* (New York: Telos Press, 2006), ed. G. L. Ulmen.
Scott, William R., *Francis Hutcheson: His Life, Teaching, and Position in the History of Philosophy* (New York: Kelley, 1966).
Scruton, Roger, *Conservative Thinkers: Essays from "The Salisbury Review"* (London and Lexington: The Claridge Press, 1989).
Scruton, Roger, 'How to be a Non-Liberal, Anti-Socialist Conservative', *The Intercollegiate Review*, 2 (Spring 1993), 19-20.
Scruton, Roger, *A Short History of Modern Philosophy From Descartes to Wittgenstein* (London and New York: Routledge, 1995).
Scruton, Roger, *The Palgrave Macmillan Dictionary of Political Thought* (London: Palgrave Macmillan, 2007).
Scruton, Roger, *How to Think Seriously About the Planet: The Case for an Environmental Conservatism* (Oxford and New York: Oxford University Press, 2012).
Scruton, Roger, *How to be a Conservative* (London: Bloomsbury Continuum, 2014).
Scruton, Roger, *Conservatism: Ideas in Profile* (London: Profile Books, 2017).
Scruton, Roger, *Conservatism: An Invitation to the Great Tradition* (New York: St-Martin's Press, 2018).
Sebastiani, Silvia, *The Scottish Enlightenment. Race, Gender, and the Limits of Progress* (New York: Palgrave Macmillan, 2013).
Sextus Empiricus, *Outlines of Pyrrhonism* (Cambridge: Harvard University Press, 1933), ed. R. G. Bury.

Sextus Empiricus, *The Outlines of Skepticism* (Cambridge: Cambridge University Press, 2002).
Sharp, Andrew, *The English Levellers* (Cambridge: Cambridge University Press, 2002).
Sidorsky, David, *The Liberal Tradition in European Thought* (New York: Putnam, 1970).
Skinner, Quentin, *The Foundations of Modern Political Thought* (Cambridge: Cambridge University Press, 1978).
Smith, Adam, *An Inquiry into the Nature and Causes of the Wealth of Nations* (London: W. Strahan and T. Cadell, 1776).
Smith, Adam, *The Theory of Moral Sentiments* (Cambridge: Cambridge University Press, 2002), ed. K. Haakonssen.
Smith, Michael J., *Realist Thought form Weber to Kissinger* (Baton Rouge: Lousiana State University, 1986).
Snare, Francis, *Morals, Motivation, and Convention: Hume's Influential Doctrines* (Cambridge: Cambridge University Press, 1991).
Soininen, Suvi, *From a «Necessary Evil» to the Art of the Contingency. Michael Oakeshott's Conception of Political Activity* (Exeter: Imprint Academic, 2005).
Spelman, Edward, *A Parallel between the Roman and the British Constitution comprehending Polybius' Curious Discourse of the Roman Senate* (London: printed by Mary Cooper, 1747).
Stephen, Leslie, *History of English Thought in the Eighteenth Century* (London: Smith, Elder & Co., 1876).
Steven A. Gerencser, *The Skeptic's Oakeshott* (New York: St. Martin's Press, 2000).
Stewart, John B., *Opinion and Reform in Hume's Political Philosophy* (Princeton: Princeton University Press, 1992).
Stewart, Michael A., and J. Wright, *Hume and Hume's Connexions* (State College: Penn State University Press, 1994).
Stone, Brad L., *Robert Nisbet: Communitarian Traditionalist* (Wilmington: ISI Books, 2002).
Strasser, Mark P., *Francis Hutcheson's Moral Theory: Its Form and Utility* (Wolfeboro: Longwood Academic, 1990).
Susato, Ryu, *Hume's Sceptical Enlightenment* (Edinburgh: Edinburgh University Press, 2015).
Temple, William, *The Works of William Temple* (Edinburgh: Printed

for G. Hamilton, J. Balfour, A. Kincaid and A. Donaldson, L. Hunter, W. Gordon, J. Yair and C. Wright; Glasgow: A. Stalker, 1754).

Thomas W. Merrill, 'The Rhetoric of Rebellion in Hume's Constitutional Thought', *The Review of Politics*, 2 (Spring 2005), 257-82.

Tierney, Brian, *The Idea of Natural Rights: Studies on Natural Rights, Natural Law and Church Law 1150-1625* (Atlanta: Scholars Press, 1997).

Trevelyan, George M., *The Two-Party System in English Political History* (Oxford: Clarendon Press, 1926).

Trevelyan, George M., *England Under the Stuarts (London and New York: Routledge, 2002)*.

Trevor-Roper Hugh, 'The Scottish Enlightenment', *Studies on Voltaire and the Eighteenth Century*, 68 (1967), 1635-1658.

Tseng, Roy, *The Sceptical Idealist. Michael Oakeshott as a Critical of the Enlightenment* (Exeter: Imprint Academic, 2003).

Tweyman, Stanley, *David Hume. Critical Assessments* (London and New York: Routlege, 1995).

Varela Suanzes-Carpegna, Joaquin, 'Estado y Monarquía en Hume', *Revista del Centro de Estudios Constitucionales*, 22 (1995), 59-90.

Viereck, Peter, 'Liberals and Conservatives, 1789-1951', *The Antioch Review*, 4 (1951), 387-396.

Voegelin, Eric, *The New Science of Politics* (Chicago: The University of Chicago Press, 1952).

Voltaire, *A Philosophical Dictionary* (Boston: Mendum, 1852).

Wand, Bernard, 'A Note on Sympathy in Hume's Moral Theory', *The Philosophical Review*, 2 (April 1955), 275-279.

Weaver, Richard M., *Ideas Have Consequences* (Chicago: University of Chicago Press, 1948).

Weaver, Richard M., 'Conservatism and Libertarianism: The Common Ground', *The Individualist*, 4 (May 1960), 1-8.

Weaver, Richard M., *Visions of Order: The Cultural Crisis of Our Time* (Baton Rouge: Louisiana State University Press, 1964).

Weaver, Richard M., *Life Without Prejudice and Other Essays* (Chicago: University of Chicago Press, Chicago 1965).

Whelan, Frederick G., *Order and Artifice in Hume's Political Philosophy* (Princeton: Princeton University Press, 1985).

Whelan, Frederick G., *Hume and Machiavelli: Political Realism and Liberal Thought* (Lanham: Lexington Books, 2004).

Wilkins, Burleigh T., *The Problem of Burke's Political Philosophy* (Oxford: Clarendon Press, 1967).

Wolin, Sheldon S., 'Hume and Conservatism', *The American Political Science Review*, 4 (1954), 999-1116.

Wolin, Sheldon S., *Politics and Vision* (Boston: Little Brown and Company, 1960).

Wright, John P., *Hume and Hume's Connexions* (State College: Penn State University Press, 1994).

Yenor, Scott, *David Hume's Humanity. The Philosophy of Common Life and its Limits* (New York: Palgrave Macmillan, 2016).

Zaretsky, Robert, and J. T. Scott, *The Philosophers' Quarrel: Rousseau, Hume and the Limits of Human Understanding* (New Haven: Yale University Press, 2009).

INDEX OF PERSONS

Abel, C., 190, 192
Adams, J., 182
Ajello, R., 151
Alembert, J. d', 80, 182, 184
Alison, A., 19
Annas, J., 130
Anne, Queen of England, 13
Aristotle, 52
Armitage, D., 107
Ashford, N., 158
Aspromourgos, T., 28
Atkinson, J. B., 58

Bacon, F., 189
Baier, A., 52
Bailey, A., 22
Balfour, J., 37, 81
Barbuto, G. M., 74
Barnes, J., 130
Bassani, L. M., 74
Bayle, P., 20, 23
Bentham, J., 44, 88-89, 129-130, 161, 193
Berkowitz, P., 175
Berlin, I., 67, 171
Berry, C. J., 19, 52, 186
Black, M., 157
Blackstone, W., 181
Blamires, C., 89
Bolingbroke, 100, 104, 106-107, 109-110, 115, 165, 185

Bonald, L. de, 36, 149, 154
Bongie, L. L., 137, 139, 148-149
Botero, G., 74
Botwinick, A., 186
Bowring, J., 88
Brahami, F., 22
Brewer, J., 15
Burke, E., 10, 55-56, 62, 86-87, 100, 110, 115-117, 132-134, 136-139, 142, 149, 153, 165-166, 169-170, 178-181, 184-185, 190, 192-193, 196-197
Burke, P., 21
Burnham, J., 58
Bury R. G., 22
Butler, J., 49-50

Cadell, T., 26, 64
Campi, A., 58, 167
Canavan, F., 55
Cantillon, R., 28
Castiglione, D., 78, 81
Chappell, V. C., 21
Charles I, King of England, 42, 119-120, 135-136, 146, 149
Chateaubriand, F.-R. de, 147
Chevallier, J.-J., 152
Cicero, 113, 181
Clephane, J., 25, 104, 146
Congdon, L., 171
Conniff, J., 99, 108, 113

Cooke, J. E., 88
Cotta, S., 99, 110-111
Cox, R. H., 144
Creech, W., 64
Croce, B., 185
Cromwell, O., 13, 135-137, 146
Crousaz, J.-P. de, 23
Cutler, F., 88

Davies, S., 158
De Luca, S., 58, 167
Descartes, R., 161, 195
Dewey, J., 52
Diderot, D., 80
Diodorus Siculus, 121
Dionysius of Halicarnassus, 111
Dodsley, J., 169
Donaldson, A., 26, 64, 81
Dooley, M., 194
Dove, J. F., 50
Dow, A., 25
Dow, S., 25
Downie, R. S., 49
Dryden, J., 135
Duncan-Jones, A., 50

Elizabeth, Queen of England, 14
Emerson, R. L., 25

Fennessy, R. R., 87
Ferrone, V., 151
Fieser, J., 26

Fitzgibbons, A., 43
Fleming, R., 19, 26
Flew, A., 134
Floridi, L., 20
Forbes, D., 20, 92, 95, 143
Formigari, L., 148
Foxley, R., 37
Franco, P., 186

Frazer, M. L., 139-140
Froude, J. A., 130
Fuller, T., 168, 189, 192

Gardiner, S. R., 130
Gaskin, J. C. A., 79
Gauthier, D., 61
Gay, P., 152
George I, King of England, 13
George II, King of England, 13
George III, King of England, 15, 131
Gerencser, S. A., 186
Giarratana, C., 15
Giarrizzo, G., 53, 67, 147-148
Gibbon, E., 28
Gibson, A., 87
Glahe, F., 178
Goldie, M., 38
Gordon, W., 81
Gray, J., 141
Green, J. R., 130
Greenleaf, W. H., 186
Greig, J. Y. T., 16
Grene, M., 130

Haakonssen, K., 43, 143
Hamilton, A., 87-88, 181
Hamilton, G., 37, 81
Hampsher-Monk, I. W., 87
Hampshire, S., 67
Hardin, R., 142
Hardy, H., 171
Harrington, J., 65-66, 68-69, 82-83
Harris, J. A., 23, 92
Harrison, W., 44
Hart, J., 134-135
Haslam, J., 58
Hayek, F. A. von, 34
Helm, P., 197
Henrie, M. C., 88, 175

Index of Persons

Henry III, King of England, 112
Henry IV, King of France, 112, 121
Herdt, J. A., 105
Herodotus, 121
Hiley, R. D., 161
Hobbes, T., 31, 40, 79, 153, 176-177, 193
Home, H., 15
Hoy, T., 52
Hudson, W. D., 157
Huet, P.-D., 23
Hunter, L., 81
Hutcheson, F., 49-50

Innocenti, P., 70
Ish-Shalom, P., 167

James I, King of England, 119
James II, King of England, 42, 120
James, M., 89
Jefferson, T., 182
Jones, P., 26, 163

Kahn, V. A., 23
Kant, I., 21
Kennan, G., 171
Keohane, N. O., 161
Kincaid, A., 26, 81
Kirk, R. A., 10, 172, 175, 179-185, 192
Kissinger, H., 58
Klibansky, R., 131
Knight, W. A., 133
Kramnick, I., 107
Kristol, I., 190

La Mothe du Vayer, F., 23
Laursen, J. C., 21-22, 52
Lay, J., 88
Leavis, F. R., 129

Legg, S., 63
Limbrick, E., 161
Livingston, D. W., 23, 52, 87, 131, 135-137
Lock, F. P., 87
Locke, J., 24, 40, 45, 49, 51, 68, 79-80, 107, 143, 178-181, 184-185
Longman, T., 19
Lucas, P., 134

Macaulay, C., 130-132, 146
Maček, J., 67
Machiavelli, N., 10, 57-58, 67-75, 94, 168
Macinnes, A. I., 17
MacIntosh, J. J., 22
Madison, J., 87-88, 178
Maia Neto, J. R., 22
Maistre, J. de, 36, 137, 149, 154, 196
Manent, P., 138
Mansfield, H. C., 115, 133
Marshall, G., 39
Marx, K., 55, 178
McArthur, N., 134
McDonald, F., 181
McDonald, W. W., 180
Merrill, T. W., 145
Meynell, H. A., 22
Mill, J. S., 44, 55, 129-130, 143, 145-146, 161, 175
Millar, A., 27, 37, 48
Millar, J., 147
Miller, D., 94
Miller, E. F., 19
Millican, P., 48, 168
Mingardi, A., 74
Montaigne, M. de, 20-21, 23, 135, 161, 189, 193

Montesquieu, C.-L. de, 64, 116, 143, 178, 180-181
Moore, J., 83
More, T., 65, 69
Morgenthau, H. J., 169-170
Morice, G. P., 20
Morrow, G. R., 40
Mosca, G., 57, 74
Mossner, E. C., 24, 74, 105, 130-131, 135, 165
Muller, J. Z., 35-36, 138, 147

Nidditch, P. H., 50
Nimmo, J. C., 170
Nisbet, R. A., 10, 55, 132, 175-179
Noelle-Neumann, E., 87
Noon, J., 19
Norman, J., 55
Norton, D. F., 22, 24, 44, 68
Norton, M. J., 24
O' Sullivan, L., 186
O'Neill, D. I., 165
Oakeshott, M., 10, 168, 171, 175, 186-194, 196
Okie, L., 130
Oswald J., 16, 163

Pafford, J. M., 180
Paganini, G., 22
Paine, T., 87
Pascal, B., 23, 193
Pease-Watkin, C., 89
Peden, J. R., 178
Penelham, T., 22
Person, J. E., 179, 181
Petty, W., 29
Phillipson, N., 78, 131
Pidgen, C. R., 157
Pitt, W., 14, 75
Plato, 65, 69 178

Pocock, J. G. A., 38, 68, 82-83, 151
Polybius, 111, 121
Popkin, R. H., 20-22, 161
Prezzolini, G., 10, 175, 185
Pupo, S., 27, 132, 183
Pyrrho, 20

Rasmussen, D. C., 26, 43, 93, 142-143
Rathbun, B. C., 167
Raynor, D. R., 75
Resnick, D., 139
Riley, P., 38
Ritchie, D. E., 86, 116
Rivingston, C., 165
Rivingston, F., 165
Robbins, C., 107
Robertson, J., 16, 29
Robson, J. M., 129
Rosen, F., 44
Rosenthal, J. H., 58
Rossi, M., 70
Rousseau, J.-J., 176, 178, 182-183

Sabine, G. H., 133
Sabl, A., 85, 93, 110
Saltel, P., 67
Sandoz, E., 88
Sartori, G., 99, 110
Savonarola, G., 20
Schmitt, C., 57, 63
Schneewind, J. B., 34
Schwab, R. N., 80
Scott, J. T., 182
Scott, W. R., 50
Scruton, R., 10, 161, 172-173, 175, 194-197
Sebastiani, S., 53, 64
Sextus Empiricus, 20, 22, 130, 161
Shaftesbury, A., 68

Sharp, A., 37
Sharpe, L., 81
Shklar, J., 67
Sidorsky, D., 143
Skinner, Q., 131, 161
Smith, A., 26, 28-29, 40, 43, 100, 105, 143, 147, 164, 178, 196
Smith, M. J., 58
Snare, F., 134
Soininen, S., 186
Spelman, E., 111
St. Clair, J., 27, 163
Stalker, A., 81
Stephen, L., 130, 132-133
Steuart, J., 28
Stewart, A., 27, 105
Stewart, J. B., 78, 141-142, 155
Stewart, M. A., 50, 78
Stone, B. L., 132, 178
Strahan, W., 26
Strasser, M. P., 50
Susato, R., 65, 81, 143, 152

Temple, W., 81
Thomson, N. H., 71
Thucydides, 57, 121
Tierney, B., 157
Titus Livius, 68, 71-72, 121
Todd, W. B., 37
Trevelyan, G. M., 15, 17
Trevor-Roper, H., 16
Tseng, R., 186
Turgot, A.-R.-J., 26, 184

Tweyman, S., 40

Ulmen, G. L., 63

Varela Suanzes-Carpegna, J., 104
Vasudevan, A., 63
Venturi, F., 151
Viereck, P., 166
Voegelin, E., 172
Voltaire, 16, 79, 138, 143

Walpole, R., 13-14, 107, 110, 182
Wand, B., 40
Weaver, R. M., 168, 172
Weber, M., 57-58, 115
Wennerlind, C., 25
Whelan, F. G., 67, 78
Wilkes, J., 91-92, 146, 197
Wilkins, B. T., 133-134
Williams, B., 67
Wittgenstein, L., 195
Wolin, S. S., 58, 137-138
Wolker, R., 38
Wright, C., 81
Wright, J. P., 50

Xenophon, 121

Yair, J., 81
Yenor, S., 125
Yolton, J. W., 49

Zaretsky, R., 182

MIMESIS GROUP
www.mimesis-group.com

MIMESIS INTERNATIONAL
www.mimesisinternational.com
info@mimesisinternational.com

MIMESIS EDIZIONI
www.mimesisedizioni.it
mimesis@mimesisedizioni.it

ÉDITIONS MIMÉSIS
www.editionsmimesis.fr
info@editionsmimesis.fr

MIMESIS COMMUNICATION
www.mim-c.net

MIMESIS EU
www.mim-eu.com

Printed by
Geca Industrie Grafiche – San Giuliano Milanese (MI)
February 2020